FIT AND PROPER PEOPLE

FIT AND PROPER PEOPLE

THE R~~I~~SE AND FALL
LIES
OF OWNAFC

MARTIN CALLADINE
AND JAMES CAVE

First published by Pitch Publishing, 2022

Pitch Publishing
A2 Yeoman Gate
Yeoman Way
Worthing
Sussex
BN13 3QZ
www.pitchpublishing.co.uk
info@pitchpublishing.co.uk

A CIP catalogue record is available for this book
from the British Library.

ISBN 978-1 80150 047 0

Typesetting and origination by Pitch Publishing
Printed and bound in Great Britain by TJ Books, Padstow

Contents

Martin:
To my mother Val Calladine (1945-2021), who I miss every day, and to my wonderful family – Jilly, Evie and Hope – whose unfailing love and support helped me through the hardest time of my life.

James:
To Daniel, Matthew and Nic, you are loved wholly and completely every day.

1

Vive la révolution

The world's most famous broadcaster carried
news of the revolution on its website. It was
Thursday, 28 February 2019 and things
were about to change forever.

'THIS IS incredible!' said one member of the public. 'Love the idea,' said a second. 'Excited to be on board, can't wait to see what the future brings,' said a third. 'It's going to be an epic journey!'

Early converts were on hand to amplify this enthusiasm. 'Only been part of this for around four weeks,' said one, 'but loving every minute of it.' Another early joiner, Martin Roberts, said, 'I saw it as a chance to bring people from around the country together and have a common goal. Here was an opportunity to change lives.'

Like all revolutions, it promised a radical redistribution of power to a marginalised group.

'I was very keen on an idea [based on] participation,' said one paid-up member. A public participation specialist at the Scottish Parliament, meanwhile, greeted the news on social media by saying, 'My two passions combined? Participatory #democracy & #football.'

A man called Steven Holland seemed to sum it up best when he said, 'I don't know all the details, I've seen big highs and big lows, but quite excited at something fresh that could take this club to the next level.'

If you're a football fan, you'll know the feeling. Because, to be a football fan is to know deep down that things aren't being done properly.

Football, we believe, is a game of simple purity repeatedly undone by those less knowledgeable than us. The players aren't working hard enough or picking the right passes. The manager isn't setting the team up to get the most of the squad. *Match of the Day* is showing the wrong games first. Above all, the owner doesn't know what he or she is doing.

There isn't a single one of us who, if we inherited great riches, doesn't reckon they'd do a decent job running their team – or at least better than the incumbent. Forget that most of us have never managed a business of any size, never had to interrogate a balance sheet, or never had to make financial projections for a company where fluctuations in performance could see next year's income soar or collapse.

If it seems ludicrous – arrogance born of deep ignorance – it can hardly be denied that, if you spend more than a decade closely supporting any club, you'll see owners making, and repeating, all kinds of seemingly basic mistakes. Hiring and firing managers on a whim. Wasting money on terrible players. Failing to invest in facilities and coaching. Short-termism and perpetual panic.

Football's graveyard is filled with wealthy people who thought they could do things differently, whose first, adulatory interviews with the local press always included talk of being in the Premier League and becoming a global brand within three to five years.

Many of these minted people were self-made, and had either founded businesses or, more recently, had been able to navigate palace intrigues or the brutal machinations of gangster capitalism long enough to expatriate their money.

Yet there's one thing they all had in common. They didn't *know* the game, they weren't a *real* football fan. The love of the club wasn't in their marrow. They'd never stood on the terraces on cold nights, warmed only by foot stamping and camaraderie, singing themselves hoarse. They'd never had to scrape together a few quid for a ticket. They'd never found themselves dancing in the centre circle, hugging strangers and crying with joy after a promotion-induced pitch invasion.

It's a different way of seeing football and football clubs; a perspective that neither players, managers nor owners can claim. And that must count for something, mustn't it? At a time when a small number of teams are worth billions, when most clubs in the professional game are running at or close to a loss, when most owners look like contestants on *It's A Knockout!*, trying desperately to run from one end of the course to another carrying a bucket riddled with holes, from which football's TV money is gushing out faster than they can refill it, mightn't fans be able to do a better job? Might all those decades of diligent attendance have stored up some untapped knowledge that could be used to run a club more effectively?

Francis Galton, a Victorian polymath whose prodigious achievements, good and bad, defy precis, gave the most famous example of the so-called wisdom of the crowd when he showed that the average answer of all the entrants in a guess-the-weight-of-the-bull contest at a country fair was within one per cent of the correct answer. It sounds impossible, a historical curiosity, but it's been successfully and repeatedly reproduced experimentally.

With the advent of the internet – and the belief in the power of technology to radically remake whole areas of society – the wisdom of the crowd is an idea that has returned to popularity. Now we can not only cheaply and instantly canvas's everyone's views, but, with easier access to information, we can perhaps draw on a better-informed population. And, again, that's not obviously wrong.

While it's still the case that there's no opinion about football so stupid that thousands of football fans can't be found to endorse it, the average supporter has access to far more knowledge than 20 years ago: dozens of live games a week, highlights from leagues across the world, inexhaustible access to statistics and analytics.

At a time when football clubs have, for all their media output, never been more remote from fans, then might not a modern, motivated group of supporters be able to judge the performance of a manager at least as well as a group of uneducated pre-WWI yokels might estimate the weight of livestock?

One man thought so. And, more than that, he thought he'd figured out how to make it work. How to choose a club, how to raise the money and how to run things afterwards.

And so, on the last day of February 2019, he appeared on the BBC News website and proclaimed his revolution. How football clubs were owned and operated was going to change forever, he announced.

This is his story, the story of the fans who got involved and the story of what happens when revolutions fail.

* * *

Every plotter of a coup d'état knows that, at some point, they'll have to take the state broadcaster. It's only this channel that shows the strength and purpose of the putsch, legitimising the message and creating a sense of inevitability. Typically, an armed contingent will be dispatched to take and hold the network offices.

Somewhat uniquely, in this case the revolution's self-proclaimed leader found he faced next to no resistance. Rather the gates were thrown open and he was welcomed, open-armed, by a network only too happy to amplify his call-to-arms.

What ought to have been a pitched battle became a coming-out party. And the revolutionary idea – OwnaFC – was launched into football's consciousness as if it were a respectable alternative programme for government rather than an untested insurgency.

No host could've been more welcoming or generous than the BBC. Subjecting the company to the kind of challenging questioning more usually seen when Vladimir Putin sits down for a Q&A on Russian state television or a record signing chat to the local paper, things could barely have gone much better.

Under the headline 'OWNAFC: Non-league football club could be run by supporters using a phone app', a man called Stuart Harvey was quoted as saying, 'This is all about people with a dream of owning a football club. To turn football on its head and take it back to the people.'[1]

Some 2,500 had already signed up, the article said, each paying £49 for a share, which would allow them to 'vote on all the club's boardroom decisions' through a phone app. 'It's the ultimate experience of being a chairman with a big board of directors – each day dealing with monumental decisions of running a club,' claimed Harvey. 'It replaces the boardroom nonsense we see at many clubs with the people that matter.'

Which club was it? Harvey couldn't reveal that, owing to an NDA (non-disclosure agreement), said the article. But it did make room for him to expand on his vision of making the club self-sustaining, with up to 10,000 shares available and with participants being guaranteed at least 51 per cent of the club. The article obligingly reproduced an extract from the company's brochure which promised fans, among other things, the power to 'make new signings', 'hire and fire staff', 'negotiate contracts', 'select the squad', 'plan training sessions' and take 'full financial control'. The only vaguely sceptical note in the whole piece came when the reporter made a comparison with the MyFootballClub project, which took over Ebbsfleet FC in 2008. Then, a welter of publicity had drawn thousands of participants, but numbers had dwindled in just a few years and the experiment collapsed, with the club eventually being handed over to its supporters' trust.

'The difference is theirs was ten years too early,' Harvey reassured readers. 'It was before iPhones became popular, before apps, and they were not using the technology we have today.'

With that, OwnaFC was open for business.

People were impressed by what they read. 'Phone app owners to take over a football club?! This is brilliant,' said one person. 'I love football, loved the concept,' said another.

The interest and enthusiasm was palpable. People were downloading the app so rapidly, and then handing over their money in such quantities, that the servers creaked. The payment system went down and others had trouble signing up. But no matter, still they came.

Fans of struggling lower and non-league clubs took to social media to invite OwnaFC into their clubs. New participants – so-called Ownas – quickly found that the app couldn't accommodate their desire for debate about every aspect of the new endeavour and sought official approval to start a Facebook group.

For many of them, there was a palpable sense of being part of something monumental. Here were a bunch of would-be revolutionaries who'd found each other and together they were going to completely remake football, transforming how clubs are owned and run, and using technology to overturn the standard model that had dominated football for over a century.

Except it didn't quite work out like that. Not at all. In hindsight, OwnaFC's big launch on the world stage wasn't the beginning of a glorious future, but rather its high point – the last time it would ever have completely positive press coverage; the brief moment when it seemed like no barrier was insurmountable and where success was inevitable.

If a week is a long time in revolutionary politics, in football it's an eternity.

* * *

A scam. A fraud. A con. The Fyre Festival of football club ownership.

These and many other terms would later be applied to OwnaFC. All offer ways of looking at what happened to the business, but perhaps the place to start is with OwnaFC's own language: the language of revolution. That tells us about how Stuart Harvey crafted his pitch and why so many found it spoke to them.

History tells us that the seeds of any revolution are sowed years before. We are often too focused on the spark – the exciting moment that everything kicks off – to recognise that it's the accumulated dry wood that's what matters. Without the right conditions, no significant undertaking stands a chance of making it off the drawing board.

Jack Goldstone, a leading academic on social change, wrote about the five factors that he said make social change possible: 'Economic or fiscal strain, alienation and opposition among the elites, widespread popular anger at injustice, a persuasive shared narrative of resistance and favourable international relations.'[2]

While the last condition doesn't apply here, it doesn't take a huge leap to see how the rest had some resonance in football. Economic and financial strain is, of course, the defining condition of lower-division and non-league football.

No matter how much money comes in, the sport has always been broke. It's only the number of zeros that change.

Not yet 30 years old, the Premier League has transformed not just English football, but the club game around the world. Harnessing Rupert Murdoch's determination to make satellite TV a success and, then, the hunger of foreign fans for the game, billions of pounds have poured into the top flight, bringing many of the finest players in the world and, more recently, many of the richest people in the world. The average Premier League player now earns over £3m a year.

While all this money has quite conspicuously not cascaded down the divisions, it has nonetheless distorted the entire professional game beneath it. The Championship has wild disparities of income as clubs gamble their futures on promotion and recently relegated clubs desperately try to climb back before their three years of parachute payments end. Beneath that, there are teams losing millions each year, the broken wrecks of former top-flight clubs and, among the smaller teams just trying to get by, a few rich upstarts – like free-spending debt machines Forest Green Rovers and Salford City – who've bought their way into the league. Below League Two is the National League, where what's traditionally called non-league football starts. There sit a host of former league clubs – Wrexham, Torquay United, Barnet, Stockport County – no longer able to simply bide their time before a return to the EFL.

All of this has made the finances of many football clubs extremely perilous. Typically, owning a club was a decent way to slowly chip away at your fortune. Now, however, it can make or break wealthy people in only a few seasons. The bets are larger and the odds are longer. As a consequence, while clubs seem to change hands with ever-greater regularity, sensible people, by and large, no longer want to buy football clubs. The result, as we'll show in this book, is that football is attracting some wildly unsuitable people into the game, imperilling the future of clubs, many of which have been at the hearts of their communities for over 100 years.

It's certainly true that, at the top end of the Premier League, Financial Fair Play (FFP) rules have helped stabilise spending a little, but as fast as money comes in, most of it goes out on ever-increasing player wages. And while bigger clubs have eased off ticket price rises in recent years, the cost of going to matches – and watching them on TV – puts a significant financial strain on fans. A season ticket and TV subscription can easily amount to more than £1,000 a year.

In 2019, Bury FC were expelled from League One over a matter of a few million pounds – a fortune to the club and its supporters, but little more than a year's salary for a top player in the Premier League. Elsewhere, North Ferriby United, in the sixth tier of football, were wound up over a debt of less than £8,000.

The sad truth is that English football's legendary pyramid, which rests on a base of thousands of semi-professional and amateur clubs, is in terrible financial stress. The average league attendance in League Two in 2019/20 was just over 4,600. Three levels below that, where North Ferriby had played, it was just over 550.

Alienation and opposition among the elites has also been clearly visible in English football. Nostalgia and perpetual complaint has long been a default setting for generations of fans, but there's a definite faction who feel bereft by the rapid changes in top-flight football.

The vast majority of clubs in the top two divisions have changed hands in the last 30 years and it's not uncommon to find teams in the lower reaches of the Championship now owned by self-proclaimed billionaires, often from abroad and frequently with an opaque path to their riches. If ever it existed, the vision of the club owned by a local businessman or woman and fielding a group of local academy graduates has long since faded.

With all this change has come the withering of football's authorities. The Premier League, under the influence of its most powerful members, has sidelined the FA and turned the EFL into a lapdog, taking for itself the role of de facto ruler of English football. The only effective restraint on the Premier League's actions comes from UEFA and FIFA, who've spent several years locked in a battle to control how the highest levels of the club game are exploited. Perhaps fearful that the supremacy of the World Cup will one day fade, FIFA has expanded its Club World Cup. UEFA, meanwhile, has been stuck between trying to restrain spending by Europe's richest clubs while also trying to stymie a breakaway European League, which it fears would destroy its Champions League cash cow.

Whoever wins the battle, it's clear that Europe's largest clubs feel they have outgrown their leagues and regard football's governing bodies as archaic and unwelcome restraints on their growth.

It's a contempt, sadly, that many owners also feel for fans. They see their clubs as their sole personal possessions and have little interest in the hopes, fears and accumulated lifetime experience of their season ticket holders. As the PR people and marketers have been engaged to help sweat the assets or polish the image, the language and practice of branding has been applied, with the owners' disregard showing in the one-sided refashioning of supporters into customers.

Kit launches and even barely notable signings have become PR events, while the EFL has sought ever-more bizarre places to hold competition draws. In place of the idea of collective ownership and stewardship, with genuine supporter representation, fans remain essentially outsiders at their own clubs. Clubs depend on their fans' unique loyalty for income but insist on the right to treat them as mere consumers in every other respect.

Football writer Martin Cloake, a long-time member of the Tottenham Hotspur Supporters' Trust, says, 'At club level, too many owners genuinely don't see why fans should have proper input. That, despite all the change in business approach, hasn't changed. It's down to, "We own it. Full stop." It's why we have to be so tremendously grateful for the merest hearing.'

Here, though, revolutionary conditions begin to ebb. Is the third present: widespread popular anger? Disenchantment among a significant group, perhaps. But one of the greatest assets club owners have – other than their own ill-gotten ones, of course – is the disunity of supporters. Protest – actual marching and campaigning, rather than complaining – tends to be focused on one's own club. It's extremely rare to find any cause that unites fans and brings them to collective action. It's perhaps this reason why politicians have been able to ignore fans for so long – instead of being a lobbying group millions strong, we are just hundreds of small, local pressure groups.

As OwnaFC demonstrated, however, there's definitely a mood for change among some. The question was, would it be strong enough and widely enough shared to create a groundswell?

Which brings us to condition number four, perhaps OwnaFC's strongest card: a persuasive shared narrative of resistance.

'This is your unique opportunity to be a part of the biggest revolution in football since the dawn of the Sky Sports era in 1992,' said its brochure. 'YOU WILL CALL THE SHOTS – LIVE AND ONLINE. THE POWER IS ALL YOURS.'

It's a call that, as we will see, many would rally to. With disastrous results.

2

A football-shaped hole

*It was a beautiful Californian afternoon,
bright and clear with a cloudless sky, when
Martin Roberts fell off a cliff.*

THE SIERRA Nevada mountains were a long way from home for the Wirral-born football coach, whose favourite hobby was ice climbing. Descending from a peak of 10,300 feet, it was also a long way down when he slipped.

Round Top is the highest point in the Eldorado National Forest, an area of the Sierra Nevada that sits above the crisp waters of Lake Tahoe. Travelling south, there's the unearthly wonders of Yosemite National Park, the giant redwood trees of the Sequoia National Park and the town of Lone Pine, the gateway to Death Valley. There, you'll find defiant outposts like Stovepipe Wells and Furnace Creek, where you can swim in a pool fed by a natural spring that delivers water straight from the ground at a steady 30°C. It's a part of California where you can start the day in sub-zero temperatures in a log cabin at 9,000ft, alert for hungry bears, and then, after a few hours' leisurely driving, end the day 40 degrees warmer, watching for rattlesnakes while you walk to a bar below sea level. East from there, across the desert and the state line, the twinkling lights of Las Vegas call to you.

Martin had always taken his climbing seriously, careful about his equipment and the weather conditions. Every Sunday for three months prior to their ascent, he and his climbing partner had returned to the mountain, going progressively higher until they felt ready to attempt the summit.

Arriving at 4am, the preparation had paid off. Despite the -7°C temperature and three feet of snow, nothing had seemed amiss that day, and Martin and his friend had completed the long and exhausting climb, which included freezing gales and almost vertical ice faces, without too much trouble. Elated but exhausted, they spent half an hour on the summit before beginning their descent. Every bit as challenging as the ascent, Martin suddenly felt his crampons slip from under him. Before he'd even had time to register his feet going, he was over the edge and falling. Things happened pretty quickly after that.

Most of us, if we are lucky, don't ever get to fall very far. Those who do, who fall any real distance, find out just how powerful a force gravity is. If you weigh about 12.5st and drop just ten metres, you'll be going faster when you hit the ground than Usain Bolt was when he set the 100m world record. Fall 26 metres – less than the length of your local swimming pool – and you could get a speeding ticket in a 50mph zone. Fall as far as Martin did, somewhere around 90 metres, and, if you don't hit anything on the way down then gravity will accelerate you to the point that you'll be travelling at over 90mph.

Fortunately for Martin, it was merely a terrifyingly steep slope rather than a sheer drop; a few degrees can make all the difference. Rocketing down the mountainside, pitching off rocks and snow, he somehow managed to swing an ice axe into the ground and bring himself to a shuddering halt close to a deep vertical drop. Cut, bruised, shaken, but miraculously still alive, Martin and his partner were forced into an exhausting trek through the forest to get back to the car. With snow falling and night closing in, Martin had to rest often and began to believe he might not make it off the mountain alive. Pulling together his last ounces of strength, they dragged themselves back to the car park and began the two-and-a-half-hour drive to hospital.

Which is where things were about to get a great deal worse. Because if ice climbing was almost his death, it was football that had been Martin's life.

A softly spoken, thoughtful man, and a lifelong Evertonian who'd spent time in the club's academy, he'd devoted every waking moment to the game since childhood. 'I loved playing,' he says. 'I knew I wasn't good enough to turn professional, but that never stopped the dream. Football's in my blood. Coaching was always the ultimate goal.' Determined to make the game his career, Martin chose to study sports technology and management at university, intending to parlay his skills into coaching. In between studying, he turned out for the university team and semi-professionally for Stafford Town, where he'd made his lone FA Cup appearance against a team that included an ageing, post-injury David Busst. Meanwhile, he'd begun his coaching badges, getting hours under his belt in academy camps and clinics for Wolves and Aston Villa.

After graduation, Martin found work as a project manager while he continued to develop his coaching skills. At the time he was in a long-distance relationship – his girlfriend was American – and it became clear that, if they were to make it work and get married, he'd have to move to the US. It was a big decision for someone who still cherished going to Everton games with his dad, but, following his heart, Martin put his ambitions on hold and immigrated to California.

At first it seemed idyllic. 'I loved the weather, loved the people,' he says. 'I was living by a lake, an hour from the mountains, two hours from the beach.' But there was a problem: American companies weren't interested in his UK work experience. Ironically, while he had had to work in project management because of the paucity of paid coaching roles in the UK, he found that, in the US, he couldn't work as a project manager, but he could walk into a gig coaching football.

'In the US, football isn't a working man's game, it's a sport that affluent kids play,' he says. 'Those who aren't wealthy really struggle, even if they're better players. The industry is so different to the UK. Parents will pay hundreds of dollars a month for their kids to be part of a youth club – so they can have good training and compete locally and state-wide.'

Working for himself and others, Martin began coaching youth football, offering professional training programmes, developing curriculums, and coaching coaches. He coached for the California Youth Soccer Association and several feeder teams for San Jose Earthquakes. Along the way, he completed a master's degree in sports psychology, which he felt was essential to help coach effectively, especially young people. After that, he moved to Folsom Lake College, where he accepted the pleasurably grand title of professor of psychology and kinesiology. At Folsom, which is a community college – a type of US tertiary education institute that provides two-year courses, typically for those who left high school with few qualifications – Martin built up first the women's football team and then the men's, becoming its first head coach. Outside of coaching, he was also working on a doctorate in organisational leadership.

If it was the US where Martin found himself as a coach, though, it was Central America which deepened his appreciation for what the game can mean to people. In 2011, he was asked to lead a volunteer group to run a 'Festival de Futbol' for refugee children in Nicaragua. When he talks about it, his voice takes on a new passion and intensity.

'That's why it's the most rewarding thing I've done in coaching,' he says. 'Forget about the sport at the top level. It's the 99 per cent of people who can see great benefit in their lives by being involved in a sport that's organised and with coaches that care.'

Martin talks fervently about the social value of football. 'I think it's a key that can transform people's lives and give opportunities to them. You see it all around the world, even in the poorest places. Where kids don't have pitches, they play against walls. Where they don't have shoes, let alone boots, they play barefoot. There's one language in this world that's universal, and that's football.'

Martin and his team ran a week-long football school. 'We had 250 refugee children under the age of 18. Twenty of them were 16 to 18. I took them aside every morning and taught them how to coach the day's topics. Ball control, passing, dribbling, that sort of thing.

'We split the remaining kids up into years and then houses, and then the kids I'd coached would spend the afternoon coaching the teams. We did that Monday to Wednesday and then had a two-day tournament on the Thursday and Friday.'

Unlike Martin's work in California, this wasn't about preparing kids for a shot at the professional game. Here the aim was to create a joyful social event, something to involve children of all ages, boys and girls alike, and their parents, and bring a much-needed sense of community to people who'd experienced great hardship.

Martin didn't want this to be a one-off event – a brief feel-good moment for the kids and coaches. He wanted it to become a lasting part of their lives. So, while there, he put together a month-by-month coaching manual to allow the tuition to develop into an ongoing programme. It's this kind of organisation and structure, he is convinced, that, when combined with belief among coaches, builds resilience and self-worth in players.

When he returned home, Martin set up a charity to finance a return trip the following year. This time he brought donated kit and boots from clubs all over California. Many of the same kids returned, this time bringing their parents, and, to his joy, it was clear they'd been keeping up with his coaching programme.

In ten years, he'd gone from semi-pro footballer in the West Midlands to an experienced, senior coach whose work – charitable and professional – was earning him acclaim around the US.

And that's when he fell off a cliff. The initial damage didn't seem too bad and he was back coaching in no time. But then Martin began to suffer from cloudy vision. Sometimes if he overheated, his vision would go completely and he'd be temporarily blinded by whiteouts.

His ophthalmologist couldn't find the problem and so referred him for an MRI. Martin had been googling his symptoms for a while, so he already had an idea, but it was still a hammer blow when the neurologist gave him the news. There were lesions on his brain; this fit young man, who, when he wasn't on the football pitch, was swimming in lakes or climbing mountains, had multiple sclerosis.

'I'd had a near fatal car crash ten years before,' says Martin. 'My doctor told me that probably did the damage and then my fall overloaded my system and triggered everything.'

At the same time, his marriage had broken down. Suddenly, everything he'd worked so hard to build for himself was under threat. The Californian sun that he'd revelled in was oppressive and damaging to his health, and the country that had welcomed his skills and allowed his career to flourish was now an unaffordably expensive place to have a chronic illness.

Deciding to start afresh again, he got divorced, quit his job, put his doctorate on hold and moved back to the Wirral.

Despite his life being turned upside down, Martin was characteristically positive and proactive, contacting the

English FA and local county associations even before he'd packed his bags in the US. There was a problem, though. For all Martin's professional skills, the FA didn't recognise his US coaching badges. 'I'd coached at a very high standard,' he says. 'UEFA recognised the badges, just not the FA.'

Having worked at college and professional level, he found his decade of experience in the US was deemed effectively worthless at home and he would have to go back to the start, unpaid, and work his way up. For someone who was no longer a recent graduate without responsibilities or a lifestyle to maintain, this just wasn't realistic.

'I wanted to continue coaching, which has always been my number one love and the best job I'd ever had,' he says. 'Having to give that up in the US was devastating. But to then find the FA wouldn't help me transition across was a slap in the face. To be told everything I'd done was worthless felt like a betrayal.'

If he couldn't earn a living in coaching, Martin was at least determined to use the skills he'd acquired in understanding, motivating and developing people's talents. He retrained as a teacher, doing a PGCE in design and technology, and began teaching in a secondary school on the Wirral. He also met and married a woman he'd gone to school with, herself also a teacher. They had a daughter and his wife had two children from her previous marriage. When his daughter was born, she was nine weeks premature, with serious health problems. Another of the family's children has a rare genetic condition, cri-du-chat syndrome, which affects fewer than 100 people in the UK. Both need round-the-clock support, which means Martin's wife put her career on hold to care for the family.

Ever practical and energetic, Martin threw himself into helping run a support group for cri-du-chat. He became a trustee of the charity and works on fundraising initiatives.

A proud father and family man, he wasn't one to bemoan his own health problems – or those of his adored children – nor the loss of his coaching career. But, for the first time since he could walk, football wasn't a regular part of his life. He loved teaching, but it was as if there was a football-shaped hole in him.

At which point, he came across OwnaFC.

'When I saw an advert saying I could become a shareholder in a football club, I thought, yeah, there's a massive hole that needs to be filled,' Martin says. It wasn't just the idea of being a part-owner that attracted him. Here was a chance to be involved in something new, and maybe even to be able to stick it to the FA.

'I thought maybe here's an opportunity, that, long term, might move me back into football,' he adds. 'I wouldn't have to start right at the beginning and all those skills I'd developed as a coach and director of football, I might be able to use them here.'

Martin wasn't the only one who read about OwnaFC and felt it call to him. It turned out there were a lot of people with a football-shaped hole of their own.

There was 21-year-old Michael Nye, who was working at a brick factory in Morecambe. A decent player when younger, injuries had set him back. Meanwhile, his local team, where he was a season ticket holder, had had a tumultuous ten years. A member of the Football League for over a decade, Morecambe were perpetually in danger of relegation. Long-term owner Peter McGuigan, who'd done some solid work, had finally tired of running a marginal club and put it up for sale in 2016. What followed was a tug-of-war so extraordinary it sounds like the distillation of the entire of the last 30 years of English football.

First, a Brazilian man in his 30s, Diego Lemos, had apparently bought the club – supposedly for somewhere in the region of £400,000. Little was known about him beyond his own claims to be an agent and to have a footballing pedigree that extended to multiple members of his family having played at a decent level, including an uncle who was in Brazil's 1974 World Cup squad.

Only a month after Lemos took over, though, Morecambe staff were paid late. A month after that, Lemos vanished – he would later be tracked down in Qatar. On buying Morecambe, Lemos had appointed Qatari businessman Abdulrahman Al-Hashemi to the board. He pretty rapidly appeared to be the only person actually propping the club up and soon walked out, claiming to have been misled by Lemos.

At this point, flamboyant Italian businessman Joseph Cala, about whom we'll hear more later, appeared on the scene claiming to have bought the club with backing from US investors. Lemos denied this, only to find that a tax consultant from Durham, Graham Burnard, who Lemos had used in his purchase of the club, was asserting that he in fact was the rightful owner. Burnard, now acting on behalf of Al-Hashemi, claimed that Lemos hadn't paid for the issue of shares in the company he used to buy Morecambe, leaving the advisor the majority owner of the company, and hence the club. A court battle followed, which Lemos lost. Left holding the baby, Burnard and Al-Hashemi stabilised the club before eventually selling it to its current owners, two southern-based businessmen who also own Worcester Warriors rugby club.[3]

If all this sounds crazy, it was exhausting for Michael and it distanced him from Morecambe. 'When I was younger, I used to go every week. But I did start to lose interest. These people don't care about the club, they probably don't even know where Morecambe is.'

With all this floating around, Michael saw an advert in November 2018 for OwnaFC. '"Do you want to own a club from as little as £99?" I thought, that's quite interesting.'

Newcastle-based accountant Liam Crowe felt the same. A son of a West Brom season ticket holder, Liam had been going to the football since he was four and had been a regular at away games since he was six. His family moved to the north-east when he was 12 and now, in his mid-20s, he was married, a new parent and was finishing his professional qualifications.

Another Owna who'd played a bit, Liam had had trials at Coventry and represented his county at cricket. 'I wasn't driven,' he says. 'I didn't push myself as a player. I'm driven at work, but I only ever really wanted to play and enjoy the game. Maybe if I'd pushed myself a bit more.'

With the demands on his time, Liam wasn't getting to many West Brom home games, though he still made some away ones. He felt vaguely discontented with much of football. 'Seeing clubs fold upsets me,' he says. 'What annoys me most is when you see how much money is being spent on older players when there are young players coming through in the Championship. Youngsters don't get promoted. You see teams getting round the homegrown player rules, with

Man City signing Scott Carson or Richard Wright. It makes a mockery of the whole idea.'

Like so many Ownas, despite the game being on television seemingly continuously, Liam was missing football. He felt an outsider to it. 'I would've done anything to be involved,' he says. 'I've looked at coaching and refereeing courses for when my kid's a bit older. Especially if you've had experience of playing at a young age, it's always something you want to be involved in.'

So when Liam saw the BBC article, he was in right away. 'It was about ten minutes between seeing the article and signing up, to be honest,' he says. 'They were saying there were not many shares left, so I thought: get in before they go.'

David Anderson, a Glasgow prison officer, was a bit more circumspect, but he too felt the emotional pull of OwnaFC. A Celtic fan born and bred, David, like many Scottish supporters, was not happy with how the game is run. 'Celtic are out of touch with their fans. I don't have any say in it. I'm just a number who pays his £500 a season,' he says. 'I'd like to be more involved in football, but Celtic are too big for that.'

So the idea of having a second team, a team he could really have a voice in – and one outside the confines of Scottish football – appealed to him. A chance to get involved in something of his own.

What seems to unite these people – and most of the Ownas we spoke to – was the desire to feel like they had a stake in football. For some, it may have been a way to recapture former glories or frustrated ambitions; for others, an attempt to arrest the gradual drift away from the game that adulthood, work and families often cause.

In David's case, it seemed like a natural complement to his other big interest: American football. David is one of the top fantasy football players in Europe. To those only familiar with soccer-based fantasy football, this might not sound like a big deal. But in the US, where sports gambling was illegal until recently, the money in NFL fantasy football can be huge. In 2018 alone, David won over $100,000. He would often spend 30 hours a week doing research and was considering leaving his job to go full-time. The idea of matching this with an investment in a small football club, to which he could devote his energy and give something back, seemed perfect.

David, Liam, Michael, Martin and thousands of others signed up to the footballing revolution. While they came to OwnaFC with similar needs, their aims and ambitions for the project varied widely.

'I just wanted an experience of running a football club,' says Liam. He wanted to be involved in signing players. 'Not scouting,' he says. 'But, say, the scouting network brings a player forward, you read the report and then vote on if to sign him.' He was similarly interested in having a say on ticket prices and other commercial decisions, like what food would be sold at the ground.

'I saw a documentary on Salford,' he says. Like many lower-division fans, he's no fan of the club run by former Manchester United greats. 'But it showed me all the things that the owners need to think about that I'd not considered.'

One thing he was clear about, though, was that he didn't want to be involved in on-pitch decisions. 'You might just end up with six players up front!' he says. 'In my head, we would decide on the manager rather than pick the team ourselves.'

Michael Nye saw things similarly. For him, it was always about strategic, off-field direction rather than on-field involvement. 'I thought it would be small decisions,' he says. 'I wouldn't want to get involved with hiring or firing managers, because 1,000 people voting on that wouldn't be fair. That's what you have a manager for. I mean, if I were a football manager, I'd want control over my team and a say over transfers. I wouldn't want to go to the board and say, "I want this" and them say, "Hang on, let's get all these people to vote on it." I'd want actual experts there to make that decision.'

Martin Roberts, who'd signed up in January 2019, when the price was £99 – rather than the later £49 – came to it with bigger ambitions than many Ownas. 'I thought there was a chance we could do something different. I felt if I was going to get involved in a club, I'd want more of a say than just handing my money over. So the way this was marketed ticked my boxes. Day-to-day influence over operations, management, administration.'

He also imagined OwnaFC as the kind of project where people could contribute according to their levels of interest and experience. A natural volunteer, Martin immediately contacted OwnaFC's founder, Stuart Harvey, to offer his services. Harvey seemed interested and requested Martin send him his CV, which he did.

Martin was impressed by Harvey. 'He came across as someone who wanted to make a difference,' he says. 'He wanted to make an impact and show the football industry that it can be done differently with like-minded people. He seemed open-minded. He admitted he didn't know everything about football operations and wanted to hear my thoughts.'

Other Ownas had wondered if they might get more than just a say over the running of a club. Liam already had one eye on making some money. 'I wondered about the potential for profit,' he says. 'It was £49. If it was successful, it was likely the shares would rocket in price.'

To his regret, he signed up immediately. 'I looked on the website and that was about as much looking into it as I did, to be honest,' he says. 'Normally I'm quite scam-aware, I look in great detail. I think it might have been because it was on the BBC, I thought, "They put it on there, they will have done their own checks."'

Liam wasn't the only one. In addition to a wave of publicity, OwnaFC had a slick-looking website, a working app, a professionally designed brochure and a presence on all the major social channels, including company videos on YouTube.

'The website looked quite classy,' says Liam. 'It looked refreshing. It looked pretty professional. I thought, "49 quid well spent!"'

David, like Martin, joined in January. 'I first saw OwnaFC on a Facebook ad. I'm naturally cautious so, rather than just diving in, I researched the website, to see if it was genuine,' he says. 'Then I sent them an email with questions.'

This led to a detailed conversation with Harvey about the technicalities of the business. Among other things, David wanted to know if his shareholding would be transferable and to get assurances that buying in wouldn't create an open-ended obligation to any debts a club might have.

'I wasn't worried about the cost,' he says, 'I just didn't want to get conned. There were a few things on the website where I didn't understand what they meant. They did try to answer my questions which made me think that, if there were problems in future, I had something in writing.'

Given how interesting he found the whole idea, £99 seemed to him like a reasonable risk. 'I thought I'm happy to get involved,' he says. 'If I lose the money, I lose the money. I'm prepared to take the element of risk.'

Michael, too, understood this wasn't a sure thing. 'I didn't sign up straight away, but when it went down to £49 I thought, "They're obviously needing people."' Michael figured that if enough people bought in, it could work.

'The only thing that was off with it,' he says, 'is that it seemed almost too good to be true.'

He wasn't wrong.

3

A childhood dream

Perhaps surprisingly for a man determined to revolutionise football, the game was not Stuart Harvey's big sporting love. That was rugby league. He gave years of his life to it.

BORN IN 1979, Harvey grew up in the Wigan area. By his own account, he was introduced to rugby league at primary school in Orrell, beginning a 25-year career across three continents which never quite caught fire. A scrum-half, at one time or another he had trials for Swinton and Hunslet Hawks, before moving to Australia. There, he turned out for semi-pro sides in Queensland and Western Australia,[4] supporting himself by working as a project manager for a fire safety company.

There, as here, he didn't make it and returned home. It was 2008 and he was in his late 20s. He wasn't ready to give up, though. Founding his own fire safety business, Harvey continued to pursue his rugby. In 2009, he had trials for

London Skolars, where he was part of the winning team in that year's Veneto 9s international nine-a-side tournament. His success wasn't to last, however, and his time in London ended after he suffered a career-limiting injury at Skolars. He bounced back two years later, though, when he turned up in the US as the coach for the semi-pro New Jersey Turnpike Titans, in the inaugural season of the USA Rugby League.

Expectations were high, with one profile claiming that 'Stuart Harvey has an impressive resume, playing all over the world ... During his career he has also coached a number of sides both in conditioning and fitness as well as preparing teams with training sessions and pre-season schedules.'[5]

Some of the hype may have appeared justified when the Turnpike Titans opened their season with a 36-16 away win against the Boston 13s. The match reporter noted, 'Credit goes to coach Stuart Harvey who has done an impressive job getting the Titans prepared for their season kickoff.'[6]

Sadly, though, that first game was the high point. The season soon tailed off and the Titans, who played their home games in Jersey City, just across the Hudson River from the tip of Manhattan, lost their seven remaining fixtures, finishing second-last in the league and folding.

Other than some short-lived junior coaching in the northwest of England, that, it seemed, was it for Harvey and rugby. As he would later reflect, 'Eventually, you realise that you aren't good enough for the pro ranks but I have always kept my interest and love for the game.'[7]

Anyone who has had some sporting talent, enough that at some point there seemed a genuine possibility of making it as a pro, will be able to recall the moment they knew it wasn't going to happen for them. For most people it comes somewhere between the ages of about 11 and 18. For some it's a decisive end; they put it behind them and get on with finding a day job and thinking about their futures. For others, it lingers a little, a flame that burns ever lower but is never quite extinguished. Perhaps they go into coaching and maraud around the Sunday leagues, dominating pub teams with a technique and intensity that shames their team-mates. A very small number, though – a rare breed – never give it up. They train and play like the call may still come, could come at any moment, even a decade or more after everyone else has accepted the end. Stuart Harvey was one such person. And so, even when sport was finished with him, he wasn't finished with sport.

Rugby had left its mark on Harvey. Compact, broad-shouldered and muscly with a nose that had seen a few breaks, he was a powerful presence. A born salesman, filled with self-assurance and a belief that he could convince people to trust him, he was a dominating force in conversation. A sports obsessive who followed boxing, horse racing, football and more, he knew how to speak to his target audience.

On the same day as the BBC profile of OwnaFC, he managed to get some more favourable coverage in the form of a two-and-a-half minute piece on the ITV news bulletins in north-west England. Facing coverage every bit as gentle as that of the national broadcaster, he had free rein to expound upon his revolution.

Interviewed at his local non-league ground, Ashton Town, where his friendship with the chairman Mark Hayes allowed him to be pictured in a football environment, he said, 'It's to enable a group of people, like-minded people, football-minded people from across the country and across the globe to come together and replace the outdated chairman. A childhood dream is to own a football club but we're just working-class people, we could never afford a football club.'

That it wasn't necessarily his childhood dream wasn't important. He knew there were thousands for whom it was.

Always an active user of social media, publishing pieces on his vision for OwnaFC on LinkedIn and answering questions on Twitter, Harvey's inexhaustible energy began to display itself. He was everywhere, engaging potential customers, giving business updates and answering every critic he came across.

There were teething problems, however. The BBC article was generating traffic at such a volume that OwnaFC's server went down on Friday, 1 March. It didn't stop people visiting the website or downloading the app – which was free – but it meant people weren't able, for a few hours, to pay their £49 and become a co-investor in the future of football.

'We are currently having technical difficulties due to the unforeseen volume of registrations,' Harvey announced. 'Boardroom decisions will be paused.'

'The boardroom' was the area of the app reserved for customers where, it was promised, details of the scheme, information about target clubs and decision-making took place. ('You will have full access to pre-sale documents and takeover proposals,' the company brochure claimed. 'You will decide which deal to close and which club we take forward.') Server migration would take place that same evening, Harvey promised, and any technical problems people were experiencing would be resolved. Until then, he said, no decisions would be made and so no one would miss out on the chance to have their say.

While the app was struggling under the weight of people's desire to join, the explosion in popularity highlighted another issue with it: while people could message the support function, there wasn't a general space where Ownas could discuss their hopes and dreams for the project. The moment OwnaFC had come into the public eye, people had begun to speculate about candidate clubs and even in some cases to invite OwnaFC to buy their teams.

Faced with more conversation than Twitter could accommodate, Harvey okayed the request of some Ownas to start an 'official' Facebook group, creating a space where people could communicate about OwnaFC without having to involve it. This would prove a fateful decision.

As questions and comments flooded in, Harvey began to expound on his plans. He announced a proposed vote on a club takeover was being postponed until the following Wednesday (6 March) owing to 'the server going down and the legals plus another club coming into the picture'. This sparked a welter of conjecture about the target clubs.

Overnight, the server migration took place and app functionality was restored. Early the next day, Harvey announced, 'It was tough having 2,000 sign up in 24 hours and crash the server.' He went on to praise his technical team for solving the problem.

It was working; 2,000 people signing up at £49 each is £98,000. Off the back of a single BBC article, he'd got nearly £100,000 of investment in just a day.

Meanwhile, some more sceptical voices were demanding more details of his plan. Harvey was keen to assure people that this was more than real-life *Football Manager* to him. He had ambitious plans both on and off the pitch for whichever club was bought.

He said he intended to create 15 new roles in the club to 'replicate that of a Premier League football club'. Harvey would, he said, 'Implement full processes and procedures in areas of events management, sponsorship, marketing, finance, psychology, analytics, scouting all at no cost to the staff.'

This was no mean promise for a business intending to take over a club with a budget of up to £8.5m a year. When people questioned how this could be achieved without incurring significant debts, Harvey assured everyone the venture would pay for itself. 'A financial investment into the infrastructure of the club that will allow the club to create revenue centres that will bring profitability and long-term revenue streams to the club planning for long-term stability,' he said.

Further, he was keen to invest in the football side of the club, claiming he would 'create a player pathway for all age groups and abilities by utilising the skill set and professionalism of the community club and enhancing and supporting that same business model and allowing them to be part of the advisory group steering the club forward'.

Chris Sharp, a sports therapist with Burton Albion, questioned OwnaFC's claim that it could get 500 kids in its youth system. 'Just to put that number into context,' said Chris, 'at the club I work for, you'd have to combine all of the academy, advanced development and development centre players from under-eights to under-18s to reach the 500-player figure. Bear in mind that's a pro club, how many non-league sides could accommodate [that]?'

Responding as rapidly as he was able to questions and, by his own admission, with his writing hampered by his dyslexia, Harvey's precise meaning wasn't always clear, but he seemed to intend a significant expansion of coaching and backroom staff at a level where many clubs are run on a shoestring.

Pressed by critics on how the club could generate the additional revenue to deliver on his vision, Harvey claimed that he expected 10,000 Ownas to attend three games a year, each bringing two friends, producing £900,000 in extra annual income for the club.

Football journalist Ron Walker was incredulous at this. 'If you get 10,000 people to bring two full-paying friends to one game at any club, let alone in non-league, well you should probably be working in fan engagement for Real Madrid,' he said.

Harvey did not take kindly to this and, while he eventually admitted that the 15 extra jobs would be graduates 'wanting work experience' rather than established, paid professionals, he allowed some frustration to surface. As Walker pressed his claim that Harvey's plans weren't realistic, Harvey responded with a volley of abuse, including 'Ron, are you over 16?'; 'Ron avoids facts, do not be like Ron'; and 'What do you do Ron? You don't like answering questions do you? How old are you?'

If there was one thing that really got Harvey's goat, though, it was people repeatedly bringing up similarities with the MyFootballClub experiment at Ebbsfleet a decade before. In some ways, he ought to have been flattered by the comparison; after all, it had attracted over 30,000 paying members and raised over £500,000 in its first ten days. Harvey, it seemed, was on course to beat this, but in hindsight Ebbsfleet's achievements might merit congratulation rather than disparagement. Setting up and running the scheme was a great deal harder back then and yet they'd bought a club – for £635,000 – and, as they promised, given fans a chance to have a say in picking the team, player sales and kit designs. Shortly after the takeover, Ebbsfleet had even won the FA Trophy. By the end of the first year, though, it became clear that there was a problem with the model. Rather than a one-off share purchase, Ebbsfleet owners were expected to pay an annual subscription of £35. Come time for renewals, many didn't, with 5,000 of the original members never making a second payment. The painful truth was that, though MyFootballClub had delivered pretty much everything it promised, there was a strong novelty appeal which faded extremely fast. Within a few years, member numbers had fallen below 1,500 and in 2013 the remaining owners voted to hand a majority holding to the supporters' trust.[8]

Harvey was adamant that OwnaFC wasn't going the same way. He made the point, fairly, that MyFootballClub didn't have smartphones or modern web technology to help them. Indeed, until Ebbsfleet fans voted to abandon picking the team, it was done by people emailing in their selections – an impossibly cumbersome procedure. Clearly the options for engagement and communication would be better now. In his view, it was this – 'the lack of day-to-day involvement' – that caused interest to wane and the project to fail.

Not everyone was convinced. Some pointed out that Ebbsfleet, for all the publicity, hadn't seen a significant increase in their gates – still the primary revenue source for most non-league clubs. Meanwhile, sports journalist David Byrom, an Ebbsfleet fan, said, 'If [OwnaFC] think the only thing wrong with MyFC was the lack of an available app, then they've completely failed to do the basic research and this project will go the same way as MyFC. MyFC nearly destroyed us and I wouldn't wish anything similar on any club.'

Harvey attempted to address every criticism, but it was a difficult day for him. He seemed hamstrung by his conviction that, if they would just listen, everyone would see it his way. This, of course, isn't how it works in any field of endeavour, least of all football.

Having tried and failed to convince his sceptics, Harvey's cause got a well-timed boost when Wigan Athletic legend Pascal Chimbonda tweeted out a photo of him with the app on his phone. 'Had the chance to look at the @OWNAFC app today and it looks good,' he said. 'Good luck all Owners.' This minor coup may have occurred because Chimbonda had just signed for Harvey's friend Mark Hayes's team, where he played four games.

The big news of the day was still to come, though: the identity of OwnaFC's current target club.

If the OwnaFC launch campaign was going pretty well – and pieces would soon appear in *The Sun* and *The Times*, along with dozens of sports websites cannibalising the BBC piece – there was a growing pushback from a small group of unhappy football fans and campaigners. Were this a Premier League club under discussion, they felt, a great deal more due diligence would be being done. And so, as so often happens these days, private individuals began to do the job that the press wasn't.

Many took particular umbrage at the way the language of fan ownership was being co-opted by a private business. Fan ownership, after all, means ownership by existing fans of the club. To their eyes, what OwnaFC was proposing was little different to standard club ownership, where a rich outsider swoops in and buys up a club, heedless of its history and heritage.

Others objected to the idea of fans having control of the team on and off the pitch, as if this were no more than a computer game. Still others were concerned about the financial viability of the scheme. Even further down the English pyramid, the living ain't cheap.

Behind the admittedly slickly designed website, app and brochure, it was notable that the company hadn't published a business plan, let alone detailed financial projections. At first glance, the numbers sound big. Thousands of people all paying £49 totals up nicely, right?

Except, we're most of us pretty poor at dealing with large numbers, struggling to visualise the difference between orders of magnitude. As we'll look at later, valuing football clubs is notoriously difficult, but OwnaFC's target – a club which owned its own ground and was debt-free – wouldn't come cheap. Not least because not many really are self-sustaining. Clubs that meet those criteria but also operate with a budget of £8.5m, which is high-end League One money, are rarer still. These are the kinds of clubs with a history and a trophy cabinet, albeit one that hasn't seen many recent additions.

Harvey had mentioned 10,000 investors. Again, it sounds big, but at £49 a head, that's not even £500,000 – and you don't get a lot of club for that. In fact, even if there were 100,000 people signed up, a veritable army, that's only £4.9m. There's a reason that football's a rich person's game.

While the pitch seemed clear – we chip in together to buy and run a club – the details were hazy. In the BBC piece, Harvey had alluded to his company retaining 51 per cent of the football club, implying some other source of funds. (Since most clubs don't make any money or pay any dividends, very few have multiple owners. It would, for example, be highly unusual to find someone prepared to sell you 51 per cent of the club, leaving them with a significant minority holding.)

But the company's terms and conditions made no mention of other investors. And the more you looked, the more Harvey's statements appeared contradictory. Was he selling equal shares in a company that would buy a football club? Or were Ownas to be business partners with an anonymous individual or individuals? In fact, just how much was Harvey himself putting in? If he was selling 9,999 of the 10,000 £1 shares in his business, with the aim of owning and running a football club, what investment, if any, had he made?

Nothing about the company's financial position was clear. What other money did the company have? How many paid staff were there? Harvey surely hadn't designed and built everything himself. Moreover, what other costs did the business have? And were fan investments being ring-fenced for the purchase of the club?

The first port of call in these situations is Companies House, which is a hugely useful resource for anyone seeking information about who owns companies and their financial position. OwnaFC Ltd had been founded less than a year before, in July 2018. It had just one director and shareholder – Stuart Harvey, who owned all 10,000 of its shares. In other words, it was essentially a blank canvas. It hadn't been trading long enough to file any accounts, so there was no clue as to its financial position.

Harvey himself was also listed as the director of a second company, however: RightTrades Management Limited. This was a slightly more interesting proposition. Founded in the middle of 2017, the business, which was a smaller version of tradesman-finding sites like Rated People and Checkatrade, had already filed its first-year accounts. These showed a seemingly healthy financial position, with the company having assets at the end of the year of over £220,000. However, because of its size, the company didn't have to file full accounts, meaning there was no indication of the business's turnover or profitability. Its status ('micro-entity') and its average number of employees in its first year (two) seemed to suggest that Harvey was not quite the successful businessman he liked to make out. If he was a man of significant wealth or of expertise in sports management, it wasn't apparent.

As ever, Harvey was unabashed. Following questions about his business model, he made contact with James Cave, who had published critical comments about OwnaFC through his Against League 3 campaign. The result was a wide-ranging nine-hour written interview, which Cave published on Wednesday, 3 March.[9]

Cave, who has long experience of both lower-league football and the mechanics of club ownership, wanted answers about just what people were getting for their money. Were customers buying a stake in Harvey's company or just in the football club?

'The company has 10,000 shares available, [all] of which will be allocated to OWNAS,' replied Harvey. 'I will dilute shareholding to OWNAS as and when they come onboard and [they] will be equal shareholder[s] in the football club. The shareholders will own the football club in its entirety.'

He went on to reject concerns about what happens to the existing fans of the purchased club. 'This model is COMPLETE community ownership,' he insisted.

When asked about all the new roles he'd be hiring for at the club, Harvey seemed to suggest that the people were all ready to go. 'This is a deal already agreed,' he said.

On the question of fans making all the decisions, however, he seemed to resile from the bold claims in the brochure that 'the club will be under YOUR full control, with every decision brought to your fingertips … with the funds used however YOU see fit to deliver success'.

Now he said, 'OWNAS do not have any say over what happens on the training ground, this is the manager's job.' He went on, '[Planning training] is a job for the manager to carry out … but OWNAS reserve the right to advise on dates and times to ensure they can visit the club just like any owner would do. They can plan sessions at the beach, plan sessions in warm weather camp.'

Asked about the headline 'up to £8.5m annual budget' figure, which was still being advertised on the website and social media feeds, Harvey said, '[This] was done with a league club in mind before we changed tactics due to huge debts within these clubs. The expected budget per year with clubs we are talking to will be approx. £2.5m.'

'So the £8.5m figure on the site is indeed currently incorrect?' asked Cave.

'No,' Harvey replied. 'It is very much correct as stated above.'

When later questioned about this on Twitter, Harvey doubled down on this, saying that the budget was now £2m, but that '£2m is up to £8.5m'.

At this point, Cave returned to the structure of the business, pointing out that community-owned clubs are rarely limited companies. As MyFootballClub was, they are more usually 'community benefit societies', which are prohibited from paying out profits to members. He asked, 'So out of the 10,000 shares you have in OwnaFC Limited, you will sell up to 9,999 of them, and will put yourself in a position where your directorship can be terminated by vote?'

In other words, who was really in control? Was this Harvey's project, or was he just setting something up to hand over to others? His answer was unmistakable. 'Yes,' Harvey said, '100 per cent that will be done. This is a concept I have founded. If I get voted out then this is fine.'

A close reading of OwnaFC's terms and conditions, however, suggested that the company wasn't quite the exercise in community democracy that it was being presented as. There was, for example, a puzzling clause in the refunds section. 'No refunds are offered or given for any reason other than if a takeover is not completed within three months of a club accepting our offer. If no offer is made to a football club by 01/06/2019 then refunds will be offered.'

In other words, once you'd paid your £49 for a share in the business, there was no way of getting it back for any other reason than if the business failed to make an offer for a club by June or, having had an offer made, failed to complete the deal within three months. This absence of a cooling-off period or a no-quibble refund appeared at odds with standard online purchases. How could this be legal, people asked?

The answer, buried further in the T&Cs, was that OwnaFC was claiming an opt-out from standard distance selling regulations on the basis that this was a 'personalised' product. This seemed a stretch as the opt-out was designed to protect businesses selling products that couldn't be returned and resold – things like an engraved necklace, a wedding cake or a family portrait. Given OwnaFC was selling a generic phone app and, presumably later, a share certificate, it was hard to see how they would be entitled to say 'sorry, no refunds!' any more than, say, a book shop or video-streaming service.

It also came to light that, in mid-December 2018, the day after OwnaFC put its pre-order facility live, a dozen Twitter accounts had sprung into existence and begun vigorously recommending to people that OwnaFC might be the perfect Christmas present for loved ones. All 12 accounts were created on the same day, used the same link-shortening service, instead of the company URL, and then failed ever to tweet again. The creation of fake internet accounts to promote a company's own products is illegal and the OwnaFC would later deny being behind the deception. Instead, they blamed an unnamed marketing agency 'company in the north-east' who they claimed to have fired.

In truth, though, no one was yet paying much attention to all this. Because something much more interesting had emerged – the identity of the target club, a club who OwnaFC claimed to be in advanced negotiations with.

The digital consortium was about to enter the real world.

4

Beware of geeks bearing gifts

Every Saturday during the football season,
the motorway service station at Norton Canes
fills up with football supporters twice a day.

A FAMILIAR scene plays out with every busload of supporters that arrives ('40 minutes, all right lads?'). About ten of the party, the smokers, set up camp by the front door. The group with the fashionable jackets will head off to the slot machines by the entrance. Half the coach rushes to the toilets. The shy lad who travels alone stands quietly in the queue at WH Smith for a sausage roll and a bottle of Lucozade.

On the return leg, the victors are easily spotted against the losers. Those who are having an impromptu kickabout against the Millwall fans in the car park with a drinks bottle probably don't support the same team as the gentlemen with furrowed brows huddled outside Costa blaming their defeat on someone called Trevor Kettle.

While the fans come and go every week at Norton Canes, a few miles away lies an incredible football club they've probably never heard of – passed and missed by thousands of supporters every week.

Hednesford is built on coal, both literally and figuratively. The town sits on the huge Cannock Chase Coalfield, an area of approximately 10,000 acres. While the sheer size of the coalfield is hard to envisage, it is helpful to consider that two acres are roughly the size of a football pitch.

There is evidence of settlers in Hednesford as early as AD1153, and by the 1500s the area's population was no larger than 50 people. The land was predominantly agricultural until the start of the 19th century, when mines started to emerge.

The Industrial Revolution saw coal become an essential commodity, and operations of the newly formed Hednesford Colliery Company attracted newcomers to the area. By 1861 the population of Hednesford reached 500. Twenty years later it was somewhere between 6,000 and 7,000. The Census for 1881 shows over 50 per cent of male villagers were employed in mining.

The local football team, Hednesford Town, was initially formed in 1880 following a merger of two other sides. Echoes of the club's history are dotted throughout the town.

When stepping off the train at Hednesford station, you are immediately faced by the Anglesey Hotel. This was the site of the club's first pitch, named 'The Tins' due to the metal sheeting surrounding the playing surface.

As you continue to walk down the main road, you'll eventually encounter the Cross Keys Inn. The pub is the oldest building in Hednesford, dating from 1746. From 1904 to the mid-1990s the club played just over the road. The pub is still owned by former player Chris Brindley, who won the FA Trophy with Hednesford in 2004.

Finally, you approach Keys Park, the current home of the Pitmen. It was built in 1995 for £1.3m – not a small sum for a club playing in the seventh tier of English football.

But, let's be clear. The sun is not breaking through the trees, dappling the pitch on an unusually warm spring morning. The Anglesey, with its rustic architecture, now houses a Wetherspoon pub. The Cross Keys Inn flies a skewed, dilapidated CAMRA banner on its faded exterior. It is wet. It is cold. It is windy.

It's an irrefutable scientific fact that the coldest place in the UK is the immediate one-mile radius of any non-league football match. So you should have brought your big coat.

Keys Park, though, stands up as one of the best facilities in the division. The stadium boasts cover on all four sides, and a sizeable main stand with changing rooms, offices of a good standard and a club bar.

The most recent information on the club website suggests that Keys Park holds an FA Grade B rating, making it compliant with the regulations required to play in the league above. In the 2019/20 season, their average home league attendance was about 400, making them the seventh-best supported team in the division.

It is easy to see why Stuart Harvey saw Hednesford Town as a prime target for a takeover for OwnaFC.

For one thing, Steve Price, the club's owner of over 25 years, was ready to sell. He was fast approaching his 70s, and supporters were ready for a change in direction. Price had been invited to the club by a former chairman in the mid-1990s and carried himself as a private and stoic man.

During his time at Hednesford, Price had provided steady if unspectacular custodianship. Price had always ensured financial stability, but it felt like a period of gradual decline for a club that might've hoped to be a division higher up the pyramid.

The jewel in the crown of Price's tenure was undoubtedly the grand FA Cup adventure in 1996/97. Victories over Southport, Blackpool and York City saw the Pitmen drawn against Middlesbrough in the fourth round. On the biggest day in the club's history, Hednesford took an early lead before conceding an own goal to level the tie in the first half. With the game level at 85 minutes, a flurry of late goals saw Middlesbrough run out 3-2 victors.

Price's time also saw Hednesford lift the FA Trophy in 2004 at Villa Park. The competition, essentially 'the FA Cup of non-league', is usually dominated heavily by National League (then Conference) clubs. A Southern League Premier Division team lifting the trophy was a rare occurrence and an exceptional achievement.

A pyramid restructure rudely added another division above them in 2004/05 and the following 15 years saw the team shuffled between the Northern and Southern Premier Leagues with an occasional spell in the Conference North before the inevitable relegation.

That's not to say that Hednesford or Steve Price were necessarily doing anything wrong. Quite the opposite; the slow and steady security provided by Price was better than many clubs have. The team was capable of promotion to the Conference North, it just wasn't capable of staying there.

It's reasonably easy to identify the reasons why Hednesford were struggling to compete and progress. Even the quaintness of non-league was not immune to the changing commercial landscape of English football. Millionaire playboys were finding it was much cheaper to buy a non-league club and achieve a steady stream of promotions to the Football League than it was to buy an established club. Crawley Town, Fleetwood Town, Forest Green Rovers, Harrogate Town and Salford City all found wealthy backers while in non-league before achieving the coveted promotion to the EFL. Wrexham, now part of the Marvel Cinematic Universe, won't be far behind. But if your town is fresh out of wealthy backers with more money than sense, competing in the brutal financial landscape of non-league is your only option.

Firstly, your average non-league club will bring in approximately zero broadcast revenue. For the 2018/19 season, all Premier League clubs received an equal part of the broadcast deal to the tune of £34m for the English rights, and then received £43m each for the international rights. A further £4.9m was added for combined commercial rights, advertising and merchandise. This is before the £1.2m each club received every time they were televised. As the new proud owner of a non-league club, your visual coverage will be limited to a work-experience student filming the game on a Handycam and uploading some shaky highlights to YouTube.

The most significant regular income for your new club will be the money received on the gate, and it's here you start to realise how fragile non-league finances can be. While some National League clubs enjoy gates of several thousand, it's much more common to find crowds a little further down the pyramid of several hundred, each punter paying just a few quid. With this money you need to pay for the team, travel, rent, ground maintenance, the pitch, insurance, media costs, equipment and kit, staff, the bar, the catering. The list goes on and on.

If playing in National League North or South, for example, your team is required by the league to purchase several dozen branded footballs at the start of the season, at £75 each. This goes some way to explaining why the team's kit man is often nominated to chase wayward balls into next door's garden. If you lose more than a ball a game on average, then you have an expensive outlay at some point before the end of the season just to carry on training. These little costs can start to mount up.

Most clubs below the Football League can't make it work. By far the most common financial model in non-league is to attempt to lose as little money as possible on an annual basis so that the owner can inject cash and make up the shortfall. It's a model employed at hundreds of non-league clubs, and it was undoubtedly applied at Hednesford.

The sad reality is that not every team can produce sustained sporting success. Football is built on losers just as much as winners.

While financial security is welcome – never more so than when it's absent – 20 years of stagnation was enough for some fans. Relations between the supporters and the chairman were becoming strained. It was time to go.

So when OwnaFC arrived on the scene, it seemed like a marriage made in heaven. Harvey was desperate to buy, and Price was desperate to sell.

The club was listed for sale in 2018 for £1.25m with a local estate agent. For a deal including both the club and the stadium, it seemed a reasonable price. The stadium was built on prime development land, and for the last 20 years, new-build houses have slowly surrounded the site. Hednesford fans were aware that Taylor Wimpey, one of Britain's most-prominent house builders, had closely monitored the club's situation for some time.

With lofty ambitions and a growing subscriber base, Harvey had initially aimed high when searching for a club to buy. Given the marketing afforded to the headline budget of 'up to £8.5m', Coventry City was initially targeted for purchase – though it's unclear how much formal contact Harvey had with the club's infamous hedge fund owners SISU. On 3 January, a journalist from the *Derbyshire Times* announced he believed that Harvey had contacted Chesterfield.

On Twitter, Harvey publicly asked for representatives from Bangor City and North Ferriby to contact him. Stockport County and Billericay were also considered. The Ownas were understandably becoming restless, and Harvey desperately needed a club to start taking him seriously.

In February, OwnaFC announced it had made representations to Norman Smurthwaite at Port Vale. The exchange did not go well, with Harvey tweeting that he thought Smurthwaite was 'a disgusting human being' and that OwnaFC would, in future, be looking at non-league clubs. What Smurthwaite felt about the conversation is not known.

OwnaFC was first publicly connected to Hednesford Town on 1 March, on a post on the club's unofficial supporters' forum. In the saga of OwnaFC, it was an important day. It was the day that Hednesford announced they were in takeover negotiations with two interested parties and also that Cave and Harvey began their marathon Q&A session. The rumours and then disclosure that OwnaFC had finally found its club crashed the website again.

Ownas had previously had the chance to vote on the app on whether they would prefer some suggested targets. Billericay, Chesterfield, Port Vale and Coventry were mentioned, but Hednesford hadn't been discussed at all.

Don't forget, Ownas had been promised 'full access to pre-sale documents and takeover proposals'. It was they who would 'decide which deal to close and which club we take forward'.

The broken promises would look worse still when OwnaFC later claimed that, even as it was fanning the flames of publicity about a potential takeover, it had already made an offer for the club on 28 February. We shall return to the significance of this claim later.

Around 1 March, staff and volunteers at the club were informed that, yes, Hednesford Town was a takeover target for OwnaFC. The internal reaction was not hugely favourable, but dissenters were invited to speak to Stuart Harvey, who was due to attend a home match against Grantham Town the next day. Comparisons to MyFC were made immediately by those involved with the club.

Harvey met several Hednesford fans ahead of the game, starting with the offer of a drink before unloading a well-rehearsed sales pitch directed at the dubious non-believers. He had an answer for everything. Unfortunately, it didn't quite wash. On the supporters' forum, one poster said they had spoken to 15 or so fans at the game, finding only one in favour of the takeover.

Another recollected that Harvey arrived with no prior knowledge of the Hednesford Town Supporters' Association, giving fans reason to question his level of due diligence. In between rehearsing his grievances against Martin Calladine, Cave and Supporters Direct, Harvey spent a great deal of effort spinning what those in attendance referred to as his 'football fairy tale', and that anyone who remained unconvinced was offered Harvey's phone number to 'hypnotise' them.

Harvey had lofty ambitions for Hednesford. As he had on social media for potential recruits, he rolled out his promises to fans in person. A Premier League-standard staff would be quickly installed; 10,000 Ownas would attend three or four times a year. His mere presence would see advertising and sponsorship revenue increase exponentially. The adoption of the OwnaFC concept would instantly earn worldwide acclaim, fame and fortune. The sky was the limit, and all the club had to do was sell its soul to Stuart Harvey.

It's hard to know exactly how many subscribers OwnaFC had by this point. Harvey contradicted himself in a short time by suggesting in a forum post there were 3,650 subscribers but over 10,000, in a Q&A. Whatever the number, OwnaFC was a fair distance short of raising the £1.25m that the club was initially advertised for. Insiders with knowledge of the deal suggest that Price reconsidered the sale and was prepared to allow OwnaFC to buy just the club, excluding the stadium and the land from the agreement.

However, it was a conversation between Harvey and members of the first-team management where things began to unravel.

With the match against Grantham ending in a 2-0 win for Hednesford, Harvey met head coach Nicky Eaden and assistant manager Gary Hayward shortly afterwards. Exactly how the meeting went is known only to the three men who were present but suffice to say, it did not go well. With this meeting, and in the space of just several hours, Harvey lost the support of the club's manager and several figures who assumed roles as key advisors to Steve Price. Nevertheless, two days later, on the Monday afternoon, Price was still informing club personnel that negotiations were continuing with OwnaFC.

By 10.30pm the following day, the deal was dead.

Before Stuart Harvey had ever set foot in Hednesford, the club had confirmed they were negotiating with two interested parties, not just OwnaFC. So who else wanted to buy Hednesford Town?

Ahead of any contact between Harvey and Price, a local consortium of existing club personnel, academy staff and local businessmen had discussed launching a group bid to take over the club. The group included secretary Terry McMahon, local businessmen Paul Jones and Andy Whitehouse, former professional footballer Matthew Fryatt, and press officer and Hednesford Town FC Supporters' Association chairman

Scott Smith, among others. While the consortium had begun informal discussions before OwnaFC, matters accelerated on Harvey's arrival. At a final meeting on the Tuesday after the Grantham match, Price agreed to accept assistance from the group, but notably, the club was not sold. By one account, McMahon seemed partially satisfied with Owna's bid until actually coming into contact with Harvey.

Harvey was informed of the new arrangement by Price that same evening, and the pair agreed to issue a statement confirming the end of OwnaFC's interest in the club, which the club accidentally published an hour ahead of schedule.

The club announced on Wednesday morning, 'Hednesford Town Football Club and OWNAFC have come to a collective decision that the deal for OWNAFC to take over the football club will not go ahead. No further statement will be made in regards to this decision.'

In a message to Ownas via the app, Harvey confirmed, 'OWNAFC and Hednesford Town have come to a collective decision that the proposed deal for OWNAFC to take over the football club will not go to an OWNA vote.'

In the days following the collapse, Harvey took to the supporters' forum to issue some final thoughts, 'On behalf of OWNAFC, we believe that having met this local consortium, the club is in very good hands. They have some really big plans and will drive the football club in the right direction. I have absolutely no doubt that this is the best option for the football club, and this became very apparent last Thursday and then confirmed on Saturday when I was with them at the game v Grantham. My comments when I first met this group which I made in the meeting with secretary and the consortium was that, "This club would be better placed with them taking over rather than OWNA."

'The football club's staff have been great to deal with and we wish them all the best in building this model of which I fully support with the club.'

Harvey's assessment of the collapse does not match with the recollections of those involved with the deal.

Despite publicly saying that the staff were 'great to deal with', Harvey confirmed privately that his first action would have been to dismiss Nicky Eaden. One Owna alleged that Harvey called Eaden 'cancerous'. Eaden himself admitted that he would have resigned had the takeover been completed. Gary Hayward was also suitably unimpressed with Harvey. Hayward later suggested on the Hednesford forum, where he was known for his gloriously unvarnished opinions, that he submitted his resignation immediately after the Grantham game, with Eaden threatening to leave if Hayward did. As vivid as it is under-punctuated and spellchecked, Hayward's account of the day went, 'Lads I'll put the record straight we had a meeting with that Stuart Harvey bloke who in my opinion couldn't look me in the eyes by the way in the meeting, but the top and bottom of the meeting was he wanted full ownership of all signings deals etc. plus all other *** so I told him from me gaz Hayward to *** and I resigned after grantham game. Nicky [Eaden], he's the quiet one out of us 2, just said if Gaz goes he goes then majority of the players will leave then so we spoke to Steve price [the owner] about getting rid of the circus which again in my opinion was OWNAFC he then saw right through his motives and we as a group blocked him coming into hednesford.'

Several days later, Harvey was asked by an Owna in a Q&A whether attending the Hednesford's game was a mistake, as the Ownas had not been informed beforehand. Harvey replied, 'Not at all, I was invited by the owner, and I willingly accepted. The club had invited journalists down and I was happy to meet them. I was there as a guest and not a representative of OwnaFC.'

It would be very hard to find anyone who agreed both that this was true and that it was a meaningful distinction.

With OwnaFC's failed negotiation being played out in public, negative press was starting to emerge. Subscribers were growing anxious that no prospective club was in sight and concerns were raised about Harvey's demeanour on social media.

While the story was by no means over, the collapse of the Hednesford deal was the start of the end for OwnaFC.

5

Stuart Harvey AFC

For a business promising to radically
democratise football and give power to
ordinary fans, it soon became clear that only
one person's voice would be heard. All decisions
were final, unless he decided otherwise.

BEHIND THE scenes, many Ownas had already begun
to have doubts about the whole scheme. But, when the bid
for Hednesford Town collapsed, there was genuine shock.
It was a huge let-down from a business that, to the outside,
had seemed to be gathering momentum. For all the doubters,
many had felt like there was a decent chance Harvey might
pull it off. When he didn't, people started heading for the
exits.

On signing up, some Ownas had been disappointed
to find the 'boardroom' was quite bare. But after the BBC
article, as more people bought in, some activity had begun
to develop. 'Things started to happen, it started ramping up,'

says David Anderson. 'There seemed to be votes every day and more comments. It created a buzz, and I thought, "Okay, something is happening here."'

Michael Nye was also initially impressed. 'There were a few people involved in football at higher levels,' he says. 'The Scottish Premiership, for example, which made you think in different ways.'

But when votes did come up, they seemed unsatisfactory. Options seemed weighted to produce a desired outcome, or with insufficient information to make an informed decision.

'When we would get a vote on something,' says David, 'it would be like, "Here are three options, two are obviously rubbish and here's the good one." It was just the illusion that this was a decision. I started getting a bit disgruntled with that. There was a vote, "Where would you want the club to be: here, here or here?" Well people are going to vote for where they're closest to. I thought, that may not be the best option. Let's get the clubs, see what the options are and take it from there. All we got was "this club is based in the Midlands, this club has this size of stadium, it's in this league and has approximately this amount of debt". It was a very brief overview. I was looking for more detail to get my teeth stuck into. I wanted as much information as I could to make an informed decision. I felt more and more concern building up. Other people were starting to question things, why nothing was really happening.'

Another Owna said they'd decided it wasn't for them once the voting started. Like David, they didn't feel the location should be a primary concern, other than as it affected the potential crowd size. 'Only 17 per cent of the membership voted club debt as the most important thing to consider when buying a club,' they said. 'Surely 100 per cent should think this?'

Trust was already deteriorating before the bid failed. Speaking the day before, when the vote hadn't yet been cancelled, another Owna said, 'I honestly believe tomorrow we will get fobbed off with a story about another club and an NDA on financial information.' They complained they just couldn't get 'info we should be privy to as shareholders to approve a deal'.

Others began to suspect that OwnaFC wasn't being straight with them on the terms of the deal. 'I think the stadium is going to get leased back to the club in a Coventry-style shit storm and cause all sorts of problems,' said one Owna. 'I wanted the idea to work, but am very suspicious now.'

Later, David would reflect, 'A lot of time I felt like he was hiding behind NDAs. In hindsight, I don't even know if he was even talking to clubs. "I can't disclose information yet, the club don't want us to." I felt like he was just stringing us along. I think some Ownas felt like they were being railroaded. They started questioning a few things. Genuine questions, nothing out of line, no swearing, no name-calling. Just asking, "What's going on with this? Why is this happening?" Harvey took offence at this and blocked them from the app. He said, "We don't need negative people like this."'

Liam Crowe was also having doubts. 'I tried to turn a blind eye to criticism of OwnaFC,' he says. 'There will be negative reactions to it. It's not everybody's cup of tea. But then more and more came out and it snowballed ... People on Facebook were getting worried and that's when I started to take note of the negative reactions.'

After the initial burst of positive coverage, the football press proper was beginning to sharpen its quills.

On Monday, 4 March, just days before the Hednesford bid was sunk, Seb White published a piece in *Mundial* titled 'OwnaFC is not the answer to non-league football's problems'. Both a seasoned football writer and a member of a supporters' trust board for a non-league club, White produced a critique of the business that was much richer than the standard 'you can't have fans voting on everything' response. He decried the way the model would undermine the bond between fans, many of whom are volunteers, and their teams, implying it would be an anathema to non-league football.[10]

By this stage, Harvey had become a dervish on social media, treating any question as an offence and delivering responses which rapidly descended into personal attacks. Nicola Cave, who is married to James, and who worked at Supporters Direct (now with the Football Supporters' Association), set out her criticisms of OwnaFC, only for Harvey to imply that, having already spoken to James, he didn't need to hear from his wife. 'I am very open to speaking to the wife of the man who interviewed me for nine hours and who she shares an opinion with,' he said with evident sarcasm. When Nicola pointed out the clear sexist overtones of this, a new Twitter account appeared and accused her of '[playing] the sexism card when there is nothing else left to say'. OwnaFC duly retweeted the attack. The account, which followed only one other – OwnaFC – would attack Nicola again before vanishing two days later.

At the same time, Harvey was badgering his critics to appear against him in a live-streamed debate, sending them dates and locations and demanding they make themselves available to answer his questions. When the Caves, Calladine and others refused, troubled by the tone of his communications, Harvey used their responses to attack them, accusing them of seeking publicity, being in the pay of Supporters Direct and being unwilling to face him.

Elsewhere, Harvey had been on a slightly more effective charm offensive on the Hednesford Town fans' forum, answering dozens of questions with varying degrees of clarity. He proclaimed that his grand plan for OwnaFC was to roll the format out across Europe, creating a group of clubs, with him taking a percentage of ad and sponsorship revenue, before exiting the business in five to seven years. All of this would be news to anyone who'd signed up on the strength of the company's PR blitz, website or brochure.

Harvey would also intriguingly claim elsewhere that he had already spoken to clubs overseas, including to an Italian club who he said had been keen on doing a deal until 'the mafia and local politicians' became involved.

Some Hednesford fans, already troubled by the idea of being a guinea pig for OwnaFC, felt this would inevitably mean that, as new teams came on board, interest by Ownas in their team would wane. Harvey denied this.

In response to other questions, Harvey revealed that he had an estimated 3,650 paid-up members, which would mean around £180,000 of funds, and said that his 'research [suggested] Ownas will on average attend five home games [a year]'. Had he been correct, that would've equated to a minimum of 18,250 extra admissions for Hednesford, more than doubling the total of 7,793 in 2018/19. Elsewhere, he claimed he expected over 50,000 people to attend games in the first season, which would increase gates ninefold.

Harvey reiterated that 'the Ownas and the community will hopefully own 100 per cent' of the club but unveiled a new element of the plan. An 'advisory group' comprising 'the supporters' association, the youth development, the academy, the manager, team captain, events manager, bar staff etc'. This body, he said, would explore, shape and present options to Ownas for their decision. In other words, while Ownas could vote, strategy would largely be made by club staff, who Harvey would presumably appoint.

He also claimed to be lining up sponsorship options, saying that he was in discussion with drinks and sportswear companies and had already rejected an approach from a betting firm.

Not everyone was won over. One Hednesford fan who'd met Harvey at the game said, 'This very much feels like Stuart Harvey AFC and not OwnaFC. You personally told me that "I have one agenda, that is to be CEO of a top Premier League football club and this is my interview process" and "I'm here to help it help me, because I'll get propelled and I'll walk into a job, a top job. That is my agenda behind it."'

Most notable of all, though, was Harvey's unilateral decision to offer Hednesford supporters a veto over the actions of his own shareholders. 'I am very happy to give the final decision to the fans,' he said. 'This is your club, you will be inviting me (us) to the party if you like what we have. We only want in if you want us in. Without the fans, football is nothing.' He went on to propose an AGM-style meeting of all fans where the takeover could be discussed and voted on.

Much of this appeared to be policy-making on the hoof, going against previous statements about the businesses seemingly in an effort to win favour with fans and get the deal over the line.

On closer inspection, however, these would turn out not to be OwnaFC's first encounters with Hednesford fans online. In mid-February a new account had been created on the forum and, on Saturday, 2 March, it began to speak up in favour of the OwnaFC bid, reposting long lists of positive features from the OwnaFC Facebook page and responding to criticisms.

Forum users are a suspicious lot and one asked if the account had anything to do with OwnaFC. The account responded, 'I actually have a foot in both camps in that I am an Owna and I am a casual HTFC fan. I signed up not knowing the clubs involved but am now under the impression that HTFC are one of three clubs of which two are further advanced.'

In response to another post, the account said, 'I am reliably informed (via direct message) that he will be at Keys Park today,' and to another, 'If as is stated he is going to be there today, why not go and ask him?' It later claimed, 'Stuart attended the game today, met with 30 people and only had 1 that didn't support it. Not a single person approached him all day to raise concerns.'

Later, the account admitted to being 'Stuart's relation working as an employee using an OwnaFC account'.

To anyone familiar with Harvey's writing, the tone and grammar of the relation's posts was enough to make one wonder if writing style is a heritable trait. Certainly no Owna was aware of any relation of Harvey's working for the company, though his fiancée made several appearances in a semi-official capacity on the company's Facebook page. Whether she was a casual fan of Hednesford Town is unknown. Whatever the explanation, it was indicative of the clumsy, ethically tenuous approach that would come to be OwnaFC's hallmark.

The last posts from the mystery account were made late on the Saturday night. The following morning, a new official OwnaFC account sprung up and began fielding questions directly. Answering to Harvey's name, its tone was markedly similar to its predecessor.

While Harvey was working a double shift to sell his plans for the future, more was beginning to emerge about his past.

Further digging at Companies House and other sources revealed that between 2008, when he returned to the UK from Australia, and 2018, when he was running RightTrades and OwnaFC, Harvey ran eight other businesses that he either founded (or were founded by a close family member), generally in the fire safety sector. His fiancée founded a further three businesses in this period. All 11 of these businesses had been dissolved, usually without filing accounts. Some had CCJs against them from creditors – court judgments to enforce debts.

One slight exception to the pattern was a business called United Fire & Safety Limited, which was formed in 2008. In 2011, it filed accounts for the year to June 2011 showing assets of over £100,000. Yet just five months later a creditor petitioned to have the company wound up over a debt. When the case was heard, neither Harvey nor any other representative or employee of United Fire & Safety Limited attended.

It should also be said that there is nothing illegal about any of this. It's not uncommon for people to start multiple businesses, some of which will never trade. Given that the vast majority of new businesses will fail in their first few years, the law of averages tells us that if you regularly open lots of companies you will likely regularly close many of them too.

However, if you are to be a successful entrepreneur – as Harvey liked to present himself – at some point you would perhaps expect some of these businesses to succeed. All of which leaves open the question of how Harvey had lived for these ten years, residing as he did in a large, luxuriously decorated house, with hot tub, electric gates and room on the drive for his brand-new Range Rover and BMW.

At this stage, a more sceptical note was also creeping into press coverage. *The Times*'s Gregor Robertson, who had parlayed a long career as a football player into a reporter covering the lower and non-leagues, published a piece on Hednesford Town and Harvey on Monday, 4 March. Carefully balanced, the piece expressed doubt about the model.

Speaking later, Gregor said he'd gone into his meeting with Harvey open-minded but had doubts about the concept based on his familiarity with what had happened at Ebbsfleet. He felt that Harvey just didn't have sufficient numbers – even on his own figures – to make it work. 'He didn't have enough people to fund the club beyond a few months, even at that level,' says Gregor. 'There was no way this was going to scale up. I kept trying to put to him the need for ongoing financial support and he kept just obfuscating, kept coming back to the same point – the bad state of football club ownership in English football. He couldn't explain how he could run it on an ongoing basis. He just made vague comments about infrastructure, but infrastructure's not cheap and youth development isn't a short-term answer either.'

Gregor tried to press Harvey, but, 'He didn't really offer any answers to any questions. It's difficult. You ask the same question in a different way and you can see you're not getting an answer.'

What did Gregor, who'd made over 300 professional appearances, make of the idea of giving fans day-to-day control over the running of a club?

'It's a nonsense,' he says. 'I've no qualms about saying that. I remember speaking to the manager on the day [Nicky Eaden]. He was in a difficult position, because he's a guy who's been involved in football for 25 years and the prospect of this happening, you felt that would be the end of the road for him. He wasn't going to stick around in those circumstances. That would be the same for a lot of people. It could never work. Despite all the flaws, the biggest one was the idea fans could make all the decisions.

'He just kept saying that this was an alternative to the current model of ownership. He was acting as if this was a model that could be rolled out across multiple clubs. He came from nowhere. No prior experience. He's going to change the face of ownership of British football and he's an electrician.'

On the same day Gregor's piece was published, the Football Supporters' Association put out a strongly worded statement on the Hednesford Town bid. The FSA had been in contact with Hednesford since Steve Price had announced he wanted to sell and was familiar with the club's situation. Its statement contained the damning line, 'Despite their doubtless enthusiasm, we are concerned that the lack of meaningful engagement with the club's existing supporters and a business model similar to that of MyFC means that a repeat of the ultimately failed takeover of Ebbsfleet United back in 2008 is likely.'[11]

This infuriated Harvey, who attacked the FSA and Supporters Direct on numerous platforms. He claimed that he had contacted Supporters Direct before Christmas 2018 to explain his plan and had been repeatedly ignored. 'The way they couldn't be bothered with us shows how much these organisations really care about the fans,' he said. 'They care about their funding and this is why the negativity on Twitter earlier, they were all representatives or contributors to this company.'

Harvey then contacted Supporters Direct, requesting he be called back. A member of Supporters Direct did contact him and a discussion took place, with Harvey described as 'agitated', followed by a series of text messages. Harvey would later claim to have recorded that call – a call, he hinted, that showed some dark truth about Supporters Direct. Despite saying he would release the recording as part of a promised dramatic exposé, he failed to do so. This call would later form a central plank of his blame game as he repeatedly told Ownas and others that Supporters Direct had, in effect, sabotaged the purchase of Hednesford. How this could be the case when, by his own account, he had withdrawn his bid on the basis that he believed the rival bid was the best for the club is not clear.

Assailed on all sides, OwnaFC also found itself on the receiving end of a piece from the bible of non-league football, the *Non-League Paper*. Under the headline 'Football is not just a plaything', Matt Badcock wrote, 'To those who follow football from the top … Non-league football maybe does seem a bit inconsequential and somehow less important. But ask anyone at this level if it matters. These clubs are part of people's lives.' That line, 'not just a plaything', would rankle Harvey and he would return to it in forthcoming months.[12]

Further bad news was to come with a piece in *The Sun*. What had perhaps seemed like a great publicity opportunity with Britain's highest-circulation paper became a disaster when it interviewed Alex Narey, editor of the *Non-League Paper* and led not with Harvey's claims for his business but with Narey describing the scheme as 'absurd and embarrassing'. 'Just wait until things unravel,' said Narey, 'it will become a laughing stock.'

Already jittery, some Ownas were angered by Harvey giving an interview to a newspaper reviled by many football fans for its smearing of victims of the Hillsborough disaster.

Harvey fought back, claiming to have been contacted by 'no fewer than five more football clubs to discuss putting this concept into clubs' from 'the UK and overseas who want to license the concept'.

The first signs of a siege mentality were also becoming apparent, with some attempts at Trumpian populism.

'Sabotage will always lose to those who take on the elite,' he announced. 'Football is for the fans, not funded groups making millions from peoples [sic] struggles. #OwnaFC allowing the working class to take on the elite... and win #WorkingClass.'

But to bring a bad day to a close, the app crashed, leaving OwnaFC blaming the server and posting repeated defensive comments comparing the business to Instagram, which had suffered a major outage the previous day.

While it seemed like the world of football was beginning to wake up to the potential danger OwnaFC might pose to a club and its supporters, there was still a story that no one seemed interested in: the threat that OwnaFC might pose to its customers.

What had started as a football story was becoming a consumer protection one.

On Tuesday, 5 March, the night before the bid failed, Ownas began getting in touch. First a trickle, but over the days that followed, they would number in the dozens.

Many felt disappointed and were beginning to doubt that the project would now work. Others expressed unease about having rushed into joining, their enthusiasm having blinded them to the need for due diligence. None had seen any documentation of any kind, none knew when or how shareholdings would be allocated, none knew the day-to-day operating budget or financial position of the company. And, despite having signed up with promises of collective decision-making, most felt they knew next to nothing about what was going on and had no involvement or control over the direction of the business.

One said, 'I've been feeling the last few days this might be a bit of a scam because it sounds like Stuart and his team will own the stadium and the land and the Ownas will only be in control of the team. A vote is meant to be tomorrow and I've been petitioning for weeks that I want to see a full business plan, finances, predictions, etc. As a shareholder of OwnaFC Ltd, I should be able to get financial information, but nothing is forthcoming. We have received no articles of [in]corporation and no bylaws in which to operate, we have been told that there will not be a board of directors appointed and that Stuart will remain sole director, but he plans to exit the club within seven years. After the excitement of the thought of being involved in owning a club has passed, the reality is that we've just handed over our money blindly.'

Another said, 'Other Ownas are getting concerned and frustrated, some are trying to be patient, others sound defeatist already. I doubt there will be a vote tomorrow at this rate, think he'll find some excuse to delay it.'

A third said, 'I felt that, if there was a bid, it wouldn't be a serious bid and it might've just been to meet the terms and conditions to stop people getting refunds. A phantom bid, one made never to be accepted but so OwnaFC could say [they] were making bids.'

These were the words of people who knew only of Harvey's business practices through direct experience. They didn't know about his eight failed businesses and they didn't know about something else that had come to light.

In 2013, Stuart Harvey had been made bankrupt.

6

All to be revealed

When the deal to buy Hednesford Town collapsed,
things began to spin rapidly out of control.

HARVEY HAD a difficult year in 2012. After his business
United Fire & Safety Limited was wound up by creditors,
he stepped down briefly as a director of another company
of which he had been a co-director with his then wife. The
pair had separated and he began work as a franchisee for
a US electrics firm. But by January 2013, a bankruptcy
petition had been filed against him in Liverpool County
Court. Confirmed in April of that year, it meant that only
six years before presenting himself to the world as a successful
entrepreneur who was going to change the entire football
industry, he'd had debts larger than he could pay and had
had to divest himself of all his assets to repay his creditors.

Despite this, in late February 2013, between the
bankruptcy petition being filed and being heard, Harvey
appears to have purchased, with two others, the five-bedroom
detached house that he was living in when he launched

RightTrades and OwnaFC. This is something that someone who is bankrupt would not normally be able to do.

Time and again, he would prove that he was not a man who let misfortune keep him down for long.

On Thursday, 7 March 2019, the day after his deal to buy a club had fallen apart and his app had fallen over, he tried to shore up support among troubled Ownas by changing the narrative.

Referring to the news that Hednesford had reached an agreement in principle with a local group to take over the running of the club, he announced, 'Ownas, during my meeting with the local consortium, I paused the meeting & advised that their option was better suited to this club … We would like to congratulate [them].'

So, while the day before had been spent raging at Supporters Direct for sabotaging his deal and telling Ownas that Hednesford had been hiding behind NDAs, he was now claiming, with the wisdom of Solomon, to have sunk the bid himself out of a deep love for the club.

Even if it were the case that Hednesford had changed hands during a round-table meeting with rival parties bidding against each other – which is not common practice in the world of football – it would be hard to reconcile this version of events with Harvey's later obsession with the wrong he felt Supporters Direct had done him.

What was being presented as an act of selflessness also appeared problematic for someone continuing to recruit paying members to a scheme which claimed fans would sweep away the redundant gatekeepers of football and place supporters in sole charge. Given what he'd said about the superiority of his model, harnessing the money and expertise of thousands of fans who'd each attend five extra games a season, what possible advantages could this rival consortium have had over OwnaFC? Many Ownas couldn't help but notice that, having paid their £49 to join this revolution, its leader was now claiming to have had repeated meetings with a club to negotiate a purchase and, having got to the final two, withdrawn OwnaFC's interest – all without Ownas having had a single vote on the subject.

Unabashed, Harvey announced an 'open day', claiming he would be shortly setting a date with Ownas in April to give the world a chance to find out more about his plans for world domination. Like the private sponsorship offer he had made to Hednesford, or his January 2019 promise to 'bring onboard a charity partner for a 12 month period and ... cycle to each of the 92 league grounds over 92 days in summer 2019', it never happened.

The morning also brought the last major piece of press coverage that OwnaFC would receive. Sadly for Harvey, it was an absolute bodying from Fleet Street heavy hitter Martin Samuel. Writing in the *Daily Mail* under the headline 'Giving power to a bunch of cyber nerds is fatally flawed', Samuel excoriated OwnaFC, dismissing it as impractical and yet another rerun of Ebbsfleet.[13]

Social media is only a small fragment of real life, and the subset of social media dealing with lower-league football, much smaller still. To a large degree, OwnaFC had been able to shrug off its critics; the BBC piece was still producing new recruits while the rest of the football media had decided that OwnaFC was simply too small a story to worry about.

We approached several national outlets with our as yet unpublished research on Harvey's business record and his bankruptcy, along with our findings about the structure of the company, its practices and its unhappy customers. Despite the company having raised several hundreds of thousands of pounds in just a few weeks, despite the owner's questionable temperament and despite the growing chorus of unhappy customers, no one felt it worth covering yet. 'The message, perhaps understandably, was: 'If they buy a club or if they collapse, then maybe it's a story.'

The *Daily Mail* going in high on OwnaFC was significant, then, but it was a column written about the concept. However bracing the tone, it said nothing that hadn't been said the week before. There was no evidence of any engagement with the evolving situation. As we'll see later, the lack of space given to reporting the business side of football had hampered coverage of the sport for decades. Essentially, in a game where £30m transfers are barely noticed, £200,000 of fan money getting scooped up simply doesn't rate much of a mention.

Ownas were concerned about it, however, and making their voices heard.

Still moderated by a small group of volunteers, the official Facebook account was becoming less official by the day as some of those who had been the company's most vocal proponents began to question the direction of the business. Harvey, who'd originally given the group his blessing to act as an adjunct for the app, found it was mutating into a meeting place, beyond his control, where dissatisfied customers could gather to voice their doubts, exchange information and band together to apply pressure to him.

'Facebook ended up being one of the main downfalls,' says David Anderson. 'People started talking and sharing things that were being said on Twitter. People were like, "What the hell is going on here?"'

People were beginning to interrogate the company's finances. How many people were working for the business? How much were they being paid? Who were the legal representatives Harvey said were advising on deals and how much were they charging? Most of all, with one big deal having crashed and burned, was their money safe? If they were investors, were their funds being held separately – ring-fenced solely for a club purchase? Or was the company using them to pay its operating costs?

It didn't help that Harvey was dealing with many members one-to-one, often giving conflicting information. He told several Ownas that he had personally invested a six-figure sum in the business, that he had three other partners and that the company had running costs of just £1,500 a month.

Attempting to placate the increasingly irate Ownas, Harvey tried to quell the anger by offering to provide a full written response to any questions they may have. However, he set a 30-minute deadline for submission and said he'd answer only the 15 he deemed most relevant.

The answers when they came, later the same day, were largely unsatisfactory. OwnaFC continued to insist that Supporters Direct were partly to blame for the Hednesford debacle, but maintained that they were going full steam ahead to take over a club by the end of April. 'No publicity is bad publicity, especially when you are looking to change the long-standing, traditional way of running a football club,' said one answer. 'The OwnaFC concept is a threat to many working within football.'

The answers went on that there was only a 'limited staff' working in the business – Harvey, a development team and an admin person – none of whom were drawing a salary. The other financial detail of note was the assertion that the business was looking to sell a 49 per cent minority stake to up to five investors, each of whom would provide £20,000 a year for five years, generating £500,000 over five years. No details were given of whether this was a staggered payment for shares over five years – valuing OwnaFC at just over £1m – or, if not, what the investors would get for their money.

There was one note of realism, however, with an admission that the structure of takeovers meant that Ownas wouldn't be able to have access to any financial information about prospective purchases. The earlier promise of 'full access' was replaced by this message: 'Ownas will need to put trust in OwnaFC and its financial and legal representatives to ensure that due diligence is completed to satisfy a takeover bid.'

For many Ownas, the key takeaways from the responses were that, one, many of the tougher questions had been ignored and, two, the fluency and tone of the writing over several pages meant that Harvey could not be the author. It seemed that there must be someone else helping him behind the scenes.

While attempting to get the papers interested in the story, we were pushing for answers about the precise nature of the contract Ownas had with the company. Almost without exception, Ownas felt that they had bought a share in the

OwnaFC business, with their £49 going into an investment pot to finance a club purchase.

'To me, if you buy shares in [the scheme], you are partial owners of [OwnaFC Ltd],' said one Owna, 'And if that company goes on to take over a club then you own a stake there.'

'Every shareholder signed up and paid to join on the understanding that we will receive one share in OwnaFC Ltd,' said Martin Roberts.

'I sent an email to say, "What are we actually getting? A share? Will we be registered at Companies House as a director or shareholder?"' said Liam. 'I got a reply, not from Stuart, saying, "Yes, you'll get a share certificate, you'll be an owner on Companies House."'

Another Owna messaged the company. 'How do we get proof that we own a share in the Owna company?' they wrote. OwnaFC replied, 'You will be sent a share certificate and a shareholders agreement once the club is taken over.'

Who could blame them for thinking they were buying into OwnaFC? After all, the BBC piece had said, 'Harvey's fellow Ownas have paid £49 per share.' *The Times*, meanwhile, had said that '3,500 Ownas … have stumped up a one-off £49 fee for a share in the venture.' On the Hednesford Town forum, Harvey himself had said, 'The limited company is the company that we propose takes ownership of the football club we take over. The Ownas will all be shareholders within the limited entity.'

And don't forget that in response to Cave's question, 'So out of the 10,000 shares you have in OWNA LTD, you will sell up to 9,999 of them, and will put yourself in a position where your directorship can be terminated by vote?', Harvey had replied, 'Yes, 100 per cent.'

However, the more you looked into it, the more it appeared there was an ambiguity about what you were getting for your money.

The company's terms and conditions on its website made no mention of shares, investments, ownership or voting rights. Instead, it referred only to the purchase of a 'licence'.

In the back of the company's brochure there was an FAQ section. One question was, 'Who is the legal owner of the club that is taken over?' The response, 'The legal entity that will own the club is OwnaFC Limited … All Ownas will have the option of buying one share within the club at the nominal value.'

OwnaFC, then, would be the club owner. And Ownas, rather than owning the business, would have a share in the club – a share with just 'nominal value'.

'Will I own a percentage of the club?' asked another question. 'You will own one share within the football club that we takeover if you choose to and are over the age of 18,' was the answer.

Putting these answers together, it seemed that – contrary to what had been claimed elsewhere – all those thousands of £49 payments made to OwnaFC were earmarked to buy a football club for the business. And OwnaFC's sole director and shareholder was Harvey.

Rather than investors or business partners, Ownas appeared to be little more than customers. OwnaFC wasn't an investment vehicle which ring-fenced money until such time as it could acquire a club. People hadn't bought an asset with a value of £49. All they had was access to the app and the promise of a single share in a football club of a 'nominal value' and from an unspecified total number of shares. The £180,000-plus of money that had flooded in wasn't shareholder funds, it was company income. In a company Ownas didn't own.

While that's not necessarily improper – Harvey, certainly, would argue that it was all dealt with in the small print – it was a structure that gave Ownas very little control over the future of the venture.

Hypothetically, for example, one company (Company A) could buy a target company (Company B), having told its 10,000 customers that they could buy a single share in Company B. At the moment of takeover, the owners of Company A have considerable control over the worth and power of those single shares. If there were, say, just 100 shares in Company B, more shares would have to be issued so that all the 10,000 customers could have one. But, with no agreement governing what percentage of Company B each customer would have (the promise, remember, was just a single share), it is entirely in the hands of the owners of Company A to decide how many shares to issue. If they issued 10,000 additional shares, every customer would have just less than one 100th of one per cent of Company B, while Company A (with 100 of the 10,100 shares) would have just less than one per cent of the company. Collectively, then, the customers would have over 99 per cent of Company B.

However, if Company A chose to issue a million new shares, allotting the promised single one to each of the 10,000 customers, then it would retain over 99 per cent of

Company B's shares, despite having kept its promise to its customers.

Company A could also issue a new class of shares in Company B. These might confer more voting rights or other benefits to their owner, leaving those single shares little more than tokens. In an arrangement like this, Company A could own not just a majority of shares and voting power in Company B, but also retain sole ownership and benefit of things that customers who thought they had been buying into Company A would expect to benefit from – for example, the intellectual property, brand equity and technology. Those could all stay with Company A, so that if its aspirations to expand its operations under that brand were realised, its owners might be able to cash out without the customers ever seeing a penny of the profits.

There is nothing criminal or otherwise contrary to law about any of the above. (Indeed, the Glazers did something similar when they listed Manchester United on the New York Stock Exchange, creating two classes of shares: A shares, which were made available to anyone but would not pay dividends, and Class B shares, which the family owned, and which have ten times the voting power of Class A shares.)

Harvey had always publicly declared his good intentions, his determination to create a business for the masses. And since he never completed the deal for Hednesford, we'll never know what he would have done or what share of the pie he would have allotted to the Ownas. But, like the opt-out from the distance selling regulations, you had to wonder why Harvey had made these decisions, designing a structure that left his Ownas dependent on the goodwill of someone who showed very little of it.

Seen through this lens, even the name 'Ownas' begins to appear suspect. A smart piece of branding becomes a clever elision of 'customer' and 'owner', a unique but legally meaningless status that promises everything and delivers nothing.

What about the club purchase, though; wouldn't that still have value if OwnaFC could make a deal? Well, the FAQs also specified that, if the club is sold, 'The shares will be transferred to the incoming owners and the nominal value of the share will be paid to you.'

In other words, if the club were to appreciate in value and be sold, Ownas might not share in the fruits of their good stewardship, instead only getting back for the share what they paid. Who, then, would get the profits? Presumably OwnaFC's owners.

'Real life *Football Manager*' had been the pitch to customers, but it was the ultimate irony of OwnaFC that, having promised Ownas they would have complete control, the structure of the business meant they weren't shareholders. They had no power to instruct, direct or sack Harvey. All their interaction and voting on the app was worthless. They were simply playing a game no more real than *Football Manager*.

The following morning, Friday, 8 March, as Ownas began digesting the truth about their status, Harvey went on the attack again, renewing his claim that both James and Nicola Cave were acting, in effect, as paid agents of Supporters Direct. He also publicised, as if it were a gotcha, that Calladine had once given a speech at a Supporters

Direct Scotland conference. Never mind that it had been four years before and that the speech had been unpaid, it was presented as proof of the malign intentions of one of OwnaFC's critics.

By now, OwnaFC's public communications were becoming increasingly bizarre. 'I was shocked by how professional the app looked to see his behaviour on Twitter,' said Liam. 'I was embarrassed. He was representing all of us,' said Michael. 'I said, "Just prove people wrong. There's always going to be people who think differently, that's just how we are as people." He ended up blocking me. He wasn't listening. He came across as a big baby; the moment he didn't get his own way, he kicked off.'

'Whoever runs the Twitter has turned it into a Donald Trump-style page where they lash out at opposition,' said another Owna. 'If I was a chairman thinking about selling, one look at the [OwnaFC] Twitter account would put me right off. It's so unprofessional.'

Another agreed, 'I still believe the concept could work at the right place, but after this week, how could anyone want this circus around their club?'

Ownas' dismay turned to fury when, during the Friday, it was noticed that the T&Cs on the OwnaFC website had changed.

The refunds clause, which, as we saw in Chapter Three, was already very narrowly drawn, had been slimmed down further. Previously, there had been sub-clause 20.1 which had read, 'Those who became Ownas on or before 6 January 2019 are able to apply for a refund if no offer is made to a club on or before 01/03/2019.'

Given it was now a week past that date and OwnaFC had dropped its attempts to buy Hednesford, that clause would seem to have entitled the early-bird Ownas – who had each paid £99, rather than the later £49 fee – to a refund. Depending on which set of numbers you believed, this could be as many as 2,000 people, creating a potential liability of up to £198,000.

For some unexplained reason, sub-clause 20.1 had been deleted from the website.

There was uproar on the Facebook site. Ownas were demanding copies of the original T&Cs from when they joined and there was talk of legal action – a 'class action suit for false advertising'.

Several Ownas who demanded refunds found their accounts were deactivated and, when challenged about it, Harvey replied, 'The two you refer to were removed from the platform for their political stance and showing hatred to others. We don't support them people.'

In response to other questions, having dismissed our work, Harvey now admitted that users were paying for a licence to use the software, the share should be considered 'a gift' and that people should not join OwnaFC believing it is an investment. 'This is not an investment. This is an experience whereby a share in the football club is offered,' he said. What kind of experience this was to be was becoming increasingly apparent. Under pressure from Ownas, Harvey and his fiancée ceased answering questions and left the Facebook group for the last time.

David Anderson, meanwhile, tackled the refunds issue directly, emailing Harvey. 'It appears that terms and conditions have been changed without notifying me. I think refunds should be offered again and you should let people decide if they want to stay in this. I personally do not and want out. You offered me half my money back. I would like it all, thank you.'

Harvey, who would doubtless say that the small print dealt with this and other scenarios, replied simply, 'David, these have not been changed since December.'

Later that evening, Harvey notified one of the moderators of the Facebook group that, unless they closed the group down or handed it over to him for moderation, he would close the OwnaFC app. Angered by this ultimatum, one of the moderators posted the message on the page and invited Ownas to vote on whether or not to accede to Harvey's demand. They voted decisively to reject it. In retrospect, this would prove to be the sole occasion in OwnaFC's history where Harvey was overruled by his own customers in a democratic vote. He was not pleased.

Despite the company's worsening relations with its own customers, it was still touting hard for new ones. Determined to put on a good face on its other social channels, OwnaFC was buoyed that evening by a piece on talkSPORT2, where leading non-league commentator Tony Incenzo made OwnaFC part of his weekly round-up. Incenzo's two-minute piece was, however, no more critical than the original BBC article that had given OwnaFC such a boost, accepting at face value the business's claims about itself and reporting it was in talks with three non-league clubs.

OwnaFC finished another torrid day with more bold claims about the future. 'Meeting eight clubs, four who are really interesting and then a wild card thrown in,' it tweeted. 'Great progress behind the scenes. All to be revealed next week. Time for a rest before we switch live on Monday.'

Little did they know that OwnaFC wouldn't survive the weekend.

At this point, it might be worth saying a little about how we felt about OwnaFC and how those feelings had changed. At first, we'd considered Harvey dangerous because of what he might achieve. We'd worried that his marketing and PR skills would allow him to buy a club and get his impractical scheme into operation, doubtless eventually leaving a club in ruins. But, as the bid for Hednesford developed, we began to worry that he was dangerously incompetent – that he had no idea what he was doing and that he'd cost thousands and thousands of people their money. Finally, though, when we saw how he behaved to his critics, to people wanting refunds and his customers asking straightforward questions, we realised the issue wasn't only one of ability.

This wasn't just a man with ideas bigger than he could deliver, willing to embellish a little to get his grand plan off the ground. He was someone who appeared ambitious only for himself, without any sense of fair dealing, whose entire business was built on artful ambiguity. OwnaFC was a footballing virtual reality machine in which, aided by Harvey's promptings, customers saw whatever future they most wanted to see.

It was clear that, this side of a collapse, no one in the press would run the story as anything more than a curio. And despite complaints to the Financial Conduct Authority

(FCA) and other regulatory and legal bodies, no one with any statutory authority had any intention of intervening.

Instead, Harvey was to be allowed to continue to recruit people, scooping up their money with promises that it was increasingly hard to imagine that even he could still believe.

To us it appeared a footballing emergency. OwnaFC was no closer to buying a club, had upset a significant proportion of its putative co-owners and was being run erratically. We were convinced it was going to collapse eventually; the only question was how many more fans would get sucked in and left poorer for it.

And so, despite Harvey's increasingly aggressive behaviour, we decided that, with no one else prepared to do anything, we would have to try.

That OwnaFC wouldn't go without a fight was immediately clear the next morning – Saturday, 9 March 2019. Another anonymous social media account appeared, claiming to be so angry at Harvey's treatment that they had reactivated an account from April 2012 to weigh in. The account's contribution was a 500-word personal attack on Martin Calladine from someone who claimed to be a completely satisfied, totally not misled customer. Rather than address any of our substantive criticisms or reporting, it instead abused Calladine, describing him as a sadist, a troll and a harasser. Unpleasant as the content was, the writing was fluent and grammatically correct. Similar in tone, in fact, to the written answers OwnaFC had given its customers two days before. Unfortunately, in its haste to start a backlash against critics, the owner of the account had missed something. They'd changed the profile image, deleted the previous posts and changed the Twitter handle, wiping out its past and anonymising it. However, they had neglected to delete the list of accounts it was following. One of those was an old account of Stuart Harvey's that had been created in October 2012 and had been used just a handful of times in a two-week period that month, when Harvey had been working as a franchise electrician after his marriage had broken down. As the account had been dormant for over six and a half years, it could only be from someone who'd known Harvey for a considerable period of time.

Recognising the account as a proxy for Harvey, Ownas began to respond. 'Mr Harvey has been asked a number of relevant questions on here,' said one. 'His responses have largely consisted of mocking, abuse, conspiracy theories, or simply blocking people. The only person damaging his credibility is Mr Harvey himself.'

At the same time, Ownas were reporting unsatisfactory or evasive exchanges with Harvey when trying to claim a refund. Others claimed to have been told that Harvey, facing the sporting equivalent of a bank run, had repeated his threat not just to close the app if the Facebook group wasn't handed over to him, but to liquidate the company, wiping out his customers.

With Harvey now threatening to punish customers by closing the business – his bad faith on display for all to see – there seemed no reason to delay publication of our research.

Ironically, for a man who'd said he was going to destroy the outdated role of chairman, Harvey now resembled nothing so much as one of the vain old men running a football club, thumbing their nose at booing fans. People like this are stubborn and hate being told what to do, but they always underestimate the staying power of supporters. Owners have money, but fans have patience. When chairmen go to war with fans, there can be only one outcome.

At 6.30pm on the Saturday, Cave published a brief, meticulous thread setting out Harvey's bombsite of a business history, detailing the companies that, at that stage, we'd been able to link him to and finishing with news of his bankruptcy.

Cave can't exactly recall how and when it was decided to publish details of Harvey's prior businesses, though he does remember the excited conversations and emails exchanged with Calladine in the build up. The pair knew it would be a significant blow to OwnaFC, but that posting the info would take them past the point of no return. They knew it would provoke a reaction, but couldn't predict how that reaction would manifest.

They couldn't, for example, have predicted that OwnaFC would announce its closure via its own app just six minutes after Cave had finished tweeting and then delete its social media accounts. OwnaFC, dead and buried in just 14 tweets. For two people who'd worked to expose the company without the backing of a newspaper, it felt like a huge victory.

We began to receive a wave of congratulations from Ownas, journalists and observers, as well as requests from Ownas for copies of the company's terms and conditions, so they could pursue the company for refunds through their credit card providers and file complaints of fraud with the police.

It was an amazing feeling and a vindication of our work. The feeling wouldn't last.

7

The owners of last resort

For a good while, the answer to the question,
'Who's the worst owner in football?' was
generally, 'Whoever owns Portsmouth this
season.' So when the Guy Ritchie cast of
unsuitables had finally done their worst, it
was left to the supporters to pick up the pieces.

A DECADE or more ago, as fans were first beginning to protest about Portsmouth's owners, Ashley Brown was persuaded to stand for election to the supporters' trust. 'After the first year, I was asked if I wanted to become chairman,' he says. 'I said, "Not really, I'm quite busy." They said, "We've just been bought, it's all going to be quiet now, isn't it?" Three months later, an extradition order was issued for our owner and a little while after that the club was back in administration.'

For some fans, supporter ownership is an aspiration. For others, it's simply the only practical option when the music's stopped, the cake's been eaten and the tears have started.

The Pompey Supporters' Trust was constituted in 2008 – around the time when fans were beginning to ask questions about the club's finances. 'How does Pompey, with a gate of 20,000, afford players like Sol Campbell, Sulley Muntari, Lassana Diarra, Glen Johnson. At one point we had four England internationals,' says Simon Colebrook, the current chair of the trust.

Simon is a chartered accountant by trade and initially joined the trust as a treasurer. 'We were on a merry-go-round,' says Simon. 'Fans think, particularly in the Championship, "It'll never happen to us, as long as people keep spinning the wheel, we'll be all right. And then suddenly the wheel stopped."'

Portsmouth had emerged, with a series of massive jolts, from a wild period in its history, with multiple owners, two administrations in two years and a long-running court battle with the taxman. Allegations swirled that arms dealers and organised crime were involved. There were spending sprees, fire sales of players, an owner who may or may not have existed and huge debts run up so quickly that it was hard to fathom how a club of Portsmouth's size could've accomplished them.

Some of the characters who passed through the club included Sacha Gaydamak, whose father (who some thought to be the source of his funds) had previously been convicted of tax evasion and arms dealing, and Vladimir Antonov, who fled to Russia when a Europe-wide extradition warrant was issued for him in connection with a banking scandal in Lithuania. There was Balram Chainrai, who took Portsmouth to relegation and administration and then, when trying to buy the club back, achieved the rare distinction of being unable to convince the EFL that he'd pass the Owners' and Directors' Test – about which more later. There was Sulaiman Al-Fahim, who was sentenced to five years in a UAE jail for stealing the money to buy Portsmouth from his wife. There was Ali al-Faraj, who bought the club with money borrowed from Chainrai, only to default on the payment and surrender it to Chainrai, leaving many wondering if he'd ever intended to run the club or was just a frontman. And, of course, there was would-be Morecambe owner Joseph Cala, best known for trying to finance a series of underwater casinos, who had owned an Italian club for less than a fortnight and would later turn up running Gateshead FC for a disastrous but mercifully brief period.

It was a calamity, with the club passed like a suitcase of stolen diamonds between warring mobsters.

'The first administration came with debts of about £50m,' says Simon. 'The second, only a year later, showed debts of about £120m.'

'I called the chief exec,' says Ashley, 'and said it was only a matter of time before the owners' businesses collapsed and we were going to be back in administration and what would we do then? I got told off for scaremongering.'

Having watched all this going on, it seemed clear to some fans that, sooner or later, the club was going to implode and they would have to act. No one else was going to come to the rescue.

The trust began to make plans, originally with the intention of providing support to help the club through its problems, rather than taking it over. 'Initially the safety net was around raising awareness,' says Ashley, 'and building our own profile both in the media and with local and national politicians. But it very quickly became apparent that we were going to have to do something more than that.

'There was a trust board meeting and I said, "Why don't we buy it?" Some people laughed. I said, "We've got to do more than we're doing because there's no knight in shining armour. No one wants to touch Portsmouth, it's a complete mess."'

Ashley, who had a long career in business consultancy for IBM, set up a working committee with two other trust members, both of whom had experience running and managing large businesses. The trust also created a separate work stream, drawing up plans for a phoenix club, which it was fortunate never to have to use. 'We spoke every day, trying to pull together a scheme. It was ridiculed by many and took a long time to win people over. That's why it mattered that we had other credible people involved.'

Those 'credible people' were a group of 13 local business people who were prepared to cover the club's running costs – £10,000 a month – during the bid. These business people, who they called 'Presidents', later converted their debt to equity, owning 50 per cent of the club with the rest held by fans. The trust raised £2.5m, with fans paying £1,000 each, and 'Presidents' matched it.

If that sounds like a lot of money, the trust's message to fans was stark, 'It was as basic as, "If we don't do this, there will not be a Pompey,"' says Simon.

This is the kind of ruthless clarity that comes when you understand the finances of many league clubs are ruinous – not the kind of things that can be covered with one-off capital injections or small annual subscriptions. 'One of the keys to Portsmouth's survival,' says Simon, 'was that it wasn't just the supporters' trust that did it. We had a collection of local businessmen, wealthy but not billionaires. Not football wealthy. Fans need to understand that someone has to write out a cheque every month to cover losses. You can't go to your members and ask them to keep throwing money into a black hole with no guarantee of a good outcome at the end of it.'

Eventually, after a legal battle over a debt secured on the ground, Pompey fans bought the club for £3m. 'There was this massive euphoria,' says Simon. 'At the next match, in blue and gold we had "Ours" spelt out in the Fratton End. It was a proper emotional moment.'

Buying a club is just the first step, of course. Running it is a far harder proposition and one that benefits from a collective understanding of what you're trying to achieve.

'There was never a time limit,' says Ashley. 'There was never a thought that we'll just buy it, stabilise it and sell it. And it was always clear to everyone involved that it would be run professionally.'

The Portsmouth experience highlights a tricky duality among a club's supporters. Fans generally know little about the operational aspects of running a football club and yet fan bases of any size have access to a host of professional skills that, if organised properly, have the potential to buy and run a club successfully.

'When people knock supporter ownership,' says Ashley, 'they're always quick to mock them with two things – what do fans know about running a club? And, you can't have fans voting on every decision. Well they're wrong about the first part and right about the second part. Every football club has a huge wealth of different experience across its supporter base. The experience is there. But you can't vote on every decision. We knew we'd appoint a chief executive and let the staff get on with running the club. We talked instead about how we'd structure the board. And what we would and wouldn't interfere with.'

The new Pompey board was constituted with three representatives from the trust, three of the 'Presidents' and one independent person to act as a tiebreaker. It was this group, not the broader fan base, who were tasked with overseeing the operations side of the business, like hiring and firing managers.

This structure would prove a crucial separation of powers. 'Most football fans don't really know how football clubs are run,' says Simon. 'And, to be honest, they're probably better off not knowing. It's a world of its own in terms of business.'

'There's a certain amount of good governance that's necessary,' says Ashley. 'Staff need to feel empowered to do their job if they're going to do them effectively. It's a basic management principle. I was asked the question countless times, "I've got a share, I own the club, what's my involvement?" Well, your power is in electing some of the board to represent you. Anyone – including you – can join the trust, be elected to the board and subsequently be elected to the club board. The people on the board will be as transparent as we can. They will listen and consult. But we can't have people vote on decisions in the football club.'

The ownership structure never caused a problem with recruitment. The board was always up front to executive or managerial hires about how it worked, to head off any worries they might have had about working for a fan-owned club.

Initially, Simon was quite relaxed about the scale of the task facing the new owners. Being in League Two meant Portsmouth had a big financial advantage from season ticket sales. 'I thought, as long as we get a chief executive who understands football and as long as we trust in managers, we should be fine,' he says.

It soon became clear, though, that years of turmoil had hurt the club, with many skilled and experienced staff quite understandably jumping ship for more secure employment. The off-field operations needed a total rebuild.

Rebuild them they did and, within 12 months of taking over, the club repaid the last of its creditors – a remarkable achievement for a fan-owned operation that, when under the stewardship of a stream of millionaire and billionaire businessmen, had done nothing but run up huge losses.

It wasn't all plain sailing, however. For a club the size of Portsmouth, a return to the Championship seemed just a matter of time. But, right now, there's no harder place to be a supporter-owned club than the Championship. On all sides you're surrounded by hugely indebted clubs gambling their futures, including ownership of their grounds, on getting promoted to the Premier League where, all the evidence suggests, they probably won't last more than a few years before dropping down again.

'The glass ceiling is probably the transition from League One to the Championship,' says Simon. 'The Championship is a casino, where people with more money than sense roll the dice to try and get into the Premier League. I struggle to see how we would've done any more than bounce between the Championship and League One without having owners that would chuck ten million quid a year into it.'

Simon wonders too whether the wages that clubs pay in the Championship might also create a natural limit to fan goodwill. Will people want to keep funding players on £10,000 or £20,000 a week if they're underperforming?

Ashley, who would later bring his experience at Pompey to Supporters Direct, where he was CEO, and the Football Supporters' Association, where he is head of supporter engagement and governance, is keen to stress that the glass ceiling is entirely artificial – a man-made product of the way the Premier League parcels out minimal support to the EFL while giving newly relegated clubs a huge handout.

'The great twist is that, if a fan-owned club got into the Premier League, they'd be fine,' he says. 'It's just the Championship you can't cope with. The Premier League and the money associated with it have delivered some good – not enough. But conversely they have put the pyramid system on the road to ruin. The clamour to move up has even reached non-league where we see clubs operating on ridiculous budgets just to try and clamber towards the Football League.'

The fault, then, is with the unsustainable financial structure of football that incentivises reckless owners to take risks that fan-owned clubs would never contemplate.

'Look at Exeter, a supporter-owned club,' says Ashley. 'They've been excellently run. They've proved they can comfortably stay in League Two, with the occasional pop into League One. Outside the Football League, supporter ownership is an excellent model when done properly. Take someone like Rushden & Diamonds. Not only that they resurrected their club, they've built it into a major part of the community. They run 70 or 80 different football teams. Attendances are up, people believe more in the club and feel part of it.

'There's a moral case for fan ownership. Football clubs should be treated differently. Historically they were typically formed and run by a little conglomerate of local business people. They weren't hugely rich people, but better off and they were people from that community and they cared for and were part of the club. But what we've seen is an influx of owners who have no association with the city, the community, with the fans. There are, of course, outside owners who've made real efforts to work with communities. And there are good owners. But there is a community responsibility for football clubs. They were formed in the heart of their communities and they should stay in the heart of their communities.

'We're often asked by politicians why football clubs should be treated differently. One of the answers we give: you look at protected buildings. They are viewed as significant in their community. We even protect trees as being significant to communities. Football clubs should be judged in that way. They are that important to the community. They must be protected.'

Against the ruthless logic of football's current set up, though, there was another more pressing issue facing Pompey. Fratton Park is an old stadium and there was a long backlog of maintenance, leading to the closure of some areas of the ground. One report suggested that the cost of bringing it up to standard was £5m.

There is some disagreement between fans about whether this was affordable – whether it would ruin the club or whether the improvements could be staged, with Portsmouth operating with a lower playing budget for a number of years.

Sharks were beginning to circle. Well-supported clubs not too far from London who, with a shove, might be able to crash the Premier League party are an attractive prospect to football's carpetbaggers.

The club was receiving regular approaches from would-be buyers. 'We'd frequently get emails or phone calls,' says Simon, 'normally from an agent, saying, "I've got someone who's interested in buying Pompey." It would be on a monthly basis. The first questions would always be, "Who is it? And can they show us they've got the money?" And nearly always it would then go quiet for a bit. And then the agent would say, "They want to keep it confidential."'

Eventually, though, the club got an interesting offer from the Eisner family. With a patriarch who'd been the long-time CEO of entertainment giant Disney, here were people with a level of wealth and professional expertise that you didn't need an Owners' and Directors' Test to assess. They were, they said, people with a long-term plan and a desire to make a deal everyone could be happy with.

Again, the value of a well-organised supporters' trust showed its worth.

'What we did was, I think, unique in football takeovers,' says Simon. 'We had written into the rules of the trust that the trust committee would not have the power to sell the shares that we owned in the football club. It was too big a decision to be made by 12 members. What that meant was that, when the Eisners approached us, they knew they couldn't just woo us. They had to woo the whole fan base.'

The separation of ownership and executive authority meant that staff could get on with their jobs, and the board theirs, without having to think about if the approach would succeed. Instead, the final say would be with the fans who'd paid to save the club and patiently allowed their representatives to get on with running it.

As part of the negotiations, the trust secured several concessions – including vetoes over relocation, name or shirt colour changes – but didn't get its way with guarantees on financing or involvement in future sales.

'We were satisfied that he [Michael Eisner] was a good guy,' says Simon. 'But you are only ever one sale away from a catastrophic owner. There are no guarantees in business and certainly not in football. Having got the best deal we thought we could get, we organised a town hall meeting and invited 2,500 people. Eisner stood on a stage and made a pitch to them to sell the club to him. I don't know of any situation where, before they've bought it, the new owner has stood before the fans like that.'

When the vote came, 80.3 per cent of shareholders in the trust voted in favour and 75 per cent of the 'Presidents'. The deal passed the trust's 75 per cent threshold and went through.

As fans who helped save and then sell a club, what have Ashley and Simon learned from the experience?

'The biggest thing holding football fans back is football fans themselves,' says Ashley. 'You've got all these people supporting the same team. And yet it's so difficult to get them to pull together behind one vision. It happened at Portsmouth because it became so bad. There really wasn't an alternative. It got to a real crisis point.'

'Football is unlike any other business,' says Simon. 'Properly recognising that and understanding that from the outset would've helped. It should be like any other business but it's the people involved that mess it up. As someone coming from a corporate background, I found all the procedures and processes and controls that you'd expect to be in place aren't. And it's a struggle to put them in place – people seem to go a bit haywire in football.

'I understand now a little bit more about the bravado and egos involved in football. You very quickly learn how to filter out the hangers-on and the bullshitters from the people who are actually well meaning and have something intelligent to say.

'OwnaFC smacked to me of Ebbsfleet. Having been involved in owning a football club and knowing how much money it needs, I thought, "How on earth is this business model going to work?" On the face of it, it was completely nonsensical. And then, as you dug into it more and more, it became even more nonsensical. You read the documentation, such as it was, and it starts throwing up all kinds of alarm bells as to what people are actually buying. Because it doesn't look like they are actually buying a share in a football club.

'If you are a private limited company you are not allowed to sell shares to the general public. The general public is protected against mis-selling on something they won't control and has a high risk of failure. Either he [Stuart Harvey] owns the business and he's trying to entice other people into that business, in which case he has to comply with share selling rules. Or, if you don't own that business – i.e. the club – you're acting as a financial intermediary, in which case you have to be registered with the FCA.* If you want to charge £49 for an app, fine. But don't dress it up as a share.'

On the practicalities of running a club as OwnaFC proposed, Simon was equally incredulous. 'You have the whole issue of running a football club by committee of thousands. How is that ever going to work? It can't,' he says.

'[At that level] it's very tough for those sorts of clubs to survive commercially. They've just got no income. In order to make it work in the way it was being pitched, he was going to have to be constantly going back to his "shareholders" for more and more money. And yet his claim was that it was a one-off payment.'

Ashley agrees. 'It varies depending on the club and there's different ways you can put money into the club. It might be by buying a season ticket and attending an annual dinner,' he says. 'It might be having £10m on a monthly standing order and trying to get to four or five games a year. There's different ways in which financing works, but you have to have

---

* On this point, the authors referred OwnaFC to the FCA – the Financial Conduct Authority – for investigation in early March 2019. A later Freedom of Information request for details of any action or investigation by the FCA was rejected on the grounds that to do so might 'prejudice the exercise by the FCA of its function for the purpose of ascertaining whether circumstances which would justify regulatory action in pursuance of any enactment exist or may arise'. Since notices of formal enforcement action are posted on its website, the FCA's response in this case sat somewhere on a spectrum with 'doing nothing at all' at one end and 'launching a formal investigation but not taking formal enforcement action' at the other.

some ongoing financial commitment, either as a customer or a donor or both.'

'Most football clubs outside the top flight are small businesses,' says Simon. 'In any SME you don't have the luxury of time when it comes to decision-making. If you're going to start involving fans in day-to-day decision-making, the time it takes to give them the opportunity to consider and make their views known is a huge delay. And there's no point in asking them unless it's an informed decision. Trying to inform the fans on the minutiae of, say, who the next manager is or whether you should sign player X or player Y. All of those decisions require so much detail that you would never get to a stage of having gathered the opinions of the fan base in time to make it. You'd be in a permanent state of paralysis.

'It seemed to me that Harvey had absolutely zero [skills to run a football club]. None whatsoever. It became very clear to me very quickly that he was an absolute chancer. Absolutely hopeless. He's the sort of person you'd see on *Watchdog* being chased by the presenter on a motorbike.

'He was never going to take over a club. So my concern was the people, many of whom I'm sure were well-meaning, who were chucking 50 quid at him for something that was going absolutely nowhere. And the damage it was going to do to Hednesford. One of the things I've gained a very strong appreciation of with being involved in Pompey is what it means to a local community to have their local club. Even if it's only 100 fans, it's everything to those 100 people and why should they have it taken away from them?

'The platform looked like it had the potential to be the sort of thing that trust-owned football clubs would make use of. One of the challenges we always had was how to effectively communicate with the wider fan base. How to engage with them and make them feel involved. I thought it was a shame he went off on one at Supporters Direct, who might have found it of use.'

Ashley thinks it's not the last we've heard of schemes like OwnaFC. 'It's been resurrected because of technology making it relatively easy to do,' he says. 'Interaction becomes easy. The trouble is the people who are resurrecting it are people who are looking to profit from it. They're not really in it in a community-spirited manner.

'There's always someone who thinks they'd like to own a football club but needs to use someone else's money. Or they think they're going to profit from it. Sadly both of those people are always hanging around in football.

'The technology has a future in working with real community clubs. I don't like the idea of loads of people from around the world buying a club, getting bored and leaving it in a mess. But if an actual community wants to chip in together and buy their club, there is a future for technology that can make fans feel properly involved in the running of a club. But that doesn't mean they are going to vote on key decisions. You could make certain decisions available – like kit design. And you use it as a consultation or market research tool.

'Depending on how you want to spin it, Portsmouth is either a brilliant example of supporter ownership in action or an example of why it doesn't work. On the positive, we took over a club in a complete mess – massive debt, a ground falling apart, no manager, no team, no kit, no shop, no sponsor. Not only did we balance the books and pay everybody off, we got promoted back into League One and attracted the interests of a very successful billionaire and then the fans decided who the next owner was to be. People felt their chance of getting back to the promised land was better with a billionaire. Now that's a problem with football, not with supporter ownership.'

8

Aggressive, intimidating, abusive or unprofessional

When OwnaFC collapsed, two questions emerged: Whose fault was it? And how would they be held accountable?

ON THE evening of 9 March, not long after OwnaFC shuttered its media channels, a statement appeared on the app. It announced that the company was ceasing trading with immediate effect and blamed an 'ongoing online smear campaign'.

Ownas were stunned, many angrily alleging they'd been defrauded. After all, if OwnaFC had really been run as frugally as had been suggested, then – having few staff and having made no club purchase – the company was closing its doors with hundreds of thousands of pounds of customer money, having provided nothing like the 'experience' it had promised.

What would now happen to that money?

The company statement made no mention of its plans for the contents of its well-stocked bank account. What it did say, however, was that it would be taking legal advice, claiming that it had been subject to 'harassment' and that 'threats [had been] made against the children of the directors' on the Facebook group. Ownas were united in condemning the idea of such threats. But they were equally at one in denying that they happened. Many struggled to understand how frustration at how the business was being run or over a failure to refund £49 could possibly result in threats against Stuart Harvey's children.

'I can guarantee I saw no threats of any sort made towards any children. At any point,' said an Owna. 'From what I can tell from the Facebook group, he's [Harvey] the only one that's been threatening [anyone],' said David Anderson.

'I've not seen anything in this group remotely untoward,' said another Owna. 'None of the moderators have a clue what he's on about,' said one of the people charged with running the group. 'We haven't seen anything and neither has anybody I've spoken to.'

This does not, of course, rule out that threats might have been made in private, but it certainly wasn't the case that there was some kind of widespread social media pile-on of Harvey with public threats against him and his family. We asked Harvey to provide evidence of such threats, but did not hear back from him. We also asked Greater Manchester Police if they had had any reports of such threats and if they had taken any statements or launched any criminal enquiries. They declined to comment.

As Ownas swarmed to the Facebook group to discuss the evening's events, the responses ranged from bewilderment to resignation. Many were hopeful the situation could still be repaired and the business resurrected, while others cried foul and began to plot a way to recover their money. Over the next few weeks, Ownas would report the company variously to Trading Standards, Action Fraud, several police forces, the Insolvency Service, the Financial Ombudsman and the National Fraud Intelligence Bureau. Not one body would take enforcement action against the business.

If the company was shutting up shop, however, it was not going quietly. While the social channels and website were down, Harvey continued to communicate directly with many of the Ownas who were bombarding him with questions.

He told one Owna requesting a refund, 'No refunds are required and this is stated clearly in the terms and conditions,' and that the business was 'for sale as a going concern for £1 and is debt-free'. Another refund request was met with a simple one-line response, 'We will pass this information on to the liquidators for you.'

Confirmation that the company had failed to ring-fence Ownas' funds came in a response to another inquiry. 'All monies going into the company from Ownas is as turnover,' said someone signing themselves OWNA Support, 'and used for the running costs.' In other words, people should not expect to get all their money back.

Miraculously, however, some people did appear to get a refund. Someone sharing Harvey's surname was already claiming to have received an unrequested refund on the Saturday night. He denied any personal connection with Harvey, but inadvertently posted a supposed text exchange with Harvey revealing they were both friends with Ashton

Town chairman Mark Hayes. The lucky refundee also turned out to have been the very first person to give Harvey's RightTrades business a Trustpilot review, several years before. He had generously awarded the business five stars. Mark Hayes himself appeared on Facebook, distancing himself from Harvey by stressing – correctly – that he was just a friend and customer, not an investor. The concept could still work, he said, if only the Ownas could control their anger. 'I know for a fact that there are still clubs out there who would have us,' he said. 'Yet due to the poison that is floating around by everyone I'm not sure we would be touched which is a shame.'

Elsewhere, an anonymous member of the Facebook group, who'd spent many days defending Harvey and urging people not to jump to conclusions, posted a screenshot which was supposed to show he'd received a refund. The following day, when called out as yet another sock puppet for OwnaFC, he direct-messaged the poster a photograph of him flipping him a V sign.

Another lucky person was a man who'd appeared in an OwnaFC promotional video. He posted a receipt showing he'd received a partial refund before going on to spend days on Facebook interacting with Harvey's sock puppets and arguing his receipt proved Harvey's integrity. Whenever a journalist was sniffing round the story on Twitter, he'd appear to 'put the other side of the story'. Unlike OwnaFC's other proxies and sock puppets, he seemed genuine in his belief that the business was above board and in his inability to grasp that there might be anything untoward about a small group of people close to the company getting refunds while the vast majority were denied them.

Meanwhile, even as Harvey was doling out preferential treatment, someone purporting to be a relative of his appeared in the Facebook group, pleading on his behalf.

'I'm not saying he's right,' said the relative, 'this whole thing was a bold move from him and it isn't the first time similar has happened. But he's not a conman simple. He's not going to return all the money until he's took legal advice, is he?'

'If he doesn't return ALL money to everyone then he'll have stolen it. It's really that simple,' replied David Anderson.

While the question of Harvey's initial intentions would never be adequately resolved, what would happen when he got legal advice and failed to return the money would soon become apparent.

Despite his family's supplications, Harvey did not appear contrite. Several Ownas received angry communications from the company threatening legal action for 'facilitating hate'.

The air of menace that had been building around the company reached a new and shocking height when one Owna posted on Facebook that, during a telephone conversation with Harvey, he'd 'threatened to rape my kids and kill my family'. The Owna declined to be interviewed for this book, saying he wanted to put the experience behind him, as did four other Ownas who found themselves contacted by Harvey over coming weeks with threats to visit their houses to 'discuss matters' with them. These communications didn't contain specific threats of violence, but the tone was menacing and several reported them to the police. One was told that 'a list' had been drawn up – for what purpose wasn't clear – and that he was to be added to it. The message implied someone could be tasked with locating his home address. We wrote to Harvey asking for his response to these claims of chilling threats and intimidation but, as with the many other serious allegations in the book, he did not respond.

Unaware of how matters were escalating, other Ownas continued to contact Harvey asking about his plans for the business. They were told that OwnaFC was not immediately being placed into liquidation, as had been suggested, but that a buyer was being sought and that interested parties would be invited to meetings in Warrington the following day – Monday, 11 March. Ownas who enquired further about buying the business were told any prospective purchasers would need to provide proof of funds of £50,000 to cover 'running costs'.

It was all change the next day, though. A message appeared on the app, 'OwnaFC Limited can confirm that, after meeting with its legal representatives, business is continuing as normal. A further statement will be made later this week in regard to privacy and media relations from OwnaFC Limited and its legal teams.'

Given what had happened in the previous two weeks, the business 'continuing as normal' was not perhaps quite as reassuring a message as the company had intended. No mention was made of how it could continue to trade and earn its customers' trust given that it hadn't been able to answer many of the basic questions about its business practices and that it had refunded only a select few customers. Beyond that, there were the questions of how it could hope to attract enough additional customers to finance the purchase of a club and how it could persuade any club that it was a suitable partner with whom to do a deal.

The message was also a significant change on Harvey's communication just a few hours before, when he'd told David Anderson that he was stepping down, was looking to sell the business and had '[written] off £100k in directors loans'.

If it were true that Harvey had lent the company £100,000 of his own money, it raised the question of why he hadn't disclosed this before – why he'd referred to the company as being 'debt-free' – and where he'd got £100,000 from. Had he borrowed it? Was it dividends from his other businesses?

The position evolved still further by the end of the week when the promised corporate update appeared. On Friday, 15 March, the company put out a statement in the name of Gunnercooke LLP, a law firm with offices in London, Leeds and Manchester. Striking a surprisingly upbeat tone, it promised to bring 'exciting news about OwnaFC'.

It asserted, among other things, that it would be appointing a 'best in class non-executive advisory board' of five unnamed professionals to 'provide a stronger link' with the 'newly appointed leadership team'. Harvey, it went on, would be 'stepping aside from the business' leaving 'all decisions' in the hands of this advisory board.

Who the members of the newly appointed leadership team were and how a 'non-executive advisory board' could run a business weren't clear.

The statement went on to provide a new explanation for the collapse of the Hednesford Town bid. Rather than it being the fault of sabotage by Supporters Direct or the decision of Harvey to pull out, the statement said that 'the club pulled out on 5 March due to internal pressures'. Intriguingly, it also claimed, 'An offer was made and accepted [for the club] on 28 February.'

This was a date with significance because the original terms and conditions had included a clause – later deleted – offering a refund to anyone who'd signed up on or before 6 January if 'no offer is made to a club on or before 01/03/2019'.

In other words, the company was now claiming that it had, in fact, had an offer accepted on the last possible day before which a refund clause would've been triggered for a substantial proportion of its customers (all of whom, by virtue of when they joined, had paid £99). This seemed like a bold claim given that 28 February was the day when the BBC article had been published – when the company had been 'in talks' with several clubs. At no point publicly – nor from what we could tell privately – had OwnaFC ever previously claimed that it had had a deal accepted by Hednesford. The state of negotiations had always appeared a great deal more provisional than that.

The company provided no evidence to substantiate its claim, going on to rewrite its terms and conditions further by saying that it was in negotiations with three clubs and that, if it couldn't conclude a deal by 1 July, it would offer a 60 per cent refund to customers. This was notable for two reasons: firstly, nowhere in the T&Cs had it specified refunds would be only a percentage of the original payment and, secondly, every version of the T&Cs had included this clause, 'The price once paid is final and no refunds are offered or given for any reason other than if a takeover is not completed within three months of a club accepting our offer. If no offer is made to a football club by 01/06/2019 then refunds will be offered.'

If, as the company claimed, a bid for Hednesford Town had been accepted on 28 February, then the three-month bid completion limit would fall due on 28 May, entitling all Ownas, not merely the early joiners, to a refund. Given Hednesford had now pursued another option, this deadline appeared all but certain to be missed. Beyond that, if in fact a bid hadn't been made and accepted, then 1 June would mark the date when refunds for all would also be due.

Either way, arbitrarily shifting the date to 1 July and offering a 60 per cent refund meant the company was unilaterally rewriting its T&Cs to the significant disadvantage of its customers. Assuming that Harvey's figures of having 2,000 Ownas in early January, each paying £99, and a further 1,650 paying £49, were true, the company might've had income in a four-month period of about £280,000 (we've used here the figures Harvey most commonly claimed; later he suggested he had many times these numbers of Ownas).

Even assuming the bid for Hednesford Town had been accepted when the business had said, its own T&Cs would make the company liable for refunding the full amount of £280,000 in just two and a half months, leaving it without a penny. By rewriting the refund provision, it could buy itself another four weeks and reduce that liability to £167,000 – leaving over £100,000 for the company. Without access to the company's books – which we were never able to obtain – we'll never know the OwnaFC's true income, nor how much these changed T&Cs stood to save it. All companies, of course, reserve the right to change their T&Cs, but that doesn't mean that any change is fair and ethical.

Beyond the specific claims of the statement, it was also unusual tonally. While it seemed too well-written to be Harvey's work, it was a notably upbeat and enthusiastic piece of drafting. Perhaps surprisingly, the statement mistook the difference between an executive and non-executive board and described OwnaFC as offering a 'once-in-a-lifetime opportunity to own a football club'.

In the absence of a named Gunnercooke partner on the statement, several Ownas contacted the firm to seek clarification on the refunds announcement. They heard back on 21 March, less than a week after the statement, that the firm was no longer representing OwnaFC. The firm's compliance director declined to say why, citing client confidentiality – the same explanation given by the firm later when it refused to answer a detailed set of questions from the authors about its involvement with OwnaFC.

Before the Gunnercooke-endorsed statement had come out, the collapse of OwnaFC had begun to attract the press's interest. On Monday, 11 March, even before OwnaFC had announced its resurrection, Daniel Storey wrote a piece about the debacle for *FourFourTwo* magazine, recounting the disappointment of Ownas and the speed with which the endeavour had collapsed.[14] It was a fair and balanced piece, measured and detailed in its criticism of both the media and OwnaFC, but it did not please Harvey.

At the same time, journalist Will Magee was speaking to a group of Ownas in preparation for putting out a long-read for *i* newspaper on OwnaFC. Published on Wednesday, 13 March under the headline 'How a fan ownership "revolution" descended into disaster', it was the first time a mainstream publication had catalogued the extent of what Magee described as Harvey's 'aggressive, intimidating, abusive or unprofessional' behaviour.[15]

'I first got interested when I started to see Ownas tweeting about it; it seemed like there might have been some injustice going on,' said Magee. He put out a call for interviewees and added, 'I had at least a dozen people contact me very quickly and more afterwards, which is quite unusual for a general request on Twitter.

'There were things I thought were fundamentally wrong – like unilaterally changing the terms and conditions. The social media presence was a tell. The tone wasn't very professional, it was erratic. I spoke to some Ownas who claimed they'd been blocked or removed from the app for asking inconvenient questions – which I felt was not a way that successful companies behave.

'I was contacted by people who showed me evidence of intimidating communications they'd had. And at that point, my suspicions that this was a failed enterprise became serious and much more worrying. It was a very brazen way to deal with unhappy customers. Highly unorthodox and highly unpleasant. Numerous sock-puppet accounts popped up sending people strange and, if you knew the context, intimidating communications.'

Before publication, Magee called Harvey to put to him what he'd been told by Ownas. Magee said, 'It was very odd. There was extensive talk of legal ramifications. He was very combative, but that's to be expected. It wasn't a good news story. It wasn't a pleasant exchange, but it didn't make me think that the escalation that was to follow was inevitable.

'He denied everything apart from, I believe, changing the terms and conditions, which he said he was allowed to do under the same terms and conditions – in other words, to change them unilaterally. He denied things that I'd seen contrary evidence of, which were true. I didn't come away from the conversation feeling that we'd had an honest exchange, but it was a telling exchange nonetheless.'

Reflecting on the affair, and what it tells us about the responsibility of the media – particularly the BBC – Magee takes a balanced but critical view, 'As journalists, people will often contact you with PR stories about new apps they've created or interesting new ideas for the game, so I can kind of understand how it happened. The problem is they should have been a lot more rigorous in the way they assessed the concept. I was surprised by how much of an effect it had in the real world. It wasn't just that they'd published something and no one had read it and it was nothing to do with the whole situation. There was several people who said, "No, it influenced me to get involved."

'As a journalist, you come into contact with a lot of people and you can't vouch for their character all the time. I don't want to burn the BBC down on account of this article, but they should've been much more robust and critical, and should've thought much more carefully about what they were writing.

'The sad reality is that short, SEO-friendly articles do much better in terms of traffic. It's a journalistic ethics issue because then do you prioritise those less-investigative pieces over something like that? I'd hope a good editor would say they wouldn't, and my editor at *i* backed me and wanted me to write it, but would that piece always get written over a more digestible, less complex, less controversial piece? There's a lot of outlets that would prioritise the very quick, digestible, inoffensive journalism.'

There is, then, a tension between what many journalists would like to be writing and what those funding journalism want them to be writing about.

When asked to comment on the quality of its original story and what responsibility, if any, the BBC felt towards the many people who'd signed up with OwnaFC, the corporation refused to acknowledge any of the criticisms of Ownas or journalists. A BBC spokesperson said, 'Like a number of other news outlets, we reported on a story about an opportunity for football fans that a significant number of people had already signed up to. The piece pointed out that a similar venture had ended in failure previously and that the owners of this venture would need to pass the Football Association's Owners' and Directors' Test before they would be allowed to take over a football club. It did not endorse the venture or suggest that fans should sign up.'

For Magee, the story goes beyond journalistic practice and tells us something about the state of football.

'OwnaFC as a story is quite an important one,' he says, 'even if it's also a niche interest, because it says a lot about how fans are feeling at the moment. People do want something idealistic and community-driven and grassroots to invest themselves in, emotionally and personally. They clearly want that and especially top-flight football doesn't really offer them that. That's a sad indictment of the way football has gone. And it means we need to be incredibly vigilant about anything that attempts to tap into that sense of collective disillusion but that doesn't solve any of those issues.

'OwnaFC co-opted a lot of the language of fan ownership, fan power, grassroots movements. It talked about a revolution in the game. It almost used left-wing language that you'd see in those interested in the [German] 50+1 system and those who want to see power returned to fans from corporations. It was quite chameleonic in that sense.

'A lot of Ownas had bought into the concept in quite an idealist vision of what it was and were very enthusiastic about it. I think most people would admit now that they were quite naïve. It says a lot about fans feeling disenfranchised and disempowered; that football no longer works for them.'

Magee is keen to highlight how there is already a channel for disillusioned supporters to get more involved in football. 'You can go and start supporting your local non-league club,' he says. 'If it has 200 fans, the likelihood is your voice will be heard. You can be an influential person. Everyone gets to know everyone. It's quite easy to get involved in football governance. Every club needs volunteers. Go and be a steward, work on the turnstile, make cups of tea. You'd be doing a genuine service to a historic community institution. It would be endlessly more beneficial than signing up for an online experiment. That's not to criticise people who bought into it, because they did so with good intentions, but I think it's been a salutary lesson for a lot of people. OwnaFC was selling something that already exists. There are grassroots clubs that desperately need people's time and expertise.'

If it had been a busy week for Ownas, Harvey and the press, it was nothing compared to that of the Caves. On

Thursday, 14 March, a heavily pregnant Nic was admitted to hospital for observation after a community midwife noted her raised blood pressure. The following day, Nic and James became parents, as their first child, Daniel, was born. Six weeks premature, Daniel would be in NICU for weeks while Nic would spend several days in intensive care.

It was a moment of both joy and worry that would wipe any thought of OwnaFC from their minds. At least temporarily.

9

Another brick in the arch

*They say that the road to hell is paved with
good intentions. At least one man will tell
you the road to football's graveyard is made
from the same material.*

CAN YOU categorise the owner of a football club as 'good'
or 'bad'? Is the problem really that simple?

Andy Holt has been speaking for nearly an hour when
he says something totally unexpected. It's Wednesday
afternoon and Holt is pulling no punches over the state of
English football, from his home office, somewhere between
Accrington and Burnley, over a Zoom call.

'You've got to remember with bad owners, there are one
or two but not that many. Very few. Bad owners are created,'
says the owner of Accrington Stanley.

It's a statement that many football fans would reject
out of hand. English football is littered with current and
historical 'bad' owners: Roland Duchâtelet (Charlton

Athletic); Karl Oyston (Blackpool); Steve Dale (Bury). You could, quite literally, fill a book. But Andy thinks we need to dig deeper.

'I don't believe that an owner gets into football to be a bad owner,' he says. 'There's some, you could say Steve Dale did. I think he got in there to make a quick buck but he didn't get in there to destroy Bury, I can guarantee that. That wasn't his intention. It might have looked like that to fans, and that was the outcome. I think he took over because he wanted to make a shilling out of it. So is that a bad owner? If they'd got through the Stewart Day period and gone forward. They got promoted didn't they? Would he have been a bad owner if he'd made a few bob out of it and a new owner came in? I don't know.

'When you get into a business, you've got a right to expect normal business rules. But football isn't a normal business. It's a cheat.'

* * *

Holt practically skips over the first question about his early life and growing up on one of the poorest estates in the country. He went to a game every now and then – Manchester United, Burnley, the odd match at Wembley – but generally in his earlier years he was focused on his business. Far too busy to watch football on a Saturday. Next question.

It was a mentality that paid off. Today, Holt's What More UK business (WHAM) produces reusable plastic storage boxes and housewares, turning over approximately £70m a year. Proudly made in Britain. Recessions? No problem. Brexit? What's that?

It was via WHAM that a file on Accrington Stanley first crossed not-really-a-football-fan Andy Holt's desk.

'My company donates to foundations that give kids activities and keeps them off the streets. When I was growing up on Stoops Estate [in Burnley] we had a similar thing that stopped us doing things that we might otherwise have done. It was important to me. So we were sponsoring cricket clubs, rugby clubs, anywhere giving kids a bit of discipline and sport and everything that came with it. I think that's how Accrington Stanley landed on my desk in the first place.

'I was approached about being a sponsor and I didn't want to do it. I didn't want to know. I was approached about half a dozen times. They must have got me on a weak day.'

Contrary to their public image, Accrington Stanley's history has been largely characterised by gentle progress. Initially founded in 1896, the club slowly moved up from the Lancashire Combination to the Football League Third Division North.

This progress gave the club big ideas. Sometime in the late 1950s, in the days when it was not uncommon for clubs to buy and sell stands like trading cards, Accrington's vice-chairman became aware that a 4,700-capacity double-decker stand was for sale in Aldershot. The asking price was just £1,450 – much lower than the market value – and so he went with chairman Bob Moore to investigate. With a current seated capacity at their Peel Park ground of just 800, it was the answer to their prayers.

Explaining the decision, Moore told the *Accrington Observer*, 'The whole future of football is in the melting pot.

There is a possibility in seasons to come of a super-European League, and with Stanley's ambition as high as the sky we wish to be "in" on the ground floor and make Accrington one of the centres of football.'

Accrington Stanley – like Tottenham Hotspur, Chelsea, Manchester City et al. in 2021 – were cruelly denied their chance to join a European Super League.

Several years later, in 1962, the club resigned from Football League Fourth Division over an unpaid £4,000 bill to the taxman. Stanley folded and were re-established in 1968, only to start again, back in the Lancashire Combination.

By the time Holt took over in 2015, Stanley had progressed to League Two, where they had established a firm presence. In that time the club had been relegated just once from the Northern Premier League Premier Division in 1999, bouncing back by winning the title at the first opportunity and ultimately reaching the Football League in 2006.

But Accrington hit a ceiling in League Two. The club had one of the lower average attendances in the division. The town of Accrington was on the smaller side in terms of population. Like many north-west clubs, fans in their catchment area were less than an hour from some of Europe's elite and just a button press if they subscribed to Sky or BT. But Stanley still had to pay League Two wages in a professional, competitive division. From a financial perspective, Holt couldn't have picked a worse time to arrive.

'I went to a friendly, the place is falling down,' he says. 'I take my lad, I'm having a couple of pints and they run out of beer at the bar. It was a desert in there, they had nothing to sell.

'We sponsored the club for three years. We gave a few hundred thousand to sponsor the shirt and name the stadium. And "stadium" is in inverted commas because it was in a real state. I don't know why I did it. Don't ask me why.

'The chairman Peter Marsden said, "Is there any way you can help us?" I got the tale of woe then. They couldn't pay the wages. Hadn't paid the suppliers. He'd spent every penny he could afford to on the club while living in London. He couldn't keep it going. It turned out they had a shortfall of about £100,000 to pay the wages that month. Foolishly, I said I would give the £100,000 and if I come in fine, and if not you can consider it a gift.

'I spent the next month doing due diligence and the more I looked, the worse it got. In that month I had my lawyers in, accountants went through everything with a fine-tooth comb. Everyone was telling me "don't do it". But while they were doing that, I talked to the academy, talked to the community trust, I talked to the fans, I talked to everybody around there and it was obvious to me that the loss of Accrington would be far more than the monetary loss.

'The monetary loss was a separate issue altogether. The community trust interacts with 10,000 people in and around Accrington every year. Talking to the academy, and the community and everyone else was the only reason I got involved in the first place.'

Holt talks about the local community with a genuine passion and enthusiasm, but he isn't just saying what people want to hear, trotting out some well-prepped line from a media advisor. He exudes a true and unconditional love for the people of Accrington.

'So it's not, "Why is the club important?"' he says. 'It's the community that's important. So we need to keep the club going. The football team is almost secondary to keeping everything that is so valuable to Accrington going. I don't think people always realise how valuable a club is to a town.

'I spoke to the council. The council said to me, "It's a problem. Every time we go past the ground we look away. We end up in court over unpaid rates and unpaid bills." My wife said, "Don't do it." My kids said, "Don't do it." My accountant said, "Don't do it." My lawyers said, "Don't do it," but I had a good feeling.

'I had a meeting with the council and said, "Look, if I do this you need to back me otherwise I'll be a nightmare for you. I'll be turning the area against you. I'll get it straight and the club can have a future."

'They were the terms of reference: keep the club going to keep the community asset running. In order to keep the kids learning, disabled kids learning how to kick their first ball, you've got 85-year-olds doing walking football. You've got the whole mix. If the club dies, that dies. So that's why I got involved, that's what I'm protecting, that's why it means a lot to me. That's why I argue football has to be sustainable. Because when I disappear, if it's not sustainable, the football club could disappear. Or you need someone else to come and lose a load of money, because there aren't that many people daft enough to waste a load of money on football.

'So the council agreed to back me. After we got through all the questions from fans asking if I was an asset-stripper, when I was the only one in the room with any assets, they voted in favour for me to take over the club; the rest is history.

'My whole reason for being there is to make Accrington a sustainable club so I can leave, otherwise I'll be there forever. I haven't approached it like other owners have approached it. The more I got into it, the more I realised there's no such thing as a sustainable club. Everything that football does, everything the EFL does, everything the Premier League does, everything the FA does, every day they make it harder.'

When asked his opinion on the state of English football as a whole, Holt delivers a simple answer, 'A disaster. It's in a bad way and it's deteriorating every year that goes by. We will get more and more clubs going out of business or into administration rather than less and less. The problem is accelerating for a reason.'

For several years, Holt has been the most outspoken owner in English football. Using social media to spread his message, he has regularly and publicly criticised the sport's governance and its financial system.

'I believe that if fans understand what you're trying to do, and they see what you're trying to do but you get it wrong, they'll forgive you. But they need to know the plan,' he says.

'I use Twitter. I'd never heard of Twitter when I started at Accrington and when I leave I'll never use it again. I've never used it for my other businesses. Now and again, I put something out about Boris Johnson because he gets on my nerves. It's all about football generally. The reason is that when I first started, my daughter came to me and said, "Dad, have you seen this?" and it was this thing called Twitter. People were saying things about me that weren't true. It wasn't right. I'd never seen social media. I said she'd better get me an account then.

'So she set me up an account. I typed my name wrong. My name is Andy Mark Holt, but I typed "Andyhholt". I thought "it'll do".

'I started answering questions. Built up a conversation so the fans could understand what we're trying to do.

'It's a brilliant tool. If you use the press, you have to wait until they decide to print it. If you use books, you're dead and gone before anyone realises what was going on. To that extent I thought Twitter was brilliant. I can tell fans what I think. I don't think you can give fans enough information. I can't disclose wages but I can disclose the budget for example. I can tell fans whether we're making money or losing money. I'm more than happy to do that, it's their club. I've got nothing to hide, and I don't believe there should be anything that's secret.'

To anyone with any interest in how football is run, no matter what level your team plays at, Holt's Twitter account is absolute box office and often the cause of major sporting news.

In April 2018, Holt revealed that the EFL had contacted Accrington Stanley over allegations of inappropriate bonuses to players that were not included in the standard player contract. A serious claim not to be taken lightly. In actual fact, said bonus was £200 given to the club captain to buy a McDonald's for the squad after a win. The matter was closed after the EFL asserted that such a treat must also be provided after all matches, not just a win. It wasn't lost on critics of the EFL that, while it disclaimed responsibility for the troubles at Blackpool, Blackburn, Charlton and elsewhere, it had swung into action like Tarzan over a midweek burger and fries.

It wasn't the first time Holt had made national news for his tweets. A year earlier, following Paul Pogba's seismic transfer to Manchester United, Holt had exploded over various financial aspects of the move, and what it revealed about the state of English football. The £89m fee for Pogba would remain the UK record transfer for five years, until Manchester City's godfather offer for Jack Grealish topped it in 2021.

The transfer was a nice little earner for 'super-agent' Mino Raiola, who reportedly trousered £41m for the deal – and it was this figure that really sent Holt into orbit. He pointed out that the fee would pay for 156,000 full-priced season tickets at Accrington. With Zlatan Ibrahimović earning £367,000 a week at Old Trafford, and Pogba netting £3.5m from his own transfer, Holt tweeted, '[The Premier League should] hang your heads in shame. You are an absolute disgrace to English football.' He added, 'You're destroying the game, not "rogue" owners,' before comparing the EFL to 'a starving peasant begging for scraps off [the Premier League's] table'.

Faster than you can say 'Big Mac Meal', the Premier League fired back. It released a sneering statement asking publicly if Holt wanted the Premier League 'to continue the support' provided to his and other EFL clubs. Nice little club you have there, shame if it got broken.

Four years on, does Holt still stand by his comments?

'I stand by it 100 per cent. One hundred per cent. You've got to put a scale alongside it. Don't forget the solidarity income payment from the Premier League for League One and League Two was £26m; £41m went to one agent for one deal for a player that half the time doesn't want to play for

Manchester United. If you double the amount of money that Man Utd get, they'll double the wages and they'll double the agent fees.

'There's a gravitational pull. It's a vortex pulling the finances so high, spreading the gap so wide that the only way club owners can keep up is to overspend. Wages go up, everything goes up with it. The break-even cost of the business keeps going up. You either keep up or you get relegated and spiral down league after league.

'When you look at what the Premier League spends on players and compare it, it's more than the top four European leagues put together. It doesn't need to spend that. The Premier League spends that because it's available. It's not necessary to pay that sort of money. It's not necessary to pay Alexis Sánchez £500,000 a week to sit on the bench at Man Utd. If there was a control mechanism, or if it was that the Premier League was spending money that owners were putting in, I could understand it. The Premier League corners and controls all of the available cash.

'I understand why they do what they do, they're spending the proceeds of their own money. It doesn't hurt.'

It's not a new argument. Economists, football writers and newspapers have consistently shown that the clubs will spend every penny of what is available and often much more. Deloitte's annual report on football finance for 2018/19 revealed that clubs in the Championship were spending, on average, 107 per cent of their turnover on wages, before any other costs – a staggering figure. Clubs have never been known for fixing the roof while the sun was shining. It makes Holt's anger, as a man trying to run a financially

FIT AND PROPER PEOPLE

sustainable football club, all the more understandable. Cheat and compete, risking it all, or play fair and sink like a stone.

Holt also speaks regularly on the 'financial doping' in the sport. His arguments with former Manchester United legend and Salford City co-owner Gary Neville regularly make headlines on the back pages.

'My paradigm of football is formed by what I saw at Accrington. Gary Neville's view of football is formed from what he saw at United. He has a different paradigm to me. We're looking at the same problem and coming out with different solutions and outcomes.

'My fundamental point is this. If a load of ex-players, or actors from Hollywood, go and buy a non-league club, traditionally run clubs that mean so much to the town will slowly but surely have their place took. They're surely going to go up the league as they're paying much higher wages, they're happy to spend their investment in that way. They're buying their way into the league. They're not earning it, they're buying it. As soon as it stops paying the money, it ends up going back down. When Neville stops spending at Salford, the club doesn't have the fan base or the income to sustain itself. So Gary Neville has to be there all the time, or Peter Lim to keep it going.

'But they take the place of someone like Grimsby, someone that tried to live within their means but failed. Often these clubs fail to come back up, and they're doomed. They have to overspend now to become one of the two clubs that come up. They're trapped. They're like zombie clubs.'

It's here we start to return to our spectrum of 'good' and 'bad' owners. While on the surface it could seem fairly simple to pigeonhole the vast majority of owners into one of those two categories, Holt asserts that the reality is quite different.

'Then owners that have a go, when it fails, it fails spectacularly. Bury. Bolton. Wigan. I spoke to a former exec at Bolton and he told me their budget was to lose £10m a year. I asked why the fuck they'd be happy losing £10m a year? Do you think you'll get to the Premier League doing that? What will it achieve? And then they end up in administration.

'At the other end of the spectrum, take Notts County. Alan Hardy was a decent guy. He had a business that was turning over 70-odd million. He invested too heavily in Notts County. He had ideas above the station. He was going to take them to the Championship, etc, etc., and he may have done that if his core business hadn't turned bad.

'When Notts County was going under, he was desperate to find money to help. He was desperate to help the club survive. He was taking a big loss. But there was no assistance. I asked the EFL what they were going to do with clubs that are going to go bust for no good reason. If an owner gets into trouble, what do you do, just let it go bust? Why can't we go into these clubs and force them to get back within sensible bounds. Do we just accept community clubs are going to go bust because the owner's gone bust? A lot of the staff at his core business were suing because they said the money he spent at Notts County ruined the core business. It was just a mess that nobody could do anything with.

'I spoke to Steve Dale at Bury. I worked with a group who were looking to buy Bury. With Bury, don't forget the EFL paid bills for Bury over 100 times. It paid money out to other clubs under Stewart Day. They had ample notice things were going wrong. They did nothing. Steve Dale took over; he couldn't believe what he saw. He shit himself. He realised that he couldn't fill that hole. He should have quantified what the situation was before he got in. All it takes is decent regulation to stop that from happening.'

It's difficult to say how likely it is that 'decent regulation' will be introduced and, indeed, what 'decent regulation' is.

'I trust the owners of clubs,' says Holt. 'The vast majority are decent people. They go bad because the underlying stability is being eroded and they have to put in more and more cash to make it work. They start off with good intentions and they realise it's a thankless task. You get criticised for doing your best, while losing money. Next year you're going to lose more money, fans want you to do more. Too many club owners have not spoken to fans and explained the reality. I determined early on it was best to explain what I was trying to do so everyone knew where they stood.'

With a lack of chairmen and owners who communicate regularly with their own fans, and with the footballing public at large, Holt believes he is generally well supported in boardrooms up and down the country.

'The most common comment I get from other owners is, "We're glad you speak out. We don't agree with everything you say but we agree with a lot of it and it needs saying." Other owners are exasperated. Football is skewed. Our votes aren't worth a damn. The big clubs keep threatening to pull away. The Big Six threaten to go to a European Super League. They keep using threats to win more ballots. "We'll form a Premier League Two", "We'll form a Championship breakaway."

'League Two recently had a vote on the Premier League bailout money. League Two voted 22 out of 24 to split the money equally in League Two. Rick Parry brought it to League One to ask what they thought. You've got bigger clubs in League One, say Sunderland, and he says that it won't work unless League One agrees to it.

'So I asked Rick Parry why League One has to agree to it? If that's what League Two want to do, why does League One have to approve it? Moreover, if League Two can't decide their own stance, what's the point of having a vote?

'I never go to any of the EFL meetings now because it's pointless. When we vote for something in League One, Rick Parry will say we need over 50 per cent of the Championship to agree. You can't get anything done. You can't change anything. You can't get anything on the agenda. The agenda is set by the Premier League. The Premier League wants to change the transfer window? Straight on the agenda. We voted against it but the EFL pushed it through saying that the Championship voted for it.'

Voting procedures in the EFL and the National League have been a considerable source of debate. In May 2019, sensing that the issue was a cause of concern for a significant number of its member teams, the EFL included the question of whether clubs should have equal voting weight in the remit of an independent governance review. The matter is no less controversial in the National League, where the top division can easily outvote the two regional divisions below combined.

'If there was one thing I could do,' says Andy, 'I would give each club a golden share, and make the value of each share the same. In football the voting is rigged towards the bigger clubs. Their share is worth more than our share.'

Holt's transparent, community-based approach has made him a popular figure among fans, even those outside of Accrington. What then, did he make of the OwnaFC concept?

'I read a bit about it at the time. To me it was a non-starter from day one. If a load of fans want to buy a football club, go and buy it. I don't like these schemes. When I was joining Accrington there was a scheme like "buy a brick". Buy a brick for £1,000. The club was going to build an arch using the bricks, and the club would put your name on it. They sold one and a half bricks. I refunded the money.

'You've got to be careful when people are investing in business, whether it's a hundred quid or a hundred million, that they're doing it for a sound reason, a business reason rather than an emotional decision. Asking fans for money over what they spend on their season tickets, and merchandise, and pies, etc,. I'd rather have their help with how we run the club rather than pestering them for money.'

But Stuart Harvey did not apply caution when asking people to 'invest' in his business. While most of OwnaFC's customers just wanted to be involved in the running of a football club, there were a few who told us that owning a share that could increase in value was a draw to the company. Harvey later backtracked, saying that he was selling an 'experience'.

There was plenty that OwnaFC could have learned from Holt about community. The votes that did make the app were minimal, trivial matters and it was clear that Owna's subscribers never really had a direct influence in the running of the company.

But just how much influence should fans have in the running of their football club? Holt says, 'I think about this a lot because I think about my end of days. What happens when I leave Accrington? When I leave, I want to leave it in such a way that the work that I've done is paid for and protected. That the stadium is paid for. That the training ground is paid for. I don't want a Steve Dale type, or an OwnaFC type to come in and ruin it all, or sell the assets, or gamble it on a run at the title and Accrington goes back to square one.

'I want fans to have more say. But it's not sensible to assume that all fan groups are as good as others. It's not a safe assumption. You see this at Bury where there's competing interests. I was invited to a meeting with the MP, [supporters' group] Forever Bury and a few others. I had background because I'd spoken to Steve Dale and Sporting Ventures. Steve Dale actually rang me in the meeting. I think that put them off because they thought I was working with Steve Dale when I was actually just trying to engineer a situation where he sold the club. I thought that's what he needed to do.

'I think there should be a charter that fans can use against a club if necessary. Fans should have someone to go to, an individual or an independent regulator.'

While Holt's approach is laudable, and has clearly been successful in that the club has achieved promotion to League One and stayed there despite its size, there is a question on whether his approach can be replicated. It is heavily reliant on one individual owner having an ethos and mentality that fits in with what fans want from the club. If Holt 'went rogue' and took an entirely different direction, he would have every right to do so. The problem is there's just not enough selfless local millionaires to go round. Too many people want to be in football for what they can get from it, not for what they can give to it.

OwnaFC was the flipside of Andy Holt. Despite the shiny marketing and the promises (that were later left in a skip somewhere in Hednesford), OwnaFC was always *The Stuart Harvey Show*. How much did Harvey care about the community that already existed at any of his target clubs. Not much, it seems. Or about transparency or sustainability.

While Holt may have a point that bad owners are made, the current framework and high levels of competitive spending make it more likely that an owner will turn bad. Owners are not supported by current regulation, and they should be, because we entrust them to look after our clubs and our communities.

To replicate Accrington would rely on replicating Holt's good nature, transparency, and prudent financial policies. That's not to say there aren't other 'good' owners out there. Mark and Nicola Palios have a similar reputation running Tranmere Rovers. Carol Shanahan has won huge plaudits during her short time at Port Vale. Luton Town fans could spend all day highlighting the positives of their 2020 Consortium owners. But they are the exceptions that prove the rule.

There's clearly a lot that football could learn from Accrington Stanley. There's a lot it could learn from Andy Holt. And they're worth far more than being the butt of the joke in that bloody milk advert.

10

The bones in my face

With hindsight, I don't know how I came to ignore the signs. Ultimately, I suppose, you just don't think things like this happen to people like you.

I'M NOT a famous sports writer; it's highly unlikely you'll have read much I've written. And that means that when I'm writing about something, there are usually dozens of vastly more-experienced, better-connected writers – better writers full stop – covering the same story for well-known media organisations.

So it's very unusual and, frankly, a little intoxicating to find yourself making the running on a story, even one that seemed to many people to be fairly insignificant. For a period, James and I were the only people working on OwnaFC – trying to call public attention to its impractical business model, its poor track record and its deceptive and unprofessional practices.

Daily, I'd find myself talking to Ownas – concerned, disillusioned, let-down people – who were having no joy getting through to anyone with any kind of a platform. With their help, we'd fit another piece of the jigsaw together. Each tip or document would confirm some part of the story or open up new avenues for investigation. It felt like detective work, as if we were slowly uncovering something huge and sinister. It didn't properly occur to me until we were already in too deep that we didn't have the protection and authority afforded to police officers, that we didn't even have the know-how and legal resources of a media organisation. By then we'd already tried to hand the investigation off to several newspapers, none of whom wanted it, so we'd decided to continue it ourselves, even as Stuart Harvey's ever-more bellicose approach to PR became increasingly menacing and unsettling. Later, when Will Magee asked me why I'd spent so much time reporting on OwnaFC, my answer was simple: we were waiting for someone to do something about them, but no one did, so we had to.

When OwnaFC collapsed, it was a huge relief. It was a triumph but also a release of tension. We felt like we'd taken the bad guy down and, though he was trying to keep the business going, we knew he was a busted flush. Now, we assumed, the press would swoop in, followed in short order by the police. I felt if not invincible then close to it. While I'd continue to monitor progress towards refunds for everyone who wanted them, my thoughts were already turning to what to write about next. There didn't seem to me to be any more to the OwnaFC story beyond a bit of mopping up – largely supplying other journalists with evidence for their work and helping Ownas out with queries about T&Cs.

Despite some of the things I'd heard about Harvey, I wasn't worried on my own account. I was just one irritation and I lived at the other end of the country. It seemed most likely that he'd be so busy fending off refund demands, creditors and Trading Standards that he wouldn't have time for anything else. Not even one of what seemed to be his favourite hobbies: online harassment and intimidation.

So when word reached us that Harvey was putting it about that he had a numbered list of people who he blamed for his company's failure, we didn't take it too seriously. James and I referred to it mockingly as 'Stuart's Big List of Bastards'.

Perhaps I should've done something about it then. It may already have been too late.

Early on Saturday, 16 March, little more than 12 hours after OwnaFC put out its statement in the name of a law firm, hailing a new and more professional era of operations, an anonymous social media account appeared and began firing off questions at critics of the business. Purporting to be from a young adult who was a fan of AFC Wimbledon, it bombarded me with a stream of inane queries. As it made little attempt to hide the person behind it, I assumed Harvey was merely bored after 'stepping back' from his business.

One thing did give me a moment's concern, however. While the account didn't have a name, it had a profile picture – a map of a part of south-west London. Anyone who scrutinised my social media for long wouldn't have much trouble finding my general location, but this map showed a square of London about 500m across – just seven or eight roads east to west. It was a very small area indeed, and it was cropped so my house was just off the edge.

I didn't know if it was a lucky guess or it indicated Harvey had my home address, but it seemed an attempt at intimidation – even if the tone of the actual messages he was sending me was relatively light-hearted. Harvey, I would later discover, is a master of subtle intimidation, of knowing just how far to go so that the police can't act.

Eventually tiring of Harvey's games, I blocked the account. My wife and I went to a friend's 40th birthday party that evening and I happily chatted to people, perhaps a little boastfully, about the work I'd been doing on OwnaFC.

The next day, Sunday, was beautiful and warm for March. I woke up feeling uneasy, though. Could Harvey know where I lived? I've never had a Facebook account and I publish very limited amounts of information about myself or my family on social media – certainly no photos. I've never been the director of a company and I always sign the closed electoral register. My digital football print largely consists of things I've written. But when I came to look a few weeks later, it took less than five minutes and a small fee to find my address online.

In the mid-morning, my wife took my youngest daughter, then six, clothes shopping. A generally uncomplaining soul, she had begun to hint that she was tired of constantly living in hand-me-downs.

They came back in the early afternoon and my youngest, now beaming, wanted to do a show-and-tell. She assembled the family in the front room and began to display what she'd got. There was a dress, some trousers, a few t-shirts and a pair of trainers. None of it was expensive, but she was delighted. Having shown us the clothes, she announced she would try them on and began to change.

While we moved to the sofa to play the audience in a fashion show, I glanced at my phone. There was a Twitter notification: a new follower. It was an account called 'DeludedMartin'. I'd usually have taken it for a coincidence or a weak attempt at trolling, but before I could decide which, I noticed the profile picture. It was something horribly familiar and I realised I was in trouble. The profile image, when I enlarged it, was a photograph of the car showroom at the end of my road, about 100 metres from my front door. Not a stock shot, but something snapped with a phone camera. I felt cold and my hands were trembling. He didn't need to do this, he knew where I lived; he could've come straight to my door. But no, he wanted me to know not just that he was after me, but that he was already here. He wanted me to feel fear first.

The account was new and had sent just one tweet a few minutes before. It read, 'Today I became a tweeter. I am deluded and think I can do and say anything without consequence.'

For a minute, I couldn't move; I just sat feeling like I might vomit. My wife knew what I'd been working on these last few weeks but, not wanting to worry her, I hadn't told her the full extent of Harvey's misdeeds. It seemed like I'd need to get the kids out of the room, talk to her urgently about what was going on, and perhaps call the police. At which point, the doorbell went.

A police officer would later ask me who'd thrown the first punch and I had to confess that I didn't know. Not that I doubted it was Harvey, but rather because my memory of what happened next is very fragmented. There's blank spells, bits that seemed to fly past and moments that happened in excruciatingly slow motion.

I remember my eldest daughter springing up to get the door. Then eight, she's hyper-sociable and is always delighted to meet people. She's the kind who makes conversation with every shop assistant, waiter or ticket inspector. Every knock at the door is an opportunity for a chat.

I was barely out of my seat when she got to the door and opened it. I heard Harvey ask if I was in. I recognised his voice even before I reached the hall and saw him.

I remember getting to the doorway and, with one arm, sweeping my daughter up and dropping her down behind me. I told her to go to the lounge and began closing the door. I barked at Harvey something to the effect that he had 30 seconds to get off my doorstep before I called the police. But I couldn't close the door; he had his foot in it. I remember pulling the door back towards me to try and get the force to slam it. But as I opened it, he reached through and dragged me outside. Holding me by a bunched-up handful of my t-shirt, he threw me against the side of the house. I felt my head crack against it. Lifting me on to my tiptoes, he pinned me against the wall and I had a momentary sensation of the cold of the bricks against my shoulder blades and the base of my spine, where my t-shirt had ridden up. After that, the beating began.

Harvey isn't much taller than me and, at the time, he was a little out of shape. But I'm slightly built and type for a living, and he was a former semi-professional rugby player.

I remember the punches and I remember swinging back, wildly furious and determined to drive him away from my house. I remember my wife crying and screaming at Harvey to get off me. I can hear her voice while she was on the phone to the police. One of his punches caught the side of my face, knocking my glasses off and, as I looked down, I realised he was still holding my t-shirt with one hand while he was moving me around and then hitting me with the other. I must have looked like a rag doll.

I remember stumbling and, as I fell forward, him pulling my t-shirt over my head. Now I was blinded and my arms were pinned. There were four or five punches, with me crouching down, helpless. I remember the strangest sensation, each time his fist struck down on me, of feeling the bones in my face move. None of it hurts; there's no pain, at least not then. All there is is adrenaline screaming through your system, turbocharging you. There's almost no noise. Even the sound of the fists connecting with your ribs are dull thuds that seem to come to you not through your ears, but through the internal vibrations of your body. You hear the assault through the rattling of your bones. There are no thoughts either, just a single overpowering primal urge: keep him out of the house and away from the children.

I remember being back on my feet somehow. The distance from our front door to our gate is no more than about five or six feet and I found myself having driven him out of the gate. I was standing against it, keeping it closed, while we exchanged blows. I wasn't doing him any damage, but it was enough, for now, to stop him advancing. He was screaming now. 'You see, there are consequences! There are consequences!' Over and over. I remember the primitive rage in his face, the spit flying from his mouth.

I remember two neighbours arrived and were trying to break things up. They pulled him back and it was as if

I'd come to for a moment. Time started flowing normally again and I was able to pick up my glasses. Suddenly, I was overcome with worry he'd run off and I'd be left with no proof against him. And so even while he was screaming, I took out my phone from my pocket and made to film him – a foolish piece of learned behaviour from the social media age. He reached over the gate and ripped it from my hand and went to put it in his jacket pocket, still yelling. I remember saying pathetically, 'Are you going to make it theft too?' and, for a moment, he hesitated. I tore the phone away from him. And even as I did it, I could hear sirens blaring and a police car and a riot van rocketed round the corner and braked hard. Two policemen exploded out and were on Harvey almost instantly, dragging him away. Another two came in to take my statement.

At the time, it had seemed to last no more than 30 seconds. I told the police he'd hit me four or five times, because the moments where I was crouched down had been the most visceral element, the only portion where I could innumerate the blows. But I later found out the beating had been administered over five minutes. Punch after punch for five long minutes.

Even then, I was lucky. It turned out that the police had been coming down the main road after a previous call-out and so we hadn't had to wait for a dispatch from the nearest station. On other days, at other times, the wait could've been much longer.

I remember the aftermath most of all. My wife quivering and crying in the hall. My youngest daughter, still in her underwear where she'd been changing outfits, huddled in a ball in the corner of the lounge. She was sobbing hysterically, while my older daughter was crouched down, cuddling her to try and comfort her and covering her ears to block out the terrifying noises.

The next few hours were spent giving a statement to the police and photographing my injuries. All told, it might've been worse. I had a black eye, a bleeding nose, swelling and bruising to the rest of my face, neck and torso, and scratches to my throat. My t-shirt was ripped from where he'd literally lifted me off my feet when he'd dragged me on to the doorstep. The next day, my GP would refer me for X-rays to check I didn't have a fractured skull. Fortunately, I didn't. The day after that I could barely move my arms; I had strained almost every muscle in my upper body fighting back as fiercely as I was able.

The police told me that he'd be taken to the station, interviewed and charged. It was a simple case, they said. He'd be in court within four weeks and that would be the end of it. They were wrong about much of that.

The police also told me that, because my children had been witness to violence in the home, they would have to inform social services, in case an investigation was necessary. After what happened the following day, my wife and I would also contact my children's school, explain the situation and ask they be alert for intruders on the premises.

The same week, we had security cameras installed around the house and, despite living in a safe, friendly neighbourhood, the children were banned from ever again opening the front door. Panic attacks and depression would follow and it would be another year – until Britain was on lockdown with Covid-19 – before I'd no longer fear every knock at the door.

Like I said, things like this aren't supposed to happen. There are supposed to be lines that decent people don't cross.

I had no idea how wrong I was.

11

Daniel

*It was a different voice on the end
of the phone this time.*

THE PAST two times that I'd been called out of work, it
was my wife who rang, apologetically asking if I could come
to the hospital. The staff were concerned, it was probably
nothing, but could I come?

It was a nurse this time, 'Mr Cave, you should make your
way to the hospital.'

When I arrived, Nic, my wife, was in the delivery suite
hooked up to every monitor they had, beeping suspiciously
but quietly. The baby wasn't due for another six weeks, but
here we were. Nic had been advised to go to the hospital after
reporting a rise in her blood pressure the day before. During
observation it was discovered that our unborn son's heart
rate was periodically crashing for reasons unknown. Every
so often the beating from the monitor slowed. And slowed.
And slowed. And slowed. And slowed. Then it returned
to normal.

Over the next couple of hours, several serious-looking medical staff all brandishing clipboards came to introduce themselves, just in case. The surgeon. The head midwife. The chief consultant. The anaesthetist.

Liam was a young, stern, bespectacled surgeon. He knelt beside my wife's bed and after yet another dip of my son's heart rate concluded, 'There's only so long we can sit and watch this.' In about 20 minutes Liam would be saving the lives of my family.

A decision was made. We were told if our son's heart rate crashed again, they would operate. Nic was prepped for surgery. Someone threw a pair of scrubs at me to put on. We were warned of 'a scene from *Holby City*' and to expect a flurry of activity with no warning and no explanation. Do we agree? Sign here, please.

The inevitable dip in heart rate came about five minutes later. Nic and I were alone, I ran to the corridor and shouted for Liam. The room filled immediately with frenzied nurses and doctors. Nic was wheeled away. I didn't even get chance to say 'goodbye' or 'I love you'. I was told I'd be called in a few minutes and I could be there for the caesarean.

No. Scratch that. There's been a complication. Wait here. Your son will be out shortly, and you can come with him to ICU.

Silence. The room was dark. It was so confusing and daunting. My life was being changed a few metres away and there was nothing I could do. Five minutes passed. Ten minutes.

Finally, a beaming grin emerged from the corridor. The head midwife poked her head around the door and announced, 'Congratulations, you're a daddy! Everything's fine, we'll bring him down in a few minutes.'

They left me there for probably another half an hour. It felt like days. What do you do in that situation? Do I text someone? Just sit and wait? I watched the clock intently.

The familiar grin of the nurse appeared again this time standing in front of an incubator. He was beautiful and perfect of course, and I instantly broke down into tears. We'd been discussing names for months. It took us nearly a day to settle on Daniel.

They wheeled my son into the neonatal ICU. The attending nurse, Tenby, was fantastic. They put him in my arms and I just happily cried some more. I'm not one for crying usually.

I wasn't aware how long it takes for someone to wake from a C-section. Ten minutes? Twenty minutes? An hour? Four hours? No one had told me of any problems with Nic and it took me about 25 minutes for me to ask, 'I assume my wife is okay, by the way? Can I see her?'

I was escorted through a maze of corridors, practically skipping at the thought of finally sharing that moment with my wife. We'd done it; we'd become parents.

Being shown through a door, it quickly became clear that no, not everything was okay. Nic was on oxygen, panting, gasping for breath.

A doctor spotted my entrance and explained that an existing infection had reacted with the anaesthetic. Nic would be fine but would need constant observation for several hours. A full recovery was expected. Neither of us would learn until later that the situation during the operation was much more serious and Nic had come very close to losing her life.

I put on a brave face for Nic but could barely string a sentence together. 'He's beautiful!' I spluttered. I explained he was healthy and being seen to by fantastic nurses, but it became clear I was in the way. I promised her to come back in 15 minutes.

I spent the next 12 hours or so flitting between them both. Nic recovered her breath and was released to a recovery room, but she wasn't well enough to see Daniel for about eight hours. After significant protests, the nurses finally agreed that Nic could come with us down to neonatal to see Daniel.

Walking in felt like the end of a years-long journey and the start of a new one. We'd wanted a family for so long. Daniel was handed to Nic and you could see, instantly, that she was just meant to be a mum.

Daniel was too premature to be released, and we were told he'd have to stay at least for a few days. Nic was recovering in hospital anyway from major surgery, so we decided I should go home, try to rest.

And then reality returned.

At some point on Sunday, I checked Twitter. Martin had messaged. Stuart had been to his house and assaulted him.

Where do you start with something like that? How do you process it? Stuart had seemingly driven from Wigan to south London, knocked on Martin's door and attacked him.

Guilt was my immediate response. I was sure this was my fault. The final decision to publish the details of Harvey's businesses was mine. We'd talked about it and discussed it, sure, but I wrote the tweets and I pressed 'send'. Had I done this? Thankfully Martin said that his injuries weren't too severe. The police had responded rapidly and Harvey had been carted off.

Fuck. Just, just fuck.

That was the first time that we'd spoken on the phone. Before that, our friendship and working relationship had been completely virtual. We'd only ever communicated on Twitter and it seemed to me that Martin had always been very careful to protect his privacy. Quite right too, clearly. We were friendly, of course, but I was just a bloke off the internet. Martin was clearly shaken by the incident but was OK in the grand scheme of things.

It's then you think, 'Are we next?'

Considering Harvey was determined enough to get in his car, drive for around four hours while planning to attack someone and at no point stopped to think 'maybe this isn't a great idea', then yeah, it's perfectly reasonable to assume we were next. We only lived 45 minutes away from him.

While I maintain we didn't do anything wrong – we published legitimate investigative journalism, most of which was based on information already freely available to anyone looking hard enough – did I stop to consider what effect going in 'studs up' would have on my unborn son? To my shame, no I didn't.

* * *

We decided that on Monday I should go back to work. Nic had an army of family around her and I was useless in the hospital, really. It would be better to start my paternity leave when Nic and Daniel were home. Because Daniel was six weeks early, we hadn't finished the house. Most of it was done; the nursery was built and decorated, but both my mum and Nic's mum offered to head round to ours to do the 'deep clean'.

For about five hours on Monday, it was the best day I'd ever had in work. Everyone was so lovely and complimentary, asking how we all were, wanting to see photos.

Though I knew I had to quit, I was still smoking by this point. Only at work, never around the wife, but Amber Leaf was still my weakness and my guilty pleasure. Every lunch hour I had the same routine. I'd sit in my office, I'd roll a smoke, I'd check the news, I'd go outside, light up, ring the wife.

And it's at that point, on Monday, 18 March at about 11.58am, that everything went to shit.

I had a Twitter DM. Even before reading it, I knew who it was from and I knew it wasn't good. The username was @ JamesDeluded and the profile pic was a Southport FC badge. With my stomach churning, I opened the message:

> Hi James, firstly congratulations to you and Nicola on the birth of your child. Nothing more amazing that [sic] children coming into the world. This is why children should never be put in danger by irresponsible action [sic] of trolls and people looking for clicks.
>
> With this in mind, visits are planned to every person that has recently put children in danger as the question of why needs to be asked.
>
> We have your address and would like to come and ask you why and discuss things as children still

remain in danger and cannot live with their father because of your actions. You have by posting tweets put people in danger of lunatics and I would invite you to consider the Jo Cox murder case. Lunatics were spurred on my [sic] idiotic and damaging tweets that were done by people like you. You may not be thinking about the damage and distress you have caused and this needs to be discussed.

You have the opportunity to attend Nando's in Southport which is a public place so that you can answer the questions on why you believe tweeting like you are doing is the right thing to do, even when children have been put in danger. If you do not then answers will still be needed and we will come knocking at your door to seek these answers.

We should stress that we are looking for a civil and open discussion to understand why you have felt the need to damage a business, target individuals and put children in danger.

This is something that needs to be resolved today or tomorrow we will be knocking on your door asking this questions.

Checking the account, there was a single public tweet, 'Twitter trolls should not be allowed to harass people, put children in danger or damage businesses for clicks and attention. If they do, they should be answerable.'

The first call I made was to my mum – who was still in our house. If Stuart was planning a 'visit' I needed to get them out as soon as possible. Mum was vaguely familiar with the situation but said she wasn't going anywhere. Typical.

The next call was to 101. I was later chastised for not ringing 999. The call was excruciating. Not only was I trying to explain a lengthy, complex situation to a call handler who was probably woefully underpaid, the poor lady then had to transcribe the entire lengthy diatribe I'd received.

And then, how on earth was I going to tell Nic? She was still an inpatient in the maternity ward at Ormskirk and just wanted to be at home with her family. It was a tough time already, news of Martin's attack had already put us on edge and this was just going to make it unbearable.

I don't remember that call. I don't want to. The human brain is extraordinarily good at alerting us to threats and purging bad memories. In this case, that suits me fine. What I do remember is that she, understandably, was incredibly upset.

At that point, the cigarette wasn't a luxury or just a poor life choice. For me at that particular moment, it was an urgent medical necessity. I went outside, sparked up, and tried to understand what in the blue fuck I'd just read.

Firstly, I had to be sure it was Harvey. This wasn't hard. It followed a similar pattern to Martin's attack just the day before. @DeludedMartin. @JamesDeluded. There was a clear motive. I was certain, immediately, that Harvey had sent the message.

Jo Cox. Why was he talking about Jo Cox? While most people will be sadly familiar with the tragic fate of Jo Cox, to anyone unaware it's worth explaining that she was a sitting Labour MP who was murdered by a right-wing extremist in 2016. Was Harvey saying he'd murder me or that the focus on Harvey could cause him to be targeted like Cox? I've had no shortage of people tell me this is a full-on death threat.

I left work early to go to the hospital. That evening an officer from the Lancashire Constabulary came to speak to us both. Security measures were put in place across the entire hospital. The whole building was usually locked at about 10pm, but this was brought forward to 7pm. Harvey's photograph was circulated around the hospital. A password would be required to entire any maternity, children's or delivery ward.

And while the officer from Lancashire was particularly helpful and understanding, a problem soon became clear. The hospital was under the jurisdiction of Lancashire Police. Our house was under the umbrella of Merseyside Police. Harvey's address was under Greater Manchester Police. There was a connection to Martin's case under the Metropolitan Police in London. Trying to get representatives from each force to talk to another was impossible.

Nic and Daniel were both seen as vulnerable patients. Daniel was a tiny, six-week-premature newborn baby. Nic was a new mother recovering from a surgery with complications. The hospital reported plenty of safeguarding issues to the police, which did help hugely in forcing them to take it seriously.

The severity of the situation was drilled into me when I was advised by the police not to return home. In a little over 24 hours, using nothing but Twitter so far, Harvey was starting to unravel my entire life. Nic and I were already emotionally exhausted before his messages, with our newborn son in the ICU, Nic still an inpatient, I couldn't get my head straight to work and now I couldn't go home. The next day @ JamesDeluded tweeted, 'Southport PR8 is todays destination for Troll Watch.' PR8 is the opening part of my postcode.

An appointment was made for me to speak to officers from Merseyside Police. I was in their interview room for what must have been approaching three hours. It was another painful conversation. How do you go about explaining this entire situation? It was a scenario Martin and I would become all too familiar with, trying to summarise one of the most distressing sagas of our lives in just a few minutes.

@JamesDeluded actually tweeted 'Door knocking again today' while I was sat with officers going through his account. Harvey was showing continuous intent to visit our home, uninvited. Martin and I had stopped any and all responses to Harvey at this point, figuring he was digging his own legal grave.

We had pets at home, so I was periodically checking in on the house, parking down the road and surveying the street for lurking, Wigan-based stalkers before opening the front door. I installed a video doorbell. I had been staying with my mum but, as lovely and as welcoming as she was, I was not coping terribly well with all the various situations I was going through and insisted on going back home. There was a guitar by the door I could smash him over the head with, if need be.

About a week later we had confirmation from the Met in Martin's case that Harvey had admitted to being @ DeludedMartin. It was already obvious it was Harvey that was messaging me, and this just seemed to confirm it.

Back at the hospital, we still weren't allowed to take Daniel home. He was a small but healthy baby. Every shift we'd ask the nurses attending what the criteria and timeline was for taking Daniel home, and the answer changed constantly. It was heartbreaking. One nurse would say, 'Oh you can go home in a day or so.' By the next shift, the answer would change to, 'You've probably got another week yet.'

One nurse told us that Daniel would be expected to stay in until he reached his original delivery date, another five weeks away, and warned us that most often, if parents insisted on taking their baby home early from NICU, a large majority end up being readmitted. And when they do, she said, they go to the standard children's ward which, and this is the exact quote, 'isn't as good as here and there are a lot of infections passing round on that ward'.

But no one could actually explain why we couldn't take him home. Eventually, a consultant decided we could leave. We'd spoken to a lot of parents who'd told us of a sense of bewilderment when you get your baby home for the first time ('Well, what now?'). We were fortunate that we'd had nurses walking us through every step of care for over a week. We fed Daniel, put him down for a nap, and just like that, he was part of the family.

Two days after Nic and Daniel arrived home, someone rooted through the wheelie bins outside our house, which were awaiting collection. Unfortunately, the camera I installed didn't cover it, and no one saw anything. Maybe it was a coincidence, but given that Harvey had boasted about using private investigators to track some Ownas, I had a strong suspicion he could have been involved. I advised 101.

Over the next few days the official OwnaFC account was tweeting about selling the business. I wasn't really paying attention by this point. We were at home looking after our son, getting to know him.

We'd had six amazing days at home together when Harvey finally turned up on our doorstep.

It was 4 April. A Thursday. Nic was sat on the couch when she received a call from a withheld number.

Caller: 'Is that Nicola?'

Nic: 'Can I ask who is speaking?'

Caller: 'It's Stuart Harvey.'

Nic: 'Sorry, who is speaking?'

Caller: 'Stuart Harvey, I want to know if you and James are available for a visit today?'

Nic hung up. We had no idea how he'd got her mobile number or our address. We were on edge all day. Stupidly, I said we should stay put. Nic rang 999 who said there was nothing they could do until something happened more serious than a phone call. Two hours later, she received another call.

Caller: 'We got cut off before. I don't want to have to come and see you at [quotes our address], can we arrange to meet off site?'

Nic: 'Sorry, who is this?'

Caller: 'Stuart Harvey.'

Four hours later, Nic received a final warning. A text from Harvey at 4.47pm.

'Hi Nicola,

'I am in [your] area on a job later today. I was wondering What time is best for both of you or at least 1 of you to a chat with me this evening. I would like to explain to you the damage your tweets caused and how my children have been threatened with rape and put in danger because of your actions.

'Also I would like to explain how posting addresses online puts people in danger and how this is wrong. Every action comes with a consequence and as online trolls and campaigners, you should understand that your actions have put children in danger and that needs to be explained'

Stuart had claimed 'threats' he had received on several occasions. But neither myself, Nic nor any Owna ever saw a threat towards Stuart or his children. All we ever saw was Stuart threatening other people.

We spotted Stuart before he knocked on the door, parked over the road in the same car he had driven to Martin's house in.

I shepherded Nic and the baby upstairs.

I'm quite a big lad. I'm 6ft, admittedly a bit overweight, I could probably ride a punch or two but I'm no fighter. The prospect of having to physically defend myself against Stuart was a reluctant final resort, but if it came to that, of course I would do anything to protect my family.

It didn't come to that. Stuart wasn't given the opportunity to evolve psychological torture into physical violence. After what happened to Martin, he knew that there was no chance we were going to open the door, but he tried anyway.

After, quite bizarrely, moving his car to a slightly closer parking position several times over the next 15 minutes, Harvey knocked on the door. Upstairs, I was watching out of the window, Nic was on the phone to the police. Harvey knocked a second time. We left the dog downstairs, barking blue murder as he always did when someone knocked on our door.

On the video footage you can see Harvey brace himself, settle up and flatten his posture. He stands there for 90 seconds. It feels like hours. Upon giving up and realising we weren't going to answer the door, he walks away but as he turns he spits, 'I'll be back. I'll be back.' He doesn't leave, and sits in his car.

Two officers arrived a short while later. It was clear that nothing was going to be done. Even with all the context and the history painstakingly explained, Harvey was not arrested but rather sent on his way with a polite request from the police not to return while the matter was investigated. Merseyside Police later admitted that the decision not to arrest Harvey at this point was a mistake.

After again being given the laborious summary of the events leading up to Harvey's attendance at our home, the officers passed on a message that Harvey's main concern was that my tweets referring to him and OwnaFC were deleted.

This posed a question that came up again and again, even ahead of the publication of this book. It's a question that my wife and I wrestled with, and a question that Martin and I wrestled with. How do we weigh the need to tell this story against the risk to our families? Harvey had shown distance wasn't a barrier to him. But should we give in for security?

Should we just let him get away with it? How much could Harvey escalate the situation if he wanted to?

With genuine hesitation, I decided against removing anything. I was certain everything I had posted was legally sound, accurate, not defamatory, and, above all, an important piece of journalism. The tweets are still available on my account today. But the risk to me, more importantly the risk to my family, and the risk to Martin and his family still feels very real, even now.

There was a strange feeling in our home after that. We were still figuring out how to be parents while constantly looking over our shoulders.

But in the various discussions with the police and the CPS in the weeks ahead, we decided we didn't want to let Harvey get away with it. We didn't want him to be able to do this to anyone else.

We were pressing charges, and we were going to court.

12

The unfailable test

*In 2018, Chesterfield fan and sometime club
historian Stuart Basson stopped going to games.
What could drive someone to boycott a club
they'd been a supporter of for over 40 years?*

IT'S AN article of faith among football fans that clubs aren't
properly protected from rogue owners and that pretty much
any two-bit conman can rock up and buy a team. The problem
for football is that supporters, for once, aren't exaggerating.
If anything, they understate the ease with which someone
unsuitable can buy a club.

It's common practice to mock the Owners' and Directors'
Test, which is still often referred to by its old name, the 'Fit
and Proper Person Test', but it's rare for people to actually sit
down and read the test. If they do, it calls to mind what JFK
said having defeated Nixon in a hard-fought battle for the
US presidency in 1960, 'When we got into office, the thing
that surprised me most was to find that things were just as

bad as we'd been saying they were.' It doesn't matter how weak you think the safeguards over football clubs are, until you actually read them you have no idea. Unless you're a fan of Chesterfield. Or Charlton. Or Blackpool. Or any one of the growing band of teams who've found themselves in the hands of people who appear incapable of running a football club successfully.

To understand how Stuart and hundreds of others stopped going to Chesterfield games, you need to understand how easily venerable clubs can become vulnerable clubs. Chesterfield fans have seen more in the last ten years than most clubs have seen in their entire history. They've had a decade that it seems impossible to believe could've happened in the Premier League era.

Stuart, a technical manager in a theatre, grew up in Portsmouth. He moved to Chesterfield over 40 years ago and began supporting his local team. 'Apart from one glorious season under fraudster Darren Brown, we were always boringly well-run,' he says.[16] 'We never made much of a loss, never made much of a profit. Never did much on the pitch.'

He's not exaggerating. Chesterfield were inaugural members of the Third Division when, in 1958/59, it and the Fourth Division were formed from what had been the Third Divisions North and South. They then spent 60 straight years in what are now League One and League Two, never winning promotion to the Championship, never getting relegated to non-league. And, while they did win the EFL Trophy in 2012, they have never won the FA Cup. If you grew up in Chesterfield, it was possible to have literally lived and died a fan of the club and never see your team play in English football's second tier or above (the Spireites were last in what is now the Championship in 1950/51).

Presented in this deliberately reductive way – where trophies and transfer fees count for more than any sense of belonging – the club reeks of mediocrity. But, of course, if that's all there was to football clubs, Chesterfield wouldn't still be going; they wouldn't be able to trace their roots back to the 1860s. They wouldn't have averaged 4,500 fans in the National League in 2018/19 – third-highest in the division despite flirting with relegation all season.

Any football fan in middle age will remember the club's glorious 1997 FA Cup run, where the then third-tier side, boasting teenage Hercules and future England international Kevin Davies, made it all the way to the semi-finals before being knocked out by Premier League Middlesbrough. That year they beat Bristol City, Nottingham Forest and Bolton – where Davies got a hat-trick in a 3-2 away win. Against a Middlesbrough team featuring star signings Gianluca Festa, Emerson, Juninho, and the White Feather himself, Fabrizio Ravanelli, they scored a 119th-minute equaliser at Old Trafford to earn a replay. It remains one of the greatest cup runs in modern history.

But, gradually, things started to go wrong for the club. At the turn of the millennium, with money fever rampaging through English football, even some Chesterfield fans began to dream of better. 'People wanted rid of the chairman Norton Lea,' says Stuart, delicately referring to him as 'somewhat parsimonious'.

Fans got what they'd wished for and then some. Parsimony, like caution and realism, was a completely alien word to new owner Darren Brown. If you remember Chesterfield's cup run, you may also have dim memories of Mr Brown. A man for whom no aspiration was too large, Brown ended the 1990s pitching himself as Britain's first multi-sports mogul. Through his UK Sports Group, and still only in his 20s, he owned the Sheffield Steelers ice hockey team and the Sheffield Sharks basketball team – both big names in their sports.

But, like Icarus with wings made of false accounts, Brown soon came crashing back to earth.

'He had no business sense,' says Stuart. 'He misrepresented the value of Luke Beckett's transfer to an FA tribunal. He had two contracts, one they saw, one they didn't. He was cavalier in how he registered players. He was alleged to have operated an illegal bonus scheme, where players were literally paid in brown envelopes.' The club was also found guilty by the FA of not correctly reporting its gate receipts, which did not appear to tally with their actual attendance figures.[17]

'It's what you'd read about happening at clubs in the 1930s,' says Stuart. 'He was an old-school football crook.'

In only months, a club that had been sold with money in the bank was in trouble and, within a year, had debts of £2m. Brown stepped down from his roles at the Sheffield Sharks and Steelers, citing the abuse of fans as a factor. 'The crunch came when I got involved with arguments with some of the fans and realised whatever I did was not going to be good enough,' he said.[18]

Shortly after, a judge called him 'entirely reckless' although also 'ambitious, plausible and persuasive' and sentenced him to four years in prison for fraud.[19] Chesterfield went into administration and Brown sold them to the supporters' trust for £6,000, which was all the money the trust had in its bank account.

That was all it took. One tumultuous year under Brown undid decades of respectable stability and set in motion a series of events with the effects still being felt today.

To make things worse, the club had a second major problem: its stadium. In use since 1871, Saltergate was literally beyond repair. 'If they hadn't put a football museum in Manchester, they could've just put a roof over our ground,' says Stuart.

In the years that followed, a series of local businessmen helped support the club, while fans raised £300,000 to help pay down debt.[20] However, just 15 miles up the road, in Sheffield, something was happening that would come to define Chesterfield for a decade. David Allen, a successful casino operator, was growing increasingly unpopular at Sheffield Wednesday, where the fans didn't take kindly to dropping down into the third tier or Allen's habit of publicly insulting them. Eventually, having resigned from the board, he was introduced to Chesterfield and decided to take the club on, promising to invest £4m.

While his time at Wednesday might've been a warning sign, not every Chesterfield fan was put off. 'As a football owner, he had a terrible reputation locally, at least with Sheffield Wednesday fans,' says Stuart. 'But that was right up the street of some Chesterfield fans. When he stands up and calls Wednesday fans cretins, Chesterfield fans are behind him giving him the thumbs up. There was a feeling among some fans that perhaps what he wanted to do was come here and show Wednesday fans what they were missing by making us successful.'

With the club so recently in administration and needing to finance a new stadium, Allen's cash looked like the only game in town. He took over in 2010, appointing Ashley Carson, Assay Master at the Sheffield Assay Office, to the board. Carson would be Allen's representative at the club for the next ten years, alongside former Sheffield Wednesday goalkeeper and manager Chris Turner, who was CEO for much of the 2010s.

Sadly, as Stuart says, while Allen is a successful businessman, 'Whenever he puts his hands on an association football club, he's got the non-Midas touch.' The club embarked on a long period of losses and suffered several relegations. 'We made regular multimillion-pound losses,' says Stuart, 'even while selling players up the divisions.'

One day a complete history of Allen's time at Chesterfield will come to be written. It'll be in three volumes and weigh many kilos. But the prevailing theme according to Stuart is the people who became associated with Chesterfield and who, in his view, sullied the club.

There was the owner of a football academy – one of those seemingly designed for children whose parents have more money than they have talent – who inveigled his way into the club, having met Chris Turner in the Middle East. Shortly afterwards, he began presenting himself as the owner of Chesterfield on his Twitter feed. Fans who by this time had increasingly taken it on themselves to do the due diligence they didn't feel the club was doing passed on a dossier about him to Chesterfield and the club cut ties.

There was a commercial manager who had been dismissed from his role at a league club after apparently fabricating a job offer from a different club, seemingly as a ploy to get higher wages. Chesterfield knew about it and hired him anyway.[21]

There was an agent, who presented himself as an international scouting consultant yet seemed to have had little on his sporting CV prior to 2014, when he briefly owned Italian club Monza. They went bankrupt (under a different owner, it should be said) in 2015. A phoenix Monza club was launched the same year and, in 2018, it was bought by former Italian prime minister and AC Milan owner Silvio Berlusconi. Chesterfield fans dug all of this up as well as obtaining legal documents from Florida that showed that the scouting consultant had been arrested for, and admitted to, defrauding a bank of $11,000 to buy a car, only then, it appeared, to skip the country. A Chesterfield fan who helped publicise this information would later be visited at his place of work by a large man who told him that he'd upset someone and that, if he did it again, the next visit would be to his home. Who sent the thug was never made public, but it all added to a sense that what was going on around the club wasn't normal. The agent would later be suspended as an intermediary by the FA for three years over a separate matter.[22]

There was also Alex May, who fronted a rejected takeover bid for Chesterfield in 2018. He would later be linked to a consortium looking to take over Notts County, when it emerged he'd formerly been known as Alick Kapikanya, the name under which he'd previously been jailed for running a multimillion-pound fraud.[23] Later still, in December 2020, it emerged he had set up a company with the owner of Grimsby Town, having been photographed attending a game at Blundell Park.[24]

There was Tommy Wright, who the club hired as assistant manager when he was under investigation for receiving a £5,000 bribe, an offence for which he was later tried and sentenced to 12 months in prison, suspended for a year.[25]

There was Liam Graham, a blameless New Zealand international, who was signed by Chesterfield, only for it to emerge that he was ineligible to play because it was his third club in a year. Nevertheless, the club fielded the then 22-year-old Graham in several reserve-team games, giving not his real name on the team sheet, but the names of existing youth-team players.[26]

There was equally blameless George Margreitter, an Austrian who played for Chesterfield on loan in their 1-0 FA Cup defeat to Milton Keynes Dons in 2014, despite the club not having completed the correct paperwork. The result was the tie had to be replayed, with Chesterfield losing 1-0 again.[27] There was Ched Evans, who Chesterfield signed while he was awaiting his retrial. He was later acquitted at this second trial, but many fans felt uneasy that the club had been the first to sign someone who, though his conviction had been quashed, was at the time accused of rape.

There were two discharged bankrupts: one was appointed head of recruitment while another ran a football academy with links to the club.

There are many, many more stories about Chesterfield to tell, but you get the picture. Such was the disquiet among fans that, when Against League 3, James Cave's campaign for lower-league football, ran its annual survey of best and worst owners in English football, David Allen was the clear winner. One respondent said simply, 'If Chesterfield FC was a dog, it would have been put down years ago, it's so unloved by its owners.'

The cumulative impact of all these events and people seemed to show itself in questionable behaviour by the club. On one occasion, a competition was run, offering the chance to anyone purchasing a £20 raffle ticket to win a place on the team's overseas pre-season tour. Unfortunately, the competition was somewhat last-minute and only four tickets were sold. Amid suggestions that some at the club hadn't thought the idea of having a fan tag along with the team was a good idea, a winner was announced: one James Higgins, a Chesterfield fan from Surrey. Sadly for James, just a week before the tour, he felt ill and wasn't able to travel. 'Spare a thought for Surrey-based Spireite James Higgins,' said the club press release, 'who won the raffle for a couple of places on the club's pre-season training camp in Hungary.'[28]

The funny thing was, no one seemed to know James Higgins – he wasn't a regular on the message boards or known to anyone who was. There was a good reason for this: he didn't exist. The club later acknowledged that the winning entry was 'falsified', cancelled the raffle and refunded £20 each to the three legitimate entrants. How this all came to happen remains a mystery.

Echoes of the aborted competition could be heard in the club's development centre. A trip was announced to Spain, including a visit to Barcelona. Shortly before it was due to depart, though, it was cancelled and parents requesting a refund were instead offered a place on a future trip to Paris.

Sadly, this was due to travel not too long after the Paris terrorist attacks of 2015. Chesterfield eventually cancelled the trip, citing safety concerns, leaving parents to threaten legal action to obtain refunds, with some alleging that they'd seen no evidence that the trip to Paris had ever been booked.[29]

The development centre itself would become a further point of contention, with former staff alleging financial irregularities, including that the academy had been directly paying some first-team players' wages. The club denied wrongdoing, but bailiffs would later be seen on the academy's premises before it went into voluntary liquidation.[30]

Hearing about all this is by turns bizarre and outrageous, but not if you've lived through it. Then it's wearying and dispiriting. Speaking of some of the things the club did, Stuart Basson says, 'I wouldn't dare! I'd be terrified of being found out! The people that ran the club had no shame – and no concept of the shame that others can feel by being associated with all of this.'

As so, in 2018, following a late-night phone call to his home from someone at the club, which ended in a row, Stuart had had enough. He stopped going.

'In one sense it was easy to stop – they were crap! But I've been watching them since the 80s. I've had years watching us being truly terrible. But I just couldn't bear to be in the same ground as some of these people. I can't support people like that. You don't have to be chanting their name. If you're putting money into their operation, you're supporting them.'

He wasn't the only one. It wasn't an organised boycott, but crowds were five or six hundred down on where they'd been. Not everyone felt the same about Allen's ownership, however.

Some long-standing fans had become associate directors of the club. 'It sets person against person,' says Stuart. 'That's how they get away with it so long. If they're fighting among themselves, they won't be looking at us.'

It's hard to imagine, though, that Allen is happy with how things went. By one estimate, with his initial investment and the club's regular losses, Allen put over £16m into the club in ten years for, effectively, no return. Many Chesterfield fans struggled to understand how the club could make such losses and why such an otherwise successful businessman like Allen would tolerate such financial failure.

It's not an abstract question, either. Once a club has been run badly, so that it's failing on the pitch and seems to have enormous debts, then it becomes especially vulnerable. Sharks sniff blood in the water and soon it becomes hard to find reputable, wealthy people who want to come to the rescue. Fans, desperate for a clean slate, become more willing to welcome almost any self-proclaimed saviour. Many people's critical faculties fail them at the time when they're most important.

Ironically, it wasn't long after Stuart began his boycott of Chesterfield that OwnaFC got the club in its sights. Although the business's contacts with Chesterfield wouldn't become public knowledge until later, in early November 2018, long before most of the rest of football had heard of them, OwnaFC replied to a Chesterfield tweet saying, 'Owners not taking the fans views onboard is dangerous. Chesterfield is a target along with 9 other clubs @OWNAFC'.

We'll get to what happened next in a moment, but first a word about the Owners' and Directors' Test. How, you may be wondering, did David Allen, who was widely disliked at Wednesday and presided over a disastrous and shocking ten years at Chesterfield, not fall foul of the ODT?

The answer is simple: because there's no reason he should. The ODT is almost impossible to fail.

Different leagues have different requirements about providing proof of funds and financial disclosures, but the Owners' and Directors' Test is a document that can be read, including all the qualifying notes, and completed in less than five minutes. It's only slightly more complicated than an aeroplane landing card and it requires no legal knowledge.

The first section requires your name, address, email address and date of birth. Cunningly, it also asks for any previous names by which the prospective owner may have been known. It's the football equivalent of the bit on a US visa where you have to sign a declaration that you've not been involved in acts of terrorism or efforts to overthrow the US government. Presumably, it must occasionally catch some people out.

The second test is a requirement to list all the clubs that you are or have been a director of in the last five years. Again, it's a pretty softball question this, but it may prove to be a very useful aide-mémoire for an owner like, say, Roland Duchâtelet, who might have more clubs than he could count on the fingers of one hand.

Finally – yes, you've almost completed the test already! – there's a list of disqualifying factors. It can look a little off-putting at first, but while it's long, the list isn't that complicated. Here, translated as best as we can into plain English, is what you need to be willing to claim.

Professional qualifications declarations:

- I am not so utterly incompetent or incredibly criminal that I am currently barred from being a director of a UK company.
- I am not *currently* bankrupt.
- I have no professional qualifications or, if I do, I have yet to be struck off.

Criminal declarations:

- I have not recently been convicted here or abroad of any of the following criminal offences: dishonesty, corruption, perverting the course of justice, running a company criminally badly, streaming football on the internet, showing the football in a pub without a Sky subscription, punting on a few spare tickets, nor am I planning on doing any of the above.
- The cops aren't currently trying to pin any of the above crimes on me, either.
- I am not a registered sex offender.

Football declarations:

- I live up to football's high standards on bribery and gambling.
- I am not currently banned by a sports governing body from participating in a sport.
- I am not a football hooligan with a current banning order.
- I don't secretly run any other clubs.
- I have never run a football club in England or Wales so badly that it has been expelled from the league.

- I haven't bankrupted two clubs (or the same club twice) in the last six and a half years.

And that's it, you've passed! Congratulations! Sign and date the form and the authorities will dispatch your new club to you by return of post.

Initially, reading down that list of declarations, you might feel that it's quite testing. But here's the thing: how many people do you actually know who'd fail it? Not David Allen. Not widely detested owners like Charlton's Roland Duchâtelet, not Orient relegator Francesco Becchetti, not Bury burier Steve Dale. And not OwnaFC's Stuart Harvey, had he got far enough to attempt it.

Put simply, the vast majority of people who you wouldn't even trust with a brief shopping list and a £10 note wouldn't fall foul of the Owners' and Directors' Test. Even repeatedly bankrupting football clubs or being barred from running a company aren't disqualifications if they happened long enough ago.

You may have heard people claim, 'Even a criminal can own a football club.' Well, it's true. The ODT applies to a very narrow range of criminal offences as well as to things we might describe as professional malpractice and 'crimes against football'. And, even then, it only disqualifies people who are prepared to admit that they did these things and were caught, found guilty and punished to a certain level.

When contacted about this in 2017, the FA's Financial Regulation Department confirmed that any criminal conviction outside those specified would not necessarily be a reason to fail the test. While the FA says it reserves the right to look at each application on a case-by-case basis, prima facie it is literally the case that there is nothing in the ODT to prevent a convicted murderer running your football club. And so it came to pass in late 2021, when the Premier League finally okayed the purchase of Newcastle United by a consortium headed by the Saudi Arabia sovereign wealth fund PIF. The chair of PIF is Saudi Crown Prince Mohammed bin Salman, the man held by separate UN and US reports to bear responsibility for the grisly murder of journalist Jamal Khashoggi in 2018. It was crimes against football – persistent piracy of Premier League TV rights by a Saudi company, and the seeming unwillingness of Saudi Arabia to prevent it – rather than crimes against humanity that had initially held up the deal. Eventually, though, a face-saving deal was announced in which the Premier League declared that it had received 'legally binding guarantees' that 'the Kingdom of Saudi Arabia will not control [the club]'. These guarantees were not made public and no mention was made of Khashoggi's murder, the hundreds of Saudis who had been executed since Bin Salman took power, the ongoing war in Yemen or the many criticisms of Saudi Arabia's record on human rights. It appeared that he had passed the ODT simply because the Premier League had agreed not to apply it to him.

If the ODT sounds hopelessly inadequate, that's not even the worst of it. The test is self-certified. You do not have to have a clean record, you merely need to be willing to claim you do. Now, obviously, if you have lied, there's a decent chance you may get caught out. But those administering the test on the FA's behalf – the EFL or the Premier League – are not obliged to actively investigate your bid and dig for evidence of your unsuitability. All they have to do is see that you have filed the appropriate paperwork.

Beyond how little evidence we demand of actual good character and relevant experience, there is also a question of how we assess compliance. By using other bodies' tests, usually legal or quasi-legal third parties, it absolves the FA, EFL and Premier League of responsibility for making any judgments about people's fitness to own and run a football club. This is an entirely negative – and negligent – form of regulation; you pass if you haven't done something.

It's this that was the root of the absurd spectacle of former Leeds owner Massimo Cellino repeatedly 'failing' and then 'passing' the ODT as various legal proceedings and appeals played out in his home country. One day he wasn't allowed to run a club, the next all was fine. One thing remained unchanged throughout, though: his utterly terrible stewardship of Leeds. As the EFL itself admits, 'The Test governs the eligibility of who is able to own a club – it does not also ensure that those individuals have the capability to manage it properly.'[31]

English football doesn't seek among its owners positive evidence of ability, knowledge, experience, temperament and ethos. In fact, if you've ever interviewed someone for a job, you've likely investigated their fitness to sit at a desk in more detail than the EFL has ever explored someone's fitness to run a club. A relatively junior office job may demand two or three interviews. Running a club with roots in a community that may go back over 100 years? A form about a tenth as testing as renewing your car insurance.

We should also recognise that the chief, though generally unacknowledged, characteristic of most rogue owners is that he or she has run out of money. If their pockets are deep enough, we tend to suspend any judgments about the individual's suitability. There are some people running clubs in England who are, not to put too fine a point on it, little more than exceptionally wealthy gangsters and thieves. For legal reasons, we can't name them here, but you'll know them. People who acquired huge amounts of wealth in surprisingly short spaces of time, people who are followed like a long shadow by allegations of impropriety.

Again, the Owners' and Directors' Test has nothing to say about them. In other sports, prospective owners are subject to a detailed, proactive investigation before they are approved and can have their team effectively sold out from under them if they are deemed no longer to be fit and proper. It has happened in the not-too-distant past in the NFL and the NBA.

Following the Bury debacle, where a financially crippled club was sold to an asset-stripper without the money to pay its bills, the EFL commissioned an independent review of its actions. However, the league set the terms of reference, excluding specific recommendations for reform to the ODT or associated financial requirements. The review concluded that the EFL had 'done all it could' within the current ODT, which the EFL paraded as an exoneration, rather overlooking the fact that no one with any knowledge of the situation had suggested it could have done any more. The failing was to not make the case for reform in the years before that. Having paid for its own whitewash, the EFL consulted its members on a tougher Owners' and Directors' Test, only to find that there seemed to be little appetite among existing club owners

– some of whom would be disbarred from their own clubs by a properly functioning ODT – for any radical change.

Essentially, then, the Owners' and Directors' Test is not meaningfully a test at all, but rather a registration form. There are those who argue it does more harm than good, because while fans mock its feebleness, the very fact that a document called the Owners' and Directors' Test exists, even one that the EFL periodically admits is useless when it's trying to shirk blame, gives fans false confidence. It gives the unfounded impression that, even if inadequately, someone is guarding the hen house. But no one is. At least, not officially. Sometimes it's just a few fans of a club armed with a laptop and a knowledge of how to use the Companies House website.

Stuart Basson is one and Mark Barton, a moderator on the Chesterfield fans' forum, is another.

'I first heard about OwnaFC in November [2018],' says Mark. 'I was told he'd [Stuart Harvey] been in touch with the club, but had been given the brush off.' Shortly after, the OwnaFC app had gone live and the business had begun building some momentum and getting sign-ups. In early January the company turned its eyes to Chesterfield again, seemingly aware that the club had an active and disenchanted fan base. Stuart Harvey reached out to Mark. 'He contacted me, saying he wanted to meet,' says Mark. 'I suppose he thought I might have some sway with other fans. I think he also hoped I might be able to get him a meeting with Ashley Carson, who I've dealt with when the club wanted to pass messages to the fans.'

As with the parade of previous suiters and hangers-on that he'd seen buzzing round Chesterfield before, Mark wasn't taken in. 'I thought it was absolutely crazy from the start,' he says. 'But I was very curious to see what it was all about.'

It wasn't all bad. 'He seemed to have the marketing side of it working well,' says Mark. 'But while there were elements of it that looked genuine, there were bits of it that didn't make any sense.'

Mark spoke to Harvey. 'He kept quoting figures at me,' says Mark. 'I didn't believe them.' Mark noticed that the numbers that Harvey was claiming to have – 2,000 people paying £99 – didn't tally with the number of downloads on the various app stores. Harvey said he expected to reach 100,000 downloads once a new advertising campaign went live on Sky.

This seemed odd because he also told Mark that he planned to limit the number of subscribers to 2,500. 'It was crazy,' says Mark. 'Why would you cap the investors?'

Harvey told him that he had already secured investment to the value of £4m to buy a club and its stadium. 'He claimed to have angel investors, but he wouldn't say who they were,' says Mark. 'I asked lots of questions and he was saying, "We'll come to that later, we'll have to sign an NDA." In previous conversations he'd said, "We have an NDA with this club, we have an NDA with that club." So it seemed like he was using the fact he has an NDA with clubs to try and give himself credibility.'

Harvey eventually offered to give Mark access to the app so he could explore it, using what he described as a 'media access code'. But this, like a promise to join the Chesterfield message board and answer fan questions, didn't materialise.

'He didn't come across like he knew much about football,' says Mark. 'But he didn't come across as much of a businessman either.' Mark was immediately troubled by the original terms and conditions of the business. While the T&Cs that most people were familiar with specified that there were no refunds except if no offer was made on or before 1 March 2019, Mark spotted that the original terms and conditions, dated 12 December 2018, specified, 'The price once paid is final and no refunds are offered or given for any reason.'

'I made an issue of that,' said Mark, 'and he said, "I'll get out lawyers to change that." It had sham written all over it. He was trying to get round distance selling regulations.'

That was on 4 January and Harvey did indeed change the refund provision on 6 January to include the 1 March caveat – which the company would later appear to breach. Nonetheless, Mark appears to have been one of the few people who Harvey paid any attention to. Despite this, though, things didn't end well.

'At one point he got really arsey with me when I started asking a few questions,' says Mark. 'He said, "Oh, you're just being negative. You'll have to buy the app if you want to know any more. You're just a time waster."'

This upset Mark, who felt he was asking genuine questions on behalf of the whole fan base. 'I was absolutely outraged by the idea of our club being taken over,' says Mark. 'I was appalled by the idea [of a digital consortium]. They've not got a feel for the club. They're so remote, they're not going to see us play. It defies belief. I didn't like that, or anything about it, really. It outrages me that there are people hanging around football, trying to exploit people.'

At the same time, the local paper ran a story on OwnaFC, noting Harvey's poor business record. Fan sentiment was overwhelmingly negative; despite all the club's troubles, enough people felt the idea wasn't sound. Even the launch of a YouTube promotional video for OwnaFC by a Chesterfield fan was wildly derided. Given previous events, many doubted the supporter was even real. He was, though, and was later one of the few people who received a voluntary partial refund from the company when it collapsed, proudly sharing his 50 per cent refund as evidence that OwnaFC were good guys.

Like Mark, Stuart was contemptuous of the whole idea. 'There was no way you could run a football team like that, or any business,' he says. 'If Mansfield did it down the road, the first 3,000 subscribers would all be Chesterfield fans voting to get rid of all their best players and get them relegated. There might be a case for small things – like man of the match – but do you really think a manager anywhere in the country would allow his team to be picked this way?'

Being a Chesterfield fan has made Stuart cynical. 'You see it often enough [prospective owners] and your reaction becomes, "What are they actually after?" They are generally one-man bands and the accounts aren't doing much. These aren't proper businessmen. You google the company names and letters come up from unhappy customers, bad reviews. It's so easy to do. Easy to spot these people if you make a small amount of effort.'

He worries too about a lack of lines of defence for small clubs. 'I think the age of the internet might have changed the nature of journalism,' Stuart says. 'There's much less investigative journalism now. Whereas a local newspaper might have had ten people working for it, it's now one person who just puts out somebody else's press releases, it seems.'

Any fan of a small or non-league club will understand the frustration. Despite the huge amount of football content produced, the public consciousness seems only to have headspace for one or two crisis clubs at a time. For a while it was Bolton, and then Bury. Before that, Charlton and Blackpool.

But ask the fans of troubled clubs, and they know if there are problems brewing. 'Every club who's in this position are waiting for David Conn to do his article,' says Stuart, referring to *The Guardian*'s formidable expert on the business of football, who's one of the few high-profile journalists producing detailed reporting on problem clubs.

This lack of bandwidth means that we rarely see the big picture – the crucial factors that connect all these clubs and that point, without significant reform, to inevitable further club collapses.

What does the future hold for Chesterfield? 'We've been run so incredibly badly that, with 3,000 fans, if we are just run properly, they should be able to hold our own in League Two and every now and then we'd go up to League One,' Stuart says. 'The National League does seem to be traditional Fourth Division clubs and more ambitious, arguably better-run clubs – like Boreham Wood. Most are living within their means. But there's no longer an inevitability about getting back into the league. Forest Green and Salford have changed the dynamic. There was a sense that you dropped down, you spent a year of two down there, you rebuilt and came back up. Now there's no guarantees even with two promotion places.'

No guarantees. That's the true state of football club ownership. No matter how well you're run today, there is nothing and no one to protect your club's tomorrow. Every club is only a heart attack or a distressed sale away from disaster.

13

Fail again. Fail bigger

Failure has never been more popular. Not least among the wildly successful, who've been busily redefining this crucial part of life out of existence.

ENTER ANY of Britain's remaining bookshops and you'll find whole tables offering libraries of praise for failure. Barely a self-help business management book or a celebrity boastography or a self-satisfied meditation on mindfulness is published which doesn't hymn the wonder of defeat.

Companies run seminars on failure; schools set aside days to celebrate it. Fail early, fail often we are exhorted, as if we were a former England international embarking on a managerial career.

It's an idea that seems appealing culturally. With our one precious shot at existence, it might be beneficial if we were less afraid of failure generally, less concerned about the judgment of others, more resilient and better able to learn from our mistakes.

195

But this is not what the books are peddling. Theirs is a strange, rebranded kind of failure. It's failure as a prelude to winning. Failure as a way to talk about the components of success. Failure as an opening to discussions of fearlessness, of the value of prototyping and iteration, of marginal gains and organisational excellence, of ambition and determination, of creativity and taking chances, and of exposing yourself to ridicule but not letting it weigh too heavily as you succeed eventually.

This is failure as a form of social control; a buttress to the continuing accumulation of wealth and opportunity by a small social group. Like being poor, not achieving your ambitions isn't a sign the system is broken. It's an indication you haven't tried hard enough, that you deserve your failure.

And now that the rich and famous have got comfortable with the idea of embracing their failures, they've turned it into a form of narcissistic exhibitionism that serves to underscore the magnitude of their triumph. The message from the winners – to us, the failures – is clear: I have suffered knocks, my life has been a struggle, my success owes nothing to others, and, no, I don't think I want to pay any more tax, thank you.

It's a message that's profoundly offensive to the many people who've drawn the short straw more often than the long in their lives. And it's wildly misleading to those who interpret it to mean that, like Noel Edmonds practising some Cosmic Ordering, it's just a question of wanting it enough.

Yes, nothing worthwhile is accomplished without effort. But what if I'm just not very good at something? What if I never learn from my failure? What if I just dust myself down and prepare, not to fail better, but simply to fail yet again? What if, in fact, I come to believe that my attitude to failure – my ability to bounce back more frequently than Ian Holloway on a trampoline – is proof that I am in fact already a success? Is it possible that deception eventually becomes a central plank of my self-image and the way I present myself to the world?

* * *

The first sign of being unsuitable to own a football club is wanting to own one.

Why would anyone want to buy into an industry where almost every business loses money and only a small number appreciate in value? Very, very occasionally, the answer is that the person is a fan of the club they want to buy or recognises – like Andy Holt, Accrington Stanley's owner – that there is a value to the community in the club persisting. Discount that disappointingly small slice of owners, and you have a few major groupings. At the top end, there are the super-wealthy for whom the club is a status symbol, a PR shield and a long-term asset. Below that, you have a large pool of extremely wealthy people who find themselves pouring tens of millions into their clubs because they mistakenly believed that they could get up into the Premier League and feast on its riches. Below that, you have the majority of owners: the common or garden wealthy people who can fund a club's losses for a few years, but don't have the pockets for an assault on the top of the Championship. Many of these owners fear for the future of their clubs and would, if the right offer came along, be happy to sell. Increasingly, though, they find it hard to make a good sale. Sensible people of reasonable means generally don't buy football clubs. There is no shortage of the final category of owners, though: chancers, dreamers, gamblers and land-hungry spivs. Failures presenting themselves as successes.

These are mostly people who have neither the means nor the skill to successfully operate a football club but believe that, with their unique combination of attitude and approach, they can achieve great things. It doesn't matter what the club's circumstances are, they believe that a promotion, even two, can be achieved in short order and the club can survive at the new level without a significant increase in expenditure. Equally, however, they believe that their new regime and the success it engenders all but guarantees major increases in crowds. Leaving aside that they are often not rich themselves, they believe that they can outmanoeuvre other, richer owners through a combination of fresh thinking, charisma and, if truth be told, a greater knowledge of football (if push came to shove, they know they could probably hold the dressing room together for a few weeks between managers). They believe that the club can bring them acclaim, notoriety and new wealth. And, typically, they aren't especially bothered about what damage they might do to the club. There will, after all, be another sucker along shortly if they need to sell it.

The tragic thing with most people in this last category is the lack of self-knowledge. Where did they get the idea that they were good at running businesses? If you don't already have lots of money, what makes you think you can make a tonne of it in one of the least-forgiving industries around?

Take Steve Dale, the man who took over Bury but seemed never able to satisfy the EFL that he actually had the money to run the club. Behind his big claims for himself, here was a man who it was reported had over 40 businesses that had been either dissolved, liquidated or entered into a Company Voluntary Arrangement (CVA) with their creditors.[32] How on earth did he convince himself, let alone anyone else, that he could complete a deal for the club and fund its running costs while he turned it around? Perhaps he didn't; the moment he took over, he stopped funding Bury and tried to push through a CVA to reduce the debts. A year later, the club was kicked out of the league and plunged into financial limbo. Even if he had a plan, it certainly wasn't a good one.

Stuart Harvey's long, tangled business record had some similarities – a combination of wishful thinking, tenacity and the belief that, eventually, one of his bets would pay off big time.

Returning to the UK from Australia, and with his rugby league career not yet fully behind him, he began to cycle through failing companies with an almost rhythmical quality.

It began in 2008, ten years before he founded OwnaFC, and it was, curiously, partly Tony Blair's fault. Because it was then that he – Harvey, not Blair – began to try and turn his experience of fire safety in Australia into his own business empire. Three years before, Blair's government, in its zeal for deregulation, had introduced the Regulatory Reform (Fire Safety) Order 2005. In its own words, the order, 'Replace[d] most fire safety legislation with one simple order. It mean[t] that any person who ha[d] some level of control in premises [had to] take reasonable steps to reduce the risk from fire and make sure people [could] safely escape if there is a fire.'[33]

In other words, at a stroke, all businesses were responsible for assessing their own state of fire safety. Naturally, most companies didn't have these skills in-house and so it became necessary for them to pay consultants for staff training on responding to fires and for guidance on how to assess and record their state of preparedness.

Many of these consultants were former firefighters, taking a well-deserved career change to work in a less dangerous and better paying field. Others were not nearly so experienced and, as anyone who's been a fire marshal at work can testify, the training can be pretty perfunctory.

Companies sprung up offering fire risk assessment, including some that offered the opportunity for people to run their own fire safety franchise.

In early June 2008, a close family member of Harvey's founded a fire safety business, United Fire & Safety Limited. In December of the same year, Harvey would be appointed director and become its sole shareholder, running it until it was wound up by a creditor in early 2012 – a year before his bankruptcy. For a while, at least, the going must've been good. In 2011, Harvey received nearly £100,000 of dividends and the company spent over £80,000, perhaps on a franchise agreement. How the company should come to be wound up less than six months after the accounts were filed remains, as we said earlier, unclear. But it was a rapid change of fortune for a business that looked very good on paper.

Equally mysterious are the other businesses that sprung up around the same time. Only a few weeks after the first fire safety company was founded, three other fire safety businesses – seemingly franchises – were registered by family members of Harvey along with the director of a nationwide fire safety franchise business.

One company appeared not to trade, while the other two, one of which Harvey was appointed a director of, did a few tens of thousands of pounds of business before they were both dissolved.

In 2009, when Harvey was living in the south-east of England and playing for London Skolars, he made his first of what would become regular attempts to branch out from fire safety and electrics into the business of sport.

In the July of that year, only a month after he'd been a member of the triumphant Southgate Skolars team at the Veneto 9s, Harvey registered a new business, Tag Rugby Sports Limited, which planned to promote 'the adult participation sport of tag rugby throughout the UK'. Tag rugby, also known as flag rugby, is the non-contact version of the sport and is frequently played by children before they're old enough for the full contact game. In a world that seems to be heading increasingly towards a reduction of contact in sport, particularly head trauma, the idea of introducing this fast, skilful game to an older audience seemed like a good one.

The business gathered pace rapidly. Just two weeks after it was registered, with Harvey the sole director and shareholder, a press release went out announcing that rugby legend Iestyn Harris, who'd been a star in both league and union, would be joining as a director. Alongside this coup, two other people who were at Skolars at the time were also announced as directors, with one being styled CEO.

Something went wrong, though, and a fortnight later the two Skolars people founded their own tag rugby business, without Harvey or Harris, leaving Harvey's enterprise stillborn. It would be struck off in 2011 without ever having filed accounts, along with one of his fire safety businesses. Meanwhile, the second tag rugby business continued to expand and trade profitably and was sold to new owners in late 2019. Its founders did not respond to repeated requests for an interview and so what happened in that month – how Harvey went from sole shareholder to being left out of a successful business venture – is yet another mystery. It might be indicative of a not-entirely cordial parting of the way that the competitor business, founded exactly a month to the day after Harvey's, changed its name after less than a week from its original to something less close to Harvey's.

Harvey had also founded another new business late 2010. While his one functioning fire safety company was seemingly trading profitably, he opened a new venture. Co-owned and directed with his then wife, United Electrical Safety Limited would file three sets of dormant accounts – showing no trading activity – followed by two sets of accounts showing the company made about £5,000 profit over two years before being struck off in 2017. During its financially uneventful life, the company would see considerable boardroom upheaval, with Harvey resigning as a director, leaving his wife in full control. A few months later, she resigned and he replaced her, before himself resigning again and being replaced by his fiancée. She would become sole director and joint-equal shareholder with Harvey.

In 2011, meanwhile, Harvey piloted a new idea, one that would fail and be replaced by two similar failures. The precursor to his RightTrades business, Zee Cat Homecare Limited was Harvey's attempt to tackle the familiar problem of inexpert householders trying to engage tradespeople for work without knowing what needs doing or what a fair price might be. Harvey's business model was an annual subscription service where, for just £189.99, you could be covered for any plumbing or electrical problems. The company promoted itself with a radio advert and a social media presence where the titular Zee Cat was styled 'the coolest cat in Wigan', given a cartoon face, a seductive persona and, with a Spanish accent, could be heard encouraging worried old ladies to 'say "here, kitty!" and call Zee Cat Homecare'. The company was struck off two years later having never filed any accounts at Companies House.

In the summer of 2011, Harvey also spent some time in the US coaching in New Jersey, so perhaps Zee Cat's failure was understandable. It was also a significant – and busy – year for the person who would later become Harvey's employee at United Electrical Safety, then his business partner and finally his fiancée.

Ten years younger than Harvey, she graduated from university in the summer of 2011 and went straight into business for herself. In May, a company called Homecall Plus, which sold household insurance for plumbing and electrical issues, collapsed. At a time when many students are worrying about their finals and how to pay off their student debts, Harvey's fiancée was linked in the trade press with the purchase of the company's database and intellectual property.

She set up a business to handle the assets in June and on 1 July, when many students are still recovering from their post-finals binge, she completed the purchase of Homecall Plus assets for £55,000 and 75 per cent of renewal sales for a year. How Harvey's fiancée managed to pull off this business coup is unclear, but her bid must've impressed liquidators Grant Thornton, who chose this recent graduate over four other bids. She was quoted as saying, 'I became interested in this business when the family policy with Homecall Plus became invalid and made some early enquiries. I completed some research and populated a detailed business plan to secure some capital to buy the assets of the company. I am now looking forward to the challenges ahead.'[34]

It was not to be. Like Harvey, she seemed blessed with the reverse Midas touch.

Within four months of running the business, the company found itself in the consumer pages of *The Guardian*.[35] The dotcom discounting sensation Groupon had attracted complaints from customers who'd used the website to book boiler inspections with Homecall. One unhappy customer had paid their money and received no service, while another alleged that the service had left their boiler leaking gas, which they'd had to pay another gas engineer to fix. The article noted that neither *The Guardian* nor Groupon had been able to contact Homecall's new owner by phone or email.

Around this time, the Homecall website changed its blurb to suggest that it was now being operated by another company which was now trading under licence from Harvey's fiancée. Having apparently disposed of the business, the following month, in December 2011, she founded a new business, seemingly with a similar purpose to Homecall. It too would fold a few years later having not filed any accounts.

In 2012, the only one of Harvey's businesses to ever show a significant profit – United Fire & Safety Limited – collapsed and Harvey went back to work as a jobbing electrician for a franchise business. The following year he was made bankrupt and he and his fiancée saw several businesses struck off. He also bought a house for him and his fiancée. Seemingly, it was a year for clearing the decks before a comeback.

That comeback was a company called The Trade Circle Limited. Majority-owned by Harvey, with his fiancée holding about five per cent, the company was the link between the Zee Cat trade subscription service and the trades-finding RightTrades website which would be the business that allowed him to style himself an entrepreneur when he set up OwnaFC.

As always, the ambitions were sky-high. 'We are a trades company with a global mission to connect customers to third party-assessed trades partners,' its bumph said. 'We aim to deliver multi trades services at fixed prices in the UK, Europe and internationally. The business is a hub for customers to make secure payments, have guaranteed work, the assurance of vetted staff and guaranteed fixed price jobs.'

The problem for an idea like this was that, even in 2014, Harvey was late to the party. Established players in this field, like Rated People and Checkatrade, had already existed in one form or another for over ten years, giving them huge advantages in scale, technology and, crucially, in brand awareness to attract both customers and tradespeople.

Just a week after Harvey formed Trade Circle, his fiancée set up another new business. While the company didn't record its area of business at formation, it included 'electrical' in its title, suggesting perhaps some link to trades. It seems never to have actually traded, however, and was struck off less than two years later, having – you know what's coming – never filed accounts.

Harvey's fiancée doesn't appear to have been idle in this period, however. By mid-2015, she was appointed a director of Trade Circle and, just a few months later, Harvey resigned and passed sole ownership of the company to her. The company would file just two sets of accounts, one for a dormant company and one, for the year to October 2016, showing an £80,000 loss before applying to have itself struck off in late 2017.

The only significant activity the company appears to have undertaken was to register some intellectual property. In July 2015, it applied to trademark the word 'REPAIRD', before withdrawing the application. Given the vogue at the time for tech businesses to misspell common words by dropping vowels, this may have been deliberate. But, as a later RightTrades piece of marketing offered 'Bolier install', 'Electrical repiar' and 'Bolier repiar' within the same advert, anything is possible.

Whatever the explanation, a new application was filed in late October 2015 for a trademark on the words 'right trades'. This was followed, in October 2016, for a trademark on the RightTrades logo and, in December 2016, by Harvey winning the Merseyside Federation of Small Businesses Entrepreneur of the Year award for his work on RightTrades.

Given that RightTrades Limited wasn't actually founded until mid-2017, with the trademarks being transferred to it by Harvey's fiancée, it seems possible that Trade Circle may have acted as a proving ground for the RightTrades concept for at least two years, paying for the creation of a brand for its successor company before being dissolved.

RightTrades' own promotional material would later give support to this idea when, in trying to establish its credibility, the company claimed that it 'was founded in 2014 … [with a] vision to revolutionise the trades industry by building the world's largest trade service business'.

In language reminiscent of Trade Circle, though with even larger ambitions, it said, 'Our mission is two-part; firstly, to be the world's leading fixed price repair service for domestic and commercial properties and secondly, to change the way people have traders carry out work. Our journey is only just beginning and we see huge opportunities for trade partners to work and grow with us.'

With everything now focused on RightTrades, Harvey and his fiancée once more cleared the decks, beginning the process of closing down all their other businesses. The only slight hitch was an objection to Trade Circle's application to have itself struck off, presumably received from a creditor.

Initially RightTrades looked as if, finally, this might be the one Harvey had been waiting for. Its first year of trading went well, extremely well, in fact. It was profitable and Harvey was able to hire staff to help manage the workload and grow the business further.

Ever impatient, Harvey wanted to attract investment to help finance growth and take on the existing giants of the industry. Having previously used family members to found companies or act as directors or company secretaries for periods of time, Harvey now went one further: borrowing £360,000 from family members, including a wealthy uncle in Canada who invested through his businesses.

You could argue that, looking solely at the business's financials, this wasn't a terrible decision. The problem came with what Harvey did with the money – decisions that would set in train his eventual ruin, even if OwnaFC hadn't come tumbling down.

More staff were hired – at one point, they numbered over ten. Smart new offices were acquired on a business park. And then, with catastrophic consequences, Harvey heard the siren call of owning a sports club again.

Once again, he wouldn't fail better. He'd fail bigger.

* * *

At this juncture you may be forgiven for wondering what the above tells us and why the need for such detail. After all, it's all pretty low-level and inconsequential; a pattern of behaviour rather than proof, a man bumping along unsuccessfully through the world of business. A serial non-entrepreneur.

To a degree, that's the point. Even the most critical profiles allowed Harvey to present himself as a successful businessman to the extent that he was able to get one foot in the boardroom door at a number of sports clubs, even though there is limited evidence of his ever having run a company successfully.

The world is full of people like Harvey. Ambitious, unethical men, often skirting the limits of the law and throwing their weight around. Others go further still, inhabiting the realm where poor business practices overlap with the social parasites of criminal gangs. Tax is avoided, creditors are routinely stiffed and intimidation becomes commonplace. They largely get away with it simply because they are relatively small-time. Proving fraud is a difficult, time-consuming activity. Likewise, intimidation and threatening behaviour. After years of austerity, the hard-pressed police forces and officers of HMRC have bigger fish to fry.

In August 2019, *The Times* ran an investigation under the headline 'Action Fraud investigation: victims misled and mocked as police fail to investigate'. The piece claimed that most reports of fraud are never reviewed by the police and, instead, poorly trained call handlers in outsourced private call centres make snap decisions about complaints, while misleading the public into thinking they are talking to police officers.[36] A later article by the BBC went on to say that fraud now accounts for a third of all reported crime but that just two per cent of reports result in prosecution.[37] To a great extent then, fraud had been quietly decriminalised in the UK. In July 2021, acknowledging criticism of the way fraud is handled, the government proposed abolishing Action Fraud entirely. Whether this will improve matters remains to be seen.

Providing they don't get too big – or go too far – dodgy business people can carry on like this for decade after decade, clocking up failures and calling themselves a success. There's people like this in every town in Britain. Many of them will, at one time or another, run their eyes over a football club and wonder if there might be a percentage in it for them.

If we're lucky, these would-be Mr Bigs will decide it's not for them. But if we're unlucky, football fans may find their clubs are halfway to being sold to someone before anyone's even had a chance to figure out who these hotshots really are.

As one former Owna, who lived not too far from Harvey said, when asked about Harvey's status as one of the north-west's top young entrepreneurs and all-round local legend, 'I had never heard of him or seen him before.'

14

The Wider Interests of Football Limited

*'How much should you pay for a football
club?' is a tricky question. 'What's a football
club worth to its fans?' is tougher still.*

IN DECEMBER 2019, with earthmovers hard at work on
the building site that was due to become the new stadium for
AFC Wimbledon, a huge hole was uncovered. It was black
and £11m deep.

Seemingly within sight of returning to Plough Lane
in Merton, London, something had gone very wrong
with Wimbledon's finances and, unless many millions of
pounds could be raised in just a few months, the club would
have to drastically descope the stadium. Contractors were
waiting, pen in hand, for Wimbledon to sign off on the final
specifications.

Within a week, unnamed investors appeared offering
£7.5m of the £11m shortfall, in exchange for 30 per cent of the

club. That would value the club at £25m – significantly less than the £31.5m cost of the new stadium itself. And, much worse in many fans' eyes, the investment was contingent on the unnamed group being able to take effective control of the club and, later, majority ownership.[38]

To a fan base who had rebuilt their club from scratch the last time it was snatched away from them, this was too much. In just weeks, a group of supporters produced a scheme called the 'Plough Lane Bond', encouraging fans of the club to lend it money at low or zero interest for terms of five, ten or 20 years.[39]

Supporters rallied to the call and, within a month of launch, over £5m had been pledged, giving the club enough cash to be able to negotiate a decent commercial rate on the rest of the shortfall and, crucially, keeping AFC Wimbledon in the hands of its fans.

At a time when clubs have entered administration over much smaller sums, it raises the questions of how fans can mobilise and fundraise to take control of their club and, when they have, how they can keep control.

* * *

Charlie Talbot joined Wimbledon in 1990 on a free transfer, as part of a package deal with his favourite footballer, Warren Barton. Barton had spent the previous season at Maidstone United where, aged nine, Charlie had first been taken to his first live football game.

Charlie and his dad were Maidstone season ticket holders for three years and, as so often happens in the lower leagues, they began to get involved in the club on a voluntary basis.

Charlie's dad became the announcer and they got to know Barton and his parents .

So when Barton was sold to Wimbledon for the very sizeable amount of £300,000, Charlie and his dad went to watch a few games at his new club on days when Maidstone weren't playing. Shortly after that, following some poor financial management and a catastrophic land deal, Maidstone weren't playing at all. The club went under in 1993.

'We went from watching a few games to watching ten games and, within 18 months of Maidstone going bust, we became season ticket holders at Wimbledon,' says Charlie. It was not the beginning of a long period of stability for his new club.

One of his first games was March 1991 – just a few months before the club relocated to Selhurst Park to become tenants of Crystal Palace. 'It was a terrible 0-0 draw with Norwich,' says Charlie. 'But it means I can say, "Yeah, yeah, of course I miss Plough Lane."'

A few years later, while still in his teens, Charlie got involved in the supporters' association, working on communications. Over the years he helped run the club's unofficial programme, became AFC Wimbledon's first in-house journalist, worked on the lobbying campaign to fight the move to Milton Keynes, helped develop AFC Wimbledon's branding and marketing, and was part of the lobbying campaign to return to the club's home borough. And, nearly 30 years after becoming a supporter, he found himself helping organise the Plough Lane Bond. 'I'm a fan but I'm also involved, but that's true of a lot of people at Wimbledon. At moments of crisis, people pitch back in,' he says. 'Like the saying goes: the price of freedom is eternal vigilance.'

When a football club, like a nuclear reactor, melts down, the focus is usually on the one final mistake: the last button push that blew the roof off. But a detailed inquiry will always show that the true cause is a long series of interconnected events stretching back years; a linked chain of smaller, individual errors which conspired to produce a disaster.

Wimbledon's problem, like so many clubs', was about land. Charlie traces it back to the 1980s and the inner-city construction boom. 'David Bostock had taken over at Fulham. It couldn't be more 80s if it tried. Here was a man in a smart suit saying, "I'm terribly sorry but this land is ripe for housing, it's ridiculous to have a football club here, Fulham and QPR should merge."'

In the 1986/87 season, rumours were floated of a possible merger with Crystal Palace, then owned by former Dons owner Ron Noades. In response, Wimbledon fans held a sit-in protest on the pitch. 'The idea went away, in part because there wasn't enough money in football to make it worth their time,' says Charlie, 'but it was a formative moment for Wimbledon fans.'

Just a few years later, the Taylor Report was published and Wimbledon owner Sam Hammam moved the club to Selhurst Park, saying they couldn't meet the cost of redeveloping Plough Lane to the standard required in the report.

Around that time, fans set up their own independent supporters' association (ISA) with a focus on putting pressure on Merton Borough Council, who Hammam claimed were being obstructive, to find land for the club to build a new stadium. The first thing they did was a campaign at the All England Club during the fortnight of the Wimbledon tennis tournament. They drove a van around saying, 'Why won't Merton Council play ball with Wimbledon Football Club?'

But what trust there was in Hammam evaporated in 1996, when it was leaked that the club was seriously exploring a move to Ireland to become the 'Dublin Dons'.

'It absolutely galvanised fans,' says Charlie. Large protests began after games and the Dublin move idea quickly died. Someone would later ask Hammam when he knew Dublin wasn't going to work. He responded, 'When I saw a thousand of you crazy fuckers hanging from the rafters.'

The following year, Hammam sold the club. Having bought it for just £70,000 less than 20 years before, he pulled a masterstroke. Plough Lane had been protected from redevelopment by a covenant, but Hammam bought the covenant for a few hundred thousand pounds from a council reluctant to finance a legal battle against him. He subsequently sold the land to a supermarket for £8m before selling 80 per cent of the club to two Norwegians for £28m. This represented an extraordinary amount for a club back then. Twenty-two years later – the richest period in football history – the offer for AFC Wimbledon was less than that.[40]

'It was an amazing deal,' says Charlie. 'We didn't even own our training ground. They bought the right to squat at Selhurst Park for £28m.'

If the new owners hadn't done their due diligence, they pretty quickly realised they'd been sold a pup. The club was relegated and, soon seeking an exit, the owners brought in Charles Koppel, a South African mining executive, to run it.

At the end of the 1999/2000 season, with rising fan anger, there emerged the first mention of a relocation to Milton Keynes.

Representatives of the ISA met with Koppel to explain their opposition. 'I offered to help him write a speech at the end of the game, to help him row back on how he'd pissed the fans off,' says Charlie. 'He didn't listen to anything I said. It's the classic thing with club owners, "Well what do I need fans to tell me how to run a football club for?" Well, a lot of people are both fans and not idiots. Look at Charlton fans, for example, and their recent battles: decidedly not idiots. There's people who work in PR, in communications, they can help you communicate better with fans. Not everyone is just going to turn up and try and set fire to your car.'

In the end, Koppel went out to give the speech flanked by six burly security guards. It was not a good look. 'However much people disliked Hammam by the end, you knew for a fact he would have just bowled out there,' says Charlie, 'stood there on his own and started up with "I'm your father and you're all my children!"'

The following August, just days after fans had renewed their season tickets, a letter went out to them saying the club was moving to Milton Keynes. Charlie continues, 'It said, in essence, "Don't worry, nothing will change. It'll still be the same club, with the same kit, same name, same badge." Nothing will change! We're just going to play our home games 70 miles away.'

By now, the independent supporters' association was well organised. It had an initial response to Wimbledon out the next day, highlighting the many inaccuracies in the report the club had commissioned. Wimbledon immediately cut off contact with fan groups and then, in the protest-filled season that followed, announced they'd create their own fan forum. Inevitably, members of the ISA stood for and won election to the new body. The club refused to meet them.

Angry as the fans were, however, they were also quietly confident. No official approval had been granted and most people expected a move to Milton Keynes to be shot down just as the Dublin switch had. After all, the FA regulations were absolutely clear: teams must play in 'the conurbation whose name the club bears'.

On and off the pitch, however, things were deteriorating. Despite the team challenging for the play-offs, fans felt the club was working against them. Out-of-sorts centre-forward David Nielsen was sent on loan to Norwich, but the Dons failed to insert a clause in the deal preventing him from playing against them. Nielsen, who'd scored just twice in 12 league starts for the Dons, would score eight in 23 league games for the Canaries, including, inevitably, against Wimbledon in a 2-1 victory for Norwich, who finished sixth that season, claiming the last First Division play-off place, while Wimbledon finished ninth.

In response to the increasingly *Pravda*-esque tone of the Wimbledon programme, supporters decided to launch and distribute their own unofficial publication. 'We had a designer from *Trinity Mirror* who went on to design the club's kits and crests as AFC Wimbledon,' says Charlie. 'We began outselling the official programme four to one so they had tannoy announcements saying "don't be fooled by rogue programmes". It was a hearts and minds campaign that set us up for what was to come later.'

Elsewhere, as the protests became more vocal and organised, other people with valuable skills presented themselves. Part of the club's submission to the FA in its request to move was a claim that the then still undeveloped Plough Lane site couldn't accommodate a 20,000-seat stadium. Several Dons fans were architects and presented a set of detailed plans showing how, in fact, it could be done, simply by placing a new stadium at 90 degrees to the old one. Fans were also able to provide evidence that the club's claim that there was literally nowhere closer to Plough Lane than Milton Keynes in which to build a stadium was completely false.

The ISA commissioned professional market research showing, contrary to the club's claim, that there was a desire for it to remain in Wimbledon. A lobbying committee, meanwhile, persuaded the leader of the council to meet the owners and reiterate that it wasn't true that they wanted the club to leave; quite the opposite, in fact.

In a PR coup, they also managed to obtain a tape of Charles Koppel addressing a local residents' association, urging them to protest about Wimbledon returning home. Badmouthing his own club's supporters, he said, 'Football fans aren't the kind of people you want on your doorstep.'

Even when the ITV Digital collapse starved the Football League of funds and appeared to blunt its appetite to keep fighting the move, the fans remained buoyant. Eventually, the league passed the final decision to an arms-length three-man commission – an MO that continues to embarrass the EFL to this day.

As the date of the hearing drew closer, the fans felt they had demolished every pillar of the club's argument and stepped up their protest action.

The second-last game of the year was at Wolves, the club to which the fans' player of the year, Kevin Cooper, had been sold. The ISA contacted Wolves, who were one of several sympathetic clubs appalled by the prospect of Wimbledon being allowed to move, and asked if they could make the trophy presentation on the pitch. Wolves said yes and the chair of the ISA, Kris Stewart, who'd later become the first chair of AFC Wimbledon and its CEO, presented Cooper with his award on the Molineux turf. The Wimbledon brass were furious.

At the last home game, with just a month until the panel would rule on the relocation, the fans decided to play their final card. They'd turn their back on the team.

'We'd always held off from encouraging people to not watch the football,' says Charlie, 'because if you did that and only 20 per cent of people did it you'd have shot yourself in the foot. We handed out t-shirts with "Back to Plough Lane" on them. When the time came, I looked over my shoulder and there were 90 per cent of fans joining in. I thought, "We've done it, we've won." We didn't know what we'd won, because if the owners put the club in the bin, we'd have to pick it up.'

Confident of victory, but determined to cover all their bases, fans had already talked to Supporters Direct about founding their own club. They didn't really think they'd need to, though. 'We expected it would be a no again,' says Charlie. 'No one wanted it to happen.'

And yet, it did. As the hearing proceeded, observers began to worry that fan submissions were being dismissed while club evidence, which seemed deeply flawed, was given undue weight. They feared that, as so often in English football, the voice of fans was regarded as inherently unreliable, little more than the shrill demands of a child for ice cream at every meal.

In the end, the panel voted two to one to allow the move. Its report concluded, infamously, with a low blow that stings Wimbledon fans even today. 'Furthermore,' it said, 'resurrecting the club from its ashes as, say, "Wimbledon Town" is, with respect to those supporters who would rather that happened so that they could go back to the position the club started in 113 years ago, not in the wider interests of football.'

Not in the wider interests of football. A club moving to Milton Keynes against all the wishes of the fans, the FA, the league and other clubs was fine, but those same fans creating a phoenix club was bad for football.

'It was devastating,' says Charlie. 'We thought they'd lose and hand over a pretty distressed asset to us. Nothing they'd done to date had even been competent, so we didn't see how they could possibly win this one. But we didn't even have much time to feel angry before we had to move on to, "What are we going to do about this?"'

The very next day, a core group of fans – Ivor Heller, Marc Jones, Kris Stewart and Trevor Williams, all of whom would remain involved in the new operation in various capacities for years to come – located two potential venues where a new club could play and phoned up the London FA. Sympathetic to their plight, the London FA walked them through a long list of requirements and registered the club right away. The only sticking point was refusing to allow the fans' preferred first name, FC Wimbledon, on the grounds it was too close to the original. They did allow the second suggestion, AFC Wimbledon, and, in a tacit show of support, allowed the club to submit its registration papers with a founding date backdated by more than a century to 1889.

The following day, there was a public meeting. The first order of business was the decision itself. As the dispute had been between the club and the league, fans had no legal standing to appeal it. Only the league could do that and it was clear they wouldn't. The fans had lost only once, but they'd lost when it counted and, as is the lot of fans in English football, they had no recourse, no one to speak for them.

At which point, Kris Stewart stood up and said, 'I just want to watch football.' Spurred on by the kicker in the report, the club that had been registered just 24 hours before was sold to the supporters' club for £2.

The £28m Wimbledon FC, now without most of its fans, moved to Milton Keynes and the fans of £2 AFC Wimbledon turned their minds to rebuilding.

'It was just a given [that it would be supporter-owned],' says Charlie. 'It wasn't even a debate. Our structure and aims and how it all should work came later. At this point it was just a given that that was what we were going to do.'

At first, the ambition was little more than to get a team out. 'Initially, the question was could we make it work,' says Charlie. 'You announce a friendly, with no kit and no team and you wonder how many people will turn up. And then there's 5,000 and 2,000 more locked outside.'

Fans began sending in money. Within two days, the brand-new club had £80,000 in the bank. It applied to play in the Ryman League, winning a majority of club votes, but falling just short of the threshold. Instead, AFC Wimbledon had to start in the Combined Counties League.

For a fan base that had been used to top-flight football, it wasn't always pretty. 'Some people came a few times and said, "It's not for me, the football's terrible,"' says Charlie. 'And it was at the beginning! Awful! There were genuinely people playing who you'd played against in a Sunday league game and any number of us could've had 45 minutes in goal and not done much worse.

'Some people dipped in and out, but there comes a moment where you aren't dreaming of the old Wimbledon, you just want to win this game. For me, it was playing Barkingside in the London Senior Cup. We won on penalties and I realised in extra time that all I really wanted was for the team that I supported to win this game of football. Your brain stops thinking, "This isn't like playing Man United" and you start thinking, "How far can we take it?" And then your thought becomes, "Can we get back into the league?"'

Eventually, the club set itself two goals: to return to the league in ten years, which would require five promotions, and to find a ground in Merton.

Initially, AFC Wimbledon was 'held together with sticky tape and goodwill', says Charlie. 'It took a while to reach a point of being able to pay people properly, but things went well enough on the pitch to cover up a lot of the rest.'

The first goal was achieved at the end of year nine. To the fans, it was a massive vindication. 'It was a huge fuck you to the panel,' says Charlie. 'Not only were they wrong, but they were proved wrong so quickly. I thought it mightn't take place in my lifetime, that I'd be boring my kids with tales of how we used to be a league club. It was mind-blowing.'

While Charlie is keen to stress that every fan base is filled with the diverse talents that are needed to fight rogue owners, there's no denying one advantage Wimbledon has. In contrast to the rough and ready reputation of Wimbledon FC and its Crazy Gang – and the run-down old stadium – the club is one of the few inner-city teams based in a relatively affluent area. There are plenty of lawyers, bankers and, yes, architects among its ranks. It's never seen itself as an exclusive place, though.

From day one, the club invested time and money in its community activities. 'It was always central to the whole plan,' says Charlie. 'We'd had a very good youth team and football in the community programme. When they moved the team away, kids were going home with no football for the summer – coaching they'd paid for. As early as the second season, we had a programme running, often with first-team players. We've always tried to have an academy in as high a tier as we could and then extensive kids coaching, walking football for the elderly. This is part of what a football club is and part of what it's for.'

All of this helps explain why, 15 years later, when AFC Wimbledon acquired the land on which it would build its new stadium, the club did so using a company which they pointedly named 'The Wider Interests of Football Limited'.

It seemed that all those years of turmoil had developed among fans a shared understanding both of what the club should be about and how to get things done. Paradoxically, all the agony of the relentless fights against owners may have benefited Wimbledon by breeding a togetherness that is absent at some clubs with more rapidly unfolding crises, especially those without a clear end point, like the club moving or going under. Without that, fans can struggle to organise effectively and develop a common viewpoint about how to take the club forward.

Over the years, other people would look to buy AFC Wimbledon, but the predators were fewer on the ground than before and they always received short shrift. Having already lost its ground, there were few assets to strip, and being in League One or Two made the club less susceptible to a silly money offer from someone with dreams of owning a Premier League club in London.

Despite this, the hiccough with the stadium financing was a stark reminder of the financial realities of modern football.

'There is more of a financial glass ceiling than there's ever been,' says Charlie. 'But part of that is to do with the level of debt that other clubs have. There's not many [supporter-owned clubs] in the league, but perversely events have shown that the perception of fans in football is pretty much the wrong way round. The idea was that you had to have businessmen running the club because fans are idiots who would spend money on players and want success today and don't care about what happens to the club. They would just spend money on a new centre-forward. And yet the evidence appears to be just the opposite: most supporter-run clubs are more concerned with husbandry and keeping everything going, possibly sometimes even to the detriment of the team.

It's the random owners who come in and say, "We'll get promotion, don't worry about being £60m in debt, because we'll get to the Premier League and get it all back again" who are the danger. No fan-owned club has tried to do that.'

Another question is how well the club listens to its owners. 'We might be fan-owned, but there is occasionally a criticism that we're not always that good at engaging with our fans,' says Charlie. 'Most clubs could do that better, however they're owned. But I don't think any club can be run by giving fans more control over football matters. It sounds like a great marketing idea, and we all like to think that we know better than the manager, but you only have to look at what happens any time a rich owner starts getting involved in playing matters to know it doesn't work. Perhaps you could use apps to improve transparency and communication, and discuss the direction of the club, but not more granular than that.'

The new stadium at Plough Lane was due to open in time for the 2020/21 season, but in March 2020 Covid-19 brought work to a standstill. The wait to return to Plough Lane would come to an end in the latter months of 2020.

How would it feel for fans to be at the first game in the new stadium, the stadium they'd built hosting the team they'd founded and refused to surrender to anyone else?

'You just probably want to take some time to stand there with all the people who worked for the club over the years and try and take stock of it being the culmination of all we've achieved,' says Charlie. 'But football fans being football fans, that won't last very long. It'll be, "Right, what do we do now? How do we get more people to come? Are we actually going to win this game?"'

15

More money than sense

Congratulations! So you want
to buy a football club

DON'T. DON'T do it. Step away from the chequebook.

Being the owner of a club is a complex and stressful role. Not only do you have to comply with the rules and responsibilities that any business is subject to, but you also have to navigate football's bizarre financial landscape.

You will regularly receive criticism for matters that aren't your fault or for which you have no direct control. Just how were you meant to prevent your star midfielder going on a cocaine binge in a KFC children's area? Why haven't you announced that new striker? Why are the burgers £4.50? You know there's been a leak for months over seat D14 in the Main Stand, right? Why haven't you fixed that? You must be some sort of asset-stripper. Why won't the website load?

Your role will go far beyond trying to put a winning team on the pitch. You'll be tasked with protecting an entire ecosystem. The vast majority of clubs, whether they are

Premier League, EFL or non-league, will have layers and layers of community projects, women's squads and youth squads alongside the first team.

And all of that is before you get to the supporters. They are not supermarket customers who can simply go elsewhere if they receive a service they're not satisfied with. Not when they could boo the supermarket owner and demand they sell to someone with greater ambitions for the shop.

Fans live and die by their club, their moods defined by the performance on and off the pitch. The relegations and cup-final defeats will be an irreparable wound. The victories, the promotions and the titles will be memories cherished for a lifetime. Trying your best won't be enough. Fans may claim that's all they want from their team, but it's a romantic notion that doesn't apply to owners. If a giant of English football like Liverpool or Manchester United was relegated despite the honest toil of their players, the players would be quietly sold and consigned to the pub quiz questions of history. But the owner who caused such a demise would never be forgotten or forgiven. If you're in the market for an already competitive club, then you will be expected to win.

The risks are enormous. You know the joke, 'How do you make a bit of money in football? Start with a lot of money.' Don't open with it at the EFL owners' meeting; they've lived it. Most clubs lose money every year; they expect it, they budget for it. You are probably going to have to inject cash every year to sustain the club.

And that's assuming you don't want to roll the dice and push for promotion. Alan Hardy at Notts County and Stewart Day at Bury both did, risking it all to deliver the dream. Both propped up their club with the profits of their core businesses, and when they went bust, so did Bury and Notts County. Notts had a lucky escape but Bury did not.

Of course, it's not impossible to make money as the owner of a club, just very unlikely. Alan Sugar became the majority shareholder at Tottenham Hotspur for £8m, selling his stake a few years later for £25m. If he'd held on, he could have made much more. The club was reportedly worth around £1bn just over a decade later, though the fortunate timing of the creation of the Premier League is not something you'll be able to bank on. Sugar later reflected that he probably could have done something more lucrative with his time.

If, after all that, you're still determined to forge ahead, then you need to determine the value of the club you're intending to buy.

Valuing any business, let alone a football club, is a complex task. There is no easy, obvious or universally agreed methodology to arrive at a valuation. For a traditional business, say a shop, or a factory, the preferred method can differ depending on the industry. You could be attempting to buy a business turning over £100,000 a year (turnover being the amount of sales in a specified period). Fantastic. But if the cost of business per year is £99,000 – the business makes £1,000 profit. Is that a great return? How do you value that company?

Bigger turnover and lower costs mean more profit received – making the business more valuable. Fine. And if a business loses money per year (turnover is lower than sales) then there's a fair indication that it is worth nothing. A nominal fee must still be paid for a business with no value, to show that 'some consideration' has been paid. The fee is symbolic and needn't be £1. While Chelsea, Portsmouth, Hull, Swansea, Notts County and Wrexham (among others) have all, at one time, been purchased for £1, Steve Morgan fished a crisp tenner out of his wallet to buy Wolves.

All that makes intuitive sense. The problem comes when clubs which lose significant sums of money are assigned serious monetary value. How can that be?

Anything that a business owns is an 'asset' while anything it owes is a 'liability'. A football club can lose money while its assets hold significant value. This is why the purchase of Bolton Wanderers cost somewhere in the region of £10m to £15m in 2019, even though the club was essentially bust. The club owns a modern stadium used not only for football but live music and other events. It has a hotel attached. Player contracts are valuable assets. The club's presence in the EFL is technically an asset that could be used to generate significant revenue. Monies received and owed from broadcasting deals are another major asset.

Valuing the club isn't just a question of totalling all this up, it's about projecting how much revenue it could generate in the future. All things considered, could Bolton be turned around to break even, maybe even generate a profit? The fact there was money exchanged for a full sale implies that both seller and owner believed that, yes, Bolton Wanderers as a legal entity can be a profitable business.

Since 2007, Forbes has published an annual list of the most valuable football clubs in the world. The list serves mainly to provide a talking point and an effective piece of marketing for Forbes rather than a robust valuation that you'd use as the basis of an offer for a club. In the first list, Manchester United were ranked top at a value of $1.4bn. In 2019, Real Madrid were rated the most valuable club in the world at a staggering $5.8bn.[41] Evidently, there has been some serious inflation in club valuations. At the exchange rate on the day of writing, you could either buy Real Madrid, or you could buy 16 and a half billion Freddos.

Forbes says that its methodology is mainly equity plus net debt, and includes matchday revenue but excludes the real-estate value of the stadium.

Manchester United and Real Madrid traded Forbes's title as 'most valuable club' back and forth for 12 years. In 2020, the list was yet one more casualty of Covid and by the time it returned in 2021, a new club topped the list: FC Barcelona.

That's the same Barcelona whose most recent annual results revealed that the club had debts of $1.4bn and had made an annual operating loss of $117m. While Barcelona said they would have essentially broken even if not for the pandemic, *El Mundo*, Spain's second-largest national newspaper, claimed that the club was on the 'verge of bankruptcy'.[42]

The report revealed that the club had a negative working equity (when a company's current liabilities exceed its current assets) of $729m. Around 74 per cent of the $1.03bn revenue was spent on player wages. So drastic were the report's findings that the club board and auditors agreed that the business's status as a 'going concern' (i.e. a steady business that can pay its bills on time) was under threat.

In the summer of 2021 it was revealed that Barcelona had reached La Liga's strict squad salary cap limit, preventing them from immediately registering the signings of Memphis

Depay, Sergio Agüero, Eric García and the contract extension of Lionel Messi (despite him agreeing a 50 per cent wage cut).

Given all this financial turmoil, which came to light three months before the new Forbes ranking, you might be surprised to find that not only were Barcelona number one, but they were given a valuation of $5.76bn. Forbes tactfully omitted mention of the club's gargantuan debts, preferring to highlight their $320m shirt sponsorship deal with Rakuten, and their social media following, the fifth-largest of any sports team in the world.

Even Forbes's own stated methodology doesn't explain the value adequately. It's supposed to focus on 'equity plus net debt' and account for the 'economics of the team's stadium'. Barcelona's (negative) equity of $729m plus a $1.4bn debt leaves a figure of -$2.1bn. The real-estate value of the Camp Nou is not taken into account according to Forbes's methodology, so this doesn't explain the figure. Neither does the value of the squad, which is listed in the financial report as €600m.

Reviewing historical lists, Forbes clearly attributes significant value to commercial revenue, matchday revenue, sponsorships and social media following but particularly in the case of Barcelona, the numbers just don't add up.

So if you do fancy buying a team, you're probably going to be looking for a more robust way of agreeing a price.

For anyone concerned with the stock market, it's worth listening when Warren Buffett speaks. He is the chairman, CEO and mastermind behind Berkshire Hathaway, an investment holding company that owns a number of household-name companies outright as well as a significant percentage in companies like Coca-Cola and Apple. You can guarantee that the stock price of Berkshire Hathaway will rise in the same way you can guarantee the sun will come up in the morning.

Buffett himself was briefly a water boy for Washington's NFL team when his father was a US congressman. Later, when asked by an American radio station why he – one of the nation's wealthiest men – hadn't bought a sports team, Buffett decried the hassle of it and the inevitability of fan complaints.[43] When asked if he thought buying a sports team was actually a good investment, Buffett compared them to works of art, driven up in value by scarcity and their profile in US society. Famously frugal and unshowy, Buffett professed to prefer investing to acquiring status symbols. Several years after that interview, however, Buffett did go on to buy a minority stake in a sports team, taking a 25 per cent ownership share of the decidedly unglamorous Minor League Baseball club Omaha Storm Chasers.

On Wall Street, where Manchester United is listed on the New York Stock Exchange, the club's market cap (the number of existing shares multiplied by the share price) is around $2.6bn. While that's fine as a quick valuation, it falls well short of the full story.

A company's board can create different types of share that grant the holder different rights. They can grant access to dividends or importantly, in the case of Manchester United, different voting rights. Manchester United's 'A shares' are listed publicly while the club's 'B shares', which carry additional voting power, are held under tight control by the Glazer family.

Even the small number of publicly traded football teams are hard to price. Want to buy a slightly smaller team, say Scunthorpe United, and you won't have either a Forbes valuation or a market cap to fall back on.

As a result, a variety of specialist football valuation models, with varying degrees of complexity, have been developed. They can produce wildly different valuations, and academic papers on the subject regularly refer to a lack of quality research in the field.

The most accessible discussion of club valuation comes in *The Price of Football: Understanding Football Club Finance*, written by the foremost expert on English football finance, Kieran Maguire.[44] Maguire says there isn't a 'correct' price for a football club any more than there's a correct price for a player, or a house, or a piece of art.

One of the methodologies that Maguire presents is called the 'Markham Multivariate Model'.

Dr Tom Markham is the current head business development strategy at Sports Interactive, the developer behind the popular *Football Manager* series of video games. In 2013 he published his PhD thesis, 'What is the optimal method to value a football club?'[45]

Finding the current models lacking, he decided to introduce his own formula.

The Markham Multivariate Model is:

Club value = (Revenue + Net Assets) * [(Net Profit + Revenue) / Revenue] * (% stadium filled) / (% wage ratio)

Markham's formula is fairly simple, though could perhaps be a little overwhelming to anyone without a grounding in accountancy. Its key determinant of value is revenue, which is multiplied by certain other variables: assets, profit, wages and how full a club's stadium is.

Revenue + Net Assets is the base of the formula and gives the primary value. Revenue is the monetary amount of sales made by a club while net assets in this case will include things like a stadium and a playing squad AFTER the amount of club debt is taken into account. (Net Profit + Revenue) / Revenue will give a figure above or below 1 depending on whether the club is making a profit or not and as such will either increase or decrease the value provided in Revenue + Net Assets.

Finally, (% stadium filled) / (% wage ratio) is the last multiplier. As most clubs in the Premier League fill their stadium, while wages hover at about 70 per cent on average, every team in the division should see this value above 1 for another boost to the formula's primary value.

It's important to note that Markham specifically designed the formula to value Premier League clubs. In his book, Maguire applies the formula to Newcastle United – arriving at a valuation of £353m, which matches the figure reportedly sought by owner Mike Ashley from any potential purchaser.

To apply the formula further down the leagues produces interesting results.

In 2017, Michael Eisner – who measures his wealth in billions – paid £5.7m to become majority shareholder at Portsmouth. We know from Portsmouth's 2018 accounts that up to June 2017 the club's financial figures were:

Revenue: £7,544,996
Net Assets: £6,657,098

Net Profit: £-508,000
Stadium Usage (League): 16,822
Stadium Capacity: 19,669
Wage Ratio percentage: 152 per cent
Stadium Capacity percentage: 85.53 per cent

This allows us to calculate a valuation of £7.4m. It seems an instinctively fair price for Portsmouth in 2017 and if the formula calculated the price of a Premier League club with only £1.7m of error, it would be particularly impressive. As a percentage, it's somewhat less outstanding, out by a margin of 22 per cent.

The further you go down the pyramid, the more actual sale prices seem to drift from Markham's formula (though, again, the formula was only designed to value Premier League clubs). To apply the formula to Hednesford produces a valuation of approximately £90,000 (though some guesswork must be applied as not all of the relevant figures are publicly available). The figure is almost certainly far too low when you consider that a full sale would also include the stadium, and that the stadium is included in the assets when applied to the formula. The main issue is that the stadium's used capacity percentage, with Hednesford getting an average attendance of 300 inside their 6,000-capacity stadium, produces a multiplier which drags down the valuation. Certainly the figure of £90,000 wouldn't have impressed the owner of Hednesford Town who was seeking over a £1m for the club at the time OwnaFC were sniffing around it.

In reality, if you want the most accurate possible value for a football club, independent valuation must be sought for all of the club's assets. It's highly likely this isn't a reasonable use of time or money, particularly lower down the pyramid, when pricing the stadium, the squad and taking account of revenue and debt will tell you 99 per cent of the story.

The elephant in the room is that you can't price a club's culture, or the community surrounding it. Certainly, you can consider some modern corporate metrics like social media following but you can't value the atmosphere at Dulwich Hamlet's Champion Hill any more than you can value the atmosphere at Anfield. To pursue a value with some sort of ruthless financial efficiency in mind misses the main point of owning a club in the first place.

Unlike other sectors where venture capitalists can strip out costs, anyone aiming to profit from buying a club and selling it will generally have to be able to show some concrete progress. There is, of course, a significant conversation to be had about what that does to the sporting integrity of a division or the pyramid as a whole.

Ultimately, many of us would hope an owner purchased a club because they loved it. Because they knew the club and it meant something. And if it means paying a little over the odds, so be it. The best owners aren't necessarily the richest, they're the ones who care about the people over the team.

The best owners are the ones who correctly identify that a club, any club, your club, is priceless.

16

A modern-day Michael Knighton

Just a year before OwnaFC collapsed,
Harvey had looked to be on to a winner.

IN MARCH 2018, RightTrades Management Limited, which had notionally been trading for only ten months, changed its ownership structure. Having had just 100 shares at launch, all owned by Harvey, it now issued 900 more, split between 700 ordinary and 200 preference shares. Harvey controlled the 200 preference shares and 300 ordinary shares. The remaining 500 ordinary shares were split between Harvey's fiancée and the family members who'd injected money – £360,000 – into the businesses.

In other words, this was structured like a proper business deal, with investors getting shares for their cash rather than just helpful relatives pitching in where the banks wouldn't lend. The expectation of the investors – or at least the promise they were made – was presumably that their stakes would increase in value as the business grew and they might benefit from dividends paid out of profits.

At the time, the business was forging ahead, both under its main brand and under at least five other sister brands, which the company had created to try and scoop up new business. By incorporating likely search terms into the URLs, websites like NewFuseBox.co.uk and ElectricianNeeded.co.uk aimed to boost their Google rankings in a crowded market and then direct customers to the parent company.

The plans for RightTrades seemed to have gone out of the window in May, though, after Harvey met up with an old friend who coached at Whitehaven rugby league club. When Harvey recounted this tale to Hednesford Town fans in March 2019, he implied that he'd already been in talks to buy a football club – which is widely believed to be Stockport County, although we've not been able to confirm this – and was essentially invited to come and rescue Whitehaven.

This bid would eventually collapse in a style that would later come to appear strikingly familiar. Crucially, it seemed to mark the beginning of a full-blown obsession with owning a sports club and a rapidly dwindling interest in the newly capitalised RightTrades.

The finances of most professional sports are pretty precarious, especially once you move outside the top flight. Whitehaven, on the west coast of Cumbria, a good two hours from Wigan, were struggling. In the third tier of English rugby league, they were running desperately short of cash and had just launched an appeal for fans to raise £60,000. Without this money, the club said, it might not even be able to finish the season. Sellers don't come much more distressed than this.

As Harvey told it, 'I made some calls and had ten people ready to put £10,000 into the club each year for five years and that was it, I made contact and offered a deal. I was welcomed with open arms into the club and it felt special.'

Just a few weeks later the bid was made official, with Harvey appearing in the papers playing the saviour. The club also announced a tie-up with Red Star Rugby League Club of Belgrade to bring some of its more promising players to England. Harvey was credited with initiating the deal, which was designed to help Whitehaven acquire much-needed talent and smooth the way for the Serbian club's attempts to join the English rugby league set up. If you don't follow rugby league, you may not be aware that, while the teams competing are largely English and Welsh, there are a small number of teams from overseas, including in recent years Toronto, Perpignan and Toulouse. There have also been ongoing discussions for years about folding several smaller teams into consolidated regional teams.

Ever eager for publicity, Harvey gave interviews to the press where he laid out the template he would later deploy with OwnaFC. He aimed to increase sponsorship, bring in new coaching, create a comprehensive player pathway ('The aim would be to eventually provide the first team with the best talent in the county'), boost fan numbers and earn a promotion. All of it, of course, with only modest investment.

His ambition he said was 'a mid-table Championship club with 1,500 minimum on these terraces and a successful pathway'. Given Whitehaven's attendances at the time, he was essentially visualising tripling the gates in just a few years. This would be a major undertaking in a large urban area, but in a small, relatively isolated Cumbrian coastal town, where its nearest neighbour – Workington – also has a rugby league team, it's close to impossible without a very wealthy, or very patient, owner. Harvey was neither of these things.

Nonetheless, the club announced that Harvey had signed a letter of intent and put on a press conference so he could unveil some of the members of his consortium. At the event, he produced a message of support from a former England rugby star and an agreement from another to play for the club to help it out and raise attendances. He also claimed to have invested money in training kit and to be at work improving the club's website.

By this time, the club's appeal for funds – which Harvey said would need to reach its target to make the investment possible – had produced an impressive £45,000. A public meeting was organised for fans and shareholders to hear from Harvey about his plans. All seemed to be proceeding well.

And yet, in the last week of June, less than a month after he became involved, the deal collapsed. Both sides initially said it was amicable, but Harvey would go on to claim that the club's debts were much larger than he'd been told, that its financial systems were a mess and that he'd been the victim of sniping on social media (he had been spotted at the races with someone who'd formerly owned a rugby club and was now being linked with buying Workington, which had, he claimed, sparked anger among Whitehaven fans about the revival of a long-mooted plan to merge the clubs). 'These were silly rumours started by people who didn't want us at the club in the first place,' Harvey would later say.

The response of fans to the collapse was mixed, with many expressing confusion as to how the deal could have fallen apart. Some fans were willing, if not to side with

Harvey, then at least to believe the club mightn't have been well-enough run to present him with accurate financials. Others were concerned with Harvey's apparent taste for press coverage. 'Mr Harvey has done more press/radio interviews since his proposed takeover than President Trump, many at inappropriate times while negotiations were supposedly on-going,' said one fan. 'He seems to be constantly putting pressure on the [board of directors] in what could be construed as basically bullying at times.' Another said, 'I'm starting to think he may be a modern-day Michael Knighton,' comparing Harvey to the man who tried to buy Manchester United before acquiring Carlisle United and, eventually, taking them into voluntary administration. (To be fair to Knighton, while he became a byword for failed football takeovers among fans, his legacy is far more interesting. His predictions, for example, about the potential of Manchester United and the future of broadcasting were amply borne out.)

It proved a lucky escape for Whitehaven. Not only did the club not go under without Harvey, they managed to finish the season and then, the following year, they won League One and were promoted to the Championship. They finished their title-winning season with a 74-6 demolition of the Llanelli-based West Wales Raiders before clinching promotion in the final game, when they hung 72 unanswered points on the Coventry Bears. For a club that had been on the brink of extinction barely a year before, it was quite a turnaround.

Even if Whitehaven wasn't to be, Harvey was dead set on owning not just a sports team but a football team. The following week, on 2 July 2018, he registered OwnaFC Limited at Companies House and bought the rights to use ownafc.

com. Two days later, OwnaFC created a Twitter account and submitted a trademark application on the word OwnaFC. As the year progressed, and his marketing plans for the company developed, he also trademarked Owna – his nickname for the company and term for his customers. While the first application covered online services and entertainment, the second included an additional category: dog breeding. Even in all of his talk of a Europe-wide, multi-club sports brand, Harvey never elaborated on where dog breeding fitted into his masterplan before OwnaFC's collapse. Football's gain might have been the canine world's loss.

The same month that Harvey founded OwnaFC, his fiancée was nominated for a Young Entrepreneur of the Year award for her work on RightTrades (it was also, by coincidence, the month that Steve Price first sought a buyer for Hednesford Town at the rather optimistic valuation of £1.25m).

In the months that followed, employees of RightTrades published videos on YouTube of them experimenting with the technical capabilities of a sports app with video streaming that they were building. Despite being the sole personal owner of OwnaFC Limited, Harvey had employees of RightTrades, a company of which he was only partial owner, working on sports ownership projects – in RightTrades offices, during office hours.

We contacted several former RightTrades employees to ask about their experience working there. Most refused to be interviewed, but one was extremely positive about having worked there in that period. 'It was a very positive vibe,' they said. 'We seriously thought we were going to change the world!'

At least three developers were working on the project and money was also being spent on external graphic design services, to produce the very smart company identity, brochure, website and app interface for OwnaFC that did so much to convince people that the business was a professional one.

It's not clear which company – RightTrades or OwnaFC – paid for the graphic design work nor whether OwnaFC reimbursed RightTrades for the substantial cost of using its staff to develop the app.

Around the same time, a post appeared on a football gaming website making the first public pitch for OwnaFC outside of its Twitter feed. Posted by someone who shared a first name with the lucky Harvey refundee – the person who would run interference for the company when it collapsed, displaying his refund as proof of its goodwill – the app claimed to have been 'developed and built alongside the creators of *Grand Theft Auto*'. Creating a video game like *Grand Theft Auto* is a huge undertaking involving teams of people, so it's possible that one or more RightTrades employees might have worked on one of the bestselling series in some capacity at some point. However, given that the OwnaFC app was coded on an industrial estate in Wigan, it is very hard to see how it could be true that it had been 'developed alongside' the *GTA* games. These are made by Rockstar North, a company proudly headquartered in Edinburgh. Competent as the app was, it seems highly unlikely anyone would be moved to remark on its similarity to the vast, immersive worlds of the games from the *Grand Theft Auto* stable.

As the autumn of 2018 came round, OwnaFC geared up for a formal launch. But even then, Harvey's head was again turned by a rugby club. This time it was Rochdale Hornets. In late November, the independent supporters' club held a public meeting to discuss fundraising initiatives. Harvey was in attendance and took part in discussions about how the club might move forward.

Accounts of the meeting vary, but the closest thing to Harvey's side of the story was posted on a rugby league forum a few weeks later by someone claiming to be 'very close to' Harvey and to have 'introduced him to the club'. This anonymous poster, who had a notably clipped and aggressive writing style, went on to claim that Harvey had made 'a six-figure cash offer to takeover the Hornets' with the intent to turn it into a supporter-owned club. The poster further claimed that Harvey had provided 'proof of funds' to the club 'in advance of such offer being made' and further that 'the RFL approved [his bid]'. The bid, they said, had collapsed for unspecified reasons at which point he'd 'resigned as a director' of the club.

How far this bid got is, as always, shrouded in claims of commercial confidentiality, but it's notable that, in September 2018, a YouTube channel had been launched called Own A Rugby Club. The channel featured Rochdale's branding and it was there that RightTrades developers posted their app test videos. Like Whitehaven, in advance of a completed deal – or perhaps to sweeten that deal – Harvey had set RightTrades company resources to work on behalf of a team he wanted.

The same month, Whitehaven's coach, who had been a supporter of Harvey's bid for the club, was appointed at Rochdale.

Harvey's anonymous online close friend, who went by the name 'Hornettillidie', joined the forum in early October and, despite his name's profession of eternal love, posted just nine times before his last message on 10 December. He spent those few weeks defending Harvey on the message boards and spoke with seeming first-hand knowledge about the appointment of the coach, saying in response to a critic, 'I am not sure you fully understand that a full robust interview process took place and that the best candidate was offered the job.'

Whether Harvey had a hand in the appointment or whether his bid had got as far as claimed, it was all done and dusted by mid-December. It was then that the OwnaFC app went live and Harvey, having failed to buy Stockport County FC, Whitehaven RLFC and Rochdale Hornets RLFC, went off in search of bigger prey.

17

He's taken us as far as he can

*No good deed goes unpunished. Football is
an industry that actively incentivises reckless
behaviour by business owners, driving clubs
towards trophies or bankruptcy. The good
guys, meanwhile, get sneered at or pitied.*

GLORY! LA gloire! It's what drove Louis XIV of France, the
Sun King. He fought wars, dictated fashions, reimagined his
nation and constructed Versailles, a building so lavish and
extraordinary that the word 'palace' seems almost inadequate
to describe it. For more than 70 years he dominated France,
his every action calculated to increase his own personal gloire
and that of the country. France would not see the like of it for
another 300 years, until Sheikh Tamim bin Hamad al-Thani
bought Paris Saint-Germain through the Qatari sovereign
wealth fund and drove the club to seven magnificent titles
in nine short years. Gloire, in all its glory.

Football has always depended on its Sun Kings, people
with money to burn who love nothing more than to put on

a bonfire for the fans. Frustratingly for them, there's more to football than a fat wallet and a thirst for glory. Part of the reason so many managers last only a year is the 'Chairman's Fallacy' – the belief common to every boardroom that it should be possible to finish at least one place higher than last year and that failing to do so is unacceptable. If this seemingly modest ambition – like being two or three places better off – is widely shared, the majority of clubs will automatically end the season feeling like it was a failure. It's a paralysing fear of being left behind that generates football's version of the fight or flight response – signings or sackings – which brings chronic instability to every corner of the game.

We fans are no better. The most damaging phrase in modern football is, 'He's taken us as far as he can.' This claim, which is rolled out after almost every dismissal of a long-serving manager, is a tangle of unvoiced assumptions, the most important of which is that managerial performance, rather than club finances, is the primary determinant of success and that clubs have no natural upper limit on their league position.

No matter how many times a club fires a solid manager, or is sold to someone with an inverse relationship between the depth of their pockets and their football knowledge, a decent proportion of fans can be relied upon to hail the decision as evidence of the club's 'ambition'.

'Ambition' is a curious word, one that modern football frequently uses, unknowingly, as a euphemism for 'greed'. The idea of being satisfied with your club's performance on and off the field is as archaic as being satisfied with one's material possessions was in the 1980s. Pre-Covid, football was still living the laissez-faire fantasy of the pre-Crash era when people who couldn't spell Schumpeter, let alone had actually read him, invoked 'creative destruction' to justify orgiastic capitalism.

If you dare suggest there's another way, if you ask questions like, 'Is it wrong not to want your club to be in the Premier League?' or, 'Is it old-fashioned to just enjoy the game and be happy your club still exists?', you are liable to be sneered at or condemned as a hippy or a relic. The game has changed; you can't fight it.

Much of this book is focused on the implications of having the wrong people in charge of football clubs. People who don't know what they're doing and don't have deep-enough pockets; unethical people; people who ruin clubs. There's no doubt this group is the most pressing problem, the owners that clubs need most immediate protection from. But it's the Sun Kings who present a different kind of challenge to football's future. They don't starve or destroy clubs, they pour money into them. They don't leave them bankrupt, they push them up the league and win trophies. Chelsea and Manchester City are obvious ones, but there are many below them who don't get as much attention because the success they're buying tends to be a place higher up the pyramid than the club would otherwise be able to afford rather than silverware. Leicester bought their way into the Premier League before their astonishing title win, overspending in breach of FFP rules. Wolves, Brighton and Cardiff have all enjoyed spells in the top flight through heavy spending on players, leaving them in debt to their owners. In the Championship in recent years, over half of the clubs were spending more on wages than they received in total income, and there are numerous clubs who measure their debts in the tens of millions of pounds.

These owners are the flip side of the coin from the disaster owners; both inevitable outcomes of the insane logic of English football. The Sun Kings are rich, competent and every bit as ambitious as the others to capture more than their fair share of success.

Football is generally quite relaxed about them. When they spend big on players, we call it 'investment', even though with the poor hit rate and low resale value, most transfers are more akin to gambling. In this way, football actively incentivises and celebrates reckless behaviour by owners – before evincing surprise when clubs are destroyed. And at the bottom, left behind, financially disadvantaged and largely ignored are the clubs trying to do things the right way.

The ultimate problem with owners spending money the club doesn't have is that, even in the rare cases where it leads to a medium-term change to its position in football's pecking order and drives up its value – as with Manchester City – football isn't a normal market where competing businesses can all grow as the market expands. Football success isn't just measured in turnover and profit. It's measured in trophies, and there's a fixed number of those, however much owners are 'investing' in their clubs. Every time a club wins a trophy it could not have competed for if it was spending its own money, then every other team in the competition who was living within their means is punished.

We're used to hearing from the fans of winning clubs and those of the teams being relegated. We know that agony and that ecstasy; it's the lifeblood of all football media. But we rarely hear from the clubs in the middle, politely paying their way, waiting for virtue to be its own reward. And knowing before the season has even begun that this won't be their season.

Glenn Tamplin was a Sun King in 2017/18. Having never managed professionally before, he somehow contrived to take Billericay Town to the Isthmian League Premier Division title. Pouring money into the club and signing a trio of former Premier League players, he brought the Blues glory such as had never been seen in England's seventh tier. They won 99 points, scoring 110 goals and finishing with a goal difference of 60. They were a force of nature, scoring four or more times in 13 of their matches. For a community club with a decaying infrastructure, it was proof that, if you wait long enough, football will eventually reward you with your day in the sun.

Not everyone remembers that season quite in the same way, though. Kieron Bridges is one such individual, a Dulwich Hamlet fan who discovered his club when he went to university in London. Even though he doesn't live there now, he still makes the long drive to get to as many games as possible.

Why Dulwich and not Crystal Palace or Millwall? 'I've always been into the non-league,' he says. 'The feeling of greater ownership, the feeling of being more a part of something. There's a feeling of commonality and everyone pulling together.'

While Dulwich Hamlet's reputation as a hipster hangout has been overstated, a huge amount of successful work has been done by the club to make it a welcome tonic to much of modern football. 'We've done a hell of a lot to attract disillusioned, disenfranchised and, in fact, quite satisfied fans of league clubs to come along and adopt us as a second club,' Kieron says.

For all the club's recent growth, becoming one of the most famous teams in non-league football, it's been a tough few years financially. The long-term wrangling about Hamlet's stadium, which led at one point to the club being evicted by its landlords and having to share with Tooting & Mitcham, meant that money had to be put aside for legal fees instead of players.

Despite this, Hamlet had been knocking on the door of promotion to National League South for a number of seasons. Heading into the 2017/18 season, they had made the play-offs for three successive seasons, with the last two ending in defeats in the final. On the pitch, they should've been able to challenge; off the pitch, just finishing out the season would be an achievement.

Enter Glenn Tamplin, owner of Billericay since late 2016. 'My eyebrows were raised by Billericay before the season had even begun,' says Kieron. 'They already had Jermaine Pennant. They were spending more money than anyone at this level – historical amounts – in trying to get out. And, to be fair, Tamplin wasn't just spending on players; he spent some money on developing the facilities. They had this huge mural of him. I mean, it's not for me to judge what's tasteful.'

The season didn't initially develop as a two-horse race, but as it began to unwind, it seemed that if anyone was going to stop Billericay it was Dulwich. 'Early on in the season, they came to our place and absolutely butchered us,' says Kieron.

'Their fans were giving it some. Partly about what they'd done to us on the pitch, which was fair enough, but it was also on our ground situation – hoping we'd go under. It left a very sour taste.

'Around about Easter time, we beat them away and it looked briefly like we had a chance. But we had a fixture pile-up, largely because of the groundshare, and we had a bad run at the end of April. They had a fixture pile-up too, but they had the greater squad depth to cope with it.'

In the end, Billericay won the title by four points, sending Dulwich into yet another round of play-off roulette. It was third time lucky for Dulwich, though, as they secured promotion after 111 years, beating the other outstanding team in the league – Hendon – on penalties. One missed spot kick and it could've been different.

'It was an amazing day,' says Kieron, 'but I did feel cheated. One of the key things about sport is that it should be a level playing field. And I just believe that the amount of money that Tamplin was spending on a pet project was so far from being a level playing field it was untrue. I get that not every club in the league is going to be spending exactly the same amount; things like crowds dictate that. But this wasn't spending an ordinary amount of money. They were rumoured to be spending three and a half times what we were on wages. It led to people saying it was a tinpot league. "Anyone can manage in it. Oh, look, someone's there winning the league despite not having any football management experience."

'Had we not got promoted, I'd have felt absolutely sick to the core. Hendon fans were very gracious, but they could say they were cheated too. It's made me feel that football is very fragile and needs to be protected. We can't have teams looking to sugar daddies. They need to do things the right way and develop a community.'

Neil Pickup is another who's seen some glory and ambition. He saw Blackpool win the play-off final in 2016/17 and Coventry do the same in 2017/18. Sadly for him, he's an Exeter City fan and, in both cases, he was at Wembley cheering on the losing team.

Neil is a teacher and lives near Oxford. He's been a supporter of Exeter for 17 years since he went to university in the city. His halls of residence were just down the road and, with the club recently relegated out of the Football League and under investigation for financial irregularities, he threw himself into helping rescue it. He joined the supporters' trust and would spend Sunday mornings helping clear the ground after the previous day's game or helping with maintenance, like repainting the training ground or keeping the nearby station tidy for visiting fans. It kindled a deep love for the club and what it represents – a connection to the community, fan ownership and a commitment to developing players and playing good football – that has persisted for nearly two decades.

For all the admiration Exeter rightly attract off the pitch, results on it haven't always been great. The defeat to Blackpool was a loss to a team whose fans were boycotting en masse yet still seemed to be able to afford to turn out a winning side. One unsuitable owner was replaced by another as hedge fund-owned and perpetually homeless Coventry put three past them the next year, leaving Exeter with just an 89th-minute goal to console themselves on the train ride home.

The following year, in 2018/19, Exeter went one worse and missed the play-offs by a single point. Ahead of them were teams like Forest Green, of whom more later, the widely despised MK Dons and, most egregiously of all, Bury. Finishing nine points ahead of Exeter and winning automatic promotion, Bury were known to be spending money they didn't have, although the full, ruinous scope of this wouldn't become clear until the next season when they were expelled from the league. Though Bury were horrendously let down by the EFL and their fans suffered the slow-motion agony of their club imploding, there's no escaping the fact that they got a promotion at other clubs' expense. Throughout this period, meanwhile, Exeter were having to sell players to make ends meet, always the bridesmaid, never the bride.

'There are so many clubs spending 150 per cent, 160 per cent of their income on wages and they're all so reliant on something to fill the hole,' says Neil. 'And when that something goes, what happens? It feels like we're playing by one set of rules – hand to mouth, making ends meet, there is no other option for us.'

Neil thinks it reflects a wider malaise in a game that's become inured to frenzied overspending. 'My interest in the Premier League has dropped off,' he says. 'You watch the Premier League but it doesn't really matter that much to me. It's disconnected with what football used to be about.

'If I look at City, the moments that have stood out, those FA Cup nights, those play-off semi-finals, winning 6-5 on aggregate with a 94th-minute goal, I don't see how you get a better high from that than you get from winning the

Champions League. It's the same adrenaline kick, just at a different level. It's that same feeling you got watching Jos Buttler take stumps at the end of the Cricket World Cup Final. The same release. You play division nine cricket in Oxfordshire and you win a game by one run with the last wicket against your local rivals, that brief moment of joy. That's what sport is. It doesn't need to be chasing the Premier League and paying some player 95 grand a week.'

Likewise, ambition for Neil doesn't mean new signings or spending big to reach for the Premier League.

'I'd rather have the club meaning what it's always meant to me,' he says, 'being part of the community, part of the city, connected to all of us in and around St James [Park, Exeter's home ground], connected to its academy. I want my club to continue to exist, I want it to hold its identity, I want it to continue to bring players through. I want us to keep playing good football and make for good days out with good support, to give you days that you remember.'

Glyn Price knows the feeling. A Shrewsbury fan since he was 13, he's seen his club growing steadily and trying to shake off its 'league minnows' reputation. Shrewsbury is that rarest of gems: a club owned by a local boy made good. A fan of the team since the 1950s, Roland Wycherley has been in charge for over 20 years, building the team on and off the pitch.

'He runs it as a traditional Shropshire business,' says Glyn. 'You live within your means and try to do the best you can and, at the end of the day, you're there to provide a spectacle to the fans and support the community.'

Over the last decade, Shrewsbury established themselves as a mid-table League One team. But in 2017/18, something happened. A club that began each season aiming for safety somehow put together a 17-match unbeaten run, not losing their first league game until the end of November.

'It was a magical journey,' says Glyn. 'We were fun to watch, we were great for scoring late goals. We went into most games with a sense of invincibility. I was finding myself wanting to travel to Doncaster on a Tuesday night! It was a really good, unifying thing for the fan base.'

What made Shrewsbury's run all the more remarkable was the club's modest finances. It broke even in a league where there is a direct correlation between the teams who lose the most and the teams that finish highest in the league (by way of context, that season West Bromwich Albion finished rock bottom of the Premier League, receiving over £90m in TV money alone, while Shrewsbury, who finished just 27 places below them in the pyramid, had a total income of £6m). For much of the season, it seemed like a small, profitable, well-run team might win automatic promotion to the Championship. They were neck and neck with the leaders at Christmas and didn't slip out of the automatic promotion places until the end of January.

Unfortunately for Shrewsbury, their title challengers were Blackburn and Wigan, two much larger teams who'd just dropped out of the Championship and were very keen to get back. The lower-league equivalent of parachute payments – the money relegated teams get when they drop out of the Premier League, which wildly distorts the Championship – is the exemption that relegated clubs get from the lower leagues' cost control measures. The Salary Cost Management Protocol (SCMP) limits League One clubs to spending no more than 60 per cent of their income on wages. Clubs who have been relegated into League One have a one-year grace period, designed to help them adjust to the financial shock of relegation and rework their contracts situation. Too often though, the exemption acts as an overwhelming incentive not to cut spending but to push for promotion, using the massive financial advantage of having one uncapped season in a salary-capped division.

Champions Wigan spent £12m on wages that year – four times what Shrewsbury did – clocking up an £8m loss, while second-placed Blackburn lost £17m.

'We were still top of the table in February,' says Glyn, 'but the January transfer window showed the difference.' Both Wigan and Blackburn brought in three established players, while Shrewsbury were able to augment their squad only with lower-league signings. In the end, Shrewsbury just couldn't keep with the pace. Glyn adds, 'The team's EFL Trophy Final and FA Cup run was too much for the squad. We played 63 games in the season. From March onwards, we couldn't keep up. Our squad size and recruitment was the difference.'

Shrewsbury's season ended in a play-off final at Wembley with an extra-time winner for Rotherham United, who had spent twice what Shrewsbury had on wages. 'People thought it was a chance, but there's this omen: we've been to Wembley five times and lost every single time,' says Glyn. 'We cannot win there. The whole thing was about "Reverse the Curse" but we couldn't. The curse was not reversed and we lost again.

'I feel like there's an element of financial doping that went on that season. I don't feel overly angry at Blackburn and Wigan because I see it happening so much in the divisions above. For them to keep up with the teams above them, they've got to push themselves to the limit. I don't think it's necessarily their fault for playing that game. There's something more fundamentally wrong with the distribution of money across football and the fairness within the model. It's symptomatic of a wider problem in football.'

Facing up to the harsh financial realities of the modern game, what does ambition mean to Glyn? 'Getting into the Championship for a club like Shrewsbury is starting to become fairly unachievable,' he says. 'We came so close. It took a miracle season and we still didn't get there.'

Two years later, Shrewsbury had their notorious FA Cup replay against Liverpool. Before the Shrews even had a chance to celebrate getting a draw, Liverpool manager Jürgen Klopp had announced that, in keeping with the Premier League's winter break rules, he'd put out a youth team for the replay and wouldn't attend himself. Later, Liverpool also declined to shift the replay's date, which would've given Shrewsbury a lucrative live TV broadcast, and slashed ticket prices, leaving Shrewsbury making almost nothing from what was supposed to be a dream tie.

'The whole Anfield experience was horrible, I hated every single minute,' says Glyn. 'Getting the late 2-2 draw [at home in the first match] was fantastic – to see some of those players, Salah, Firmino, on our pitch. Brilliant, you couldn't be any higher. At the replay we filled the away end but there was no real atmosphere. It was a youth-team game. We left jaded by the whole experience.

'You hear the phrase "the football family", but I don't really feel it from fans of larger clubs. Football's broken. You can see it at the coal face of the grassroots and non-league football. At some point, post-Covid, a lot more clubs than Bury will go bust and there won't be anyone to save them. If it pushes clubs to the wall who've been overspending, we wouldn't have much sympathy. You wouldn't wish anything on the fans, but it makes you wonder if some clubs do need to go under to show there should be a different approach.'

What would Glyn do if a sugar daddy came in and took Shrewsbury over? 'The first thing I'd do is make sure my subscription was up to date with Shrewsbury Town Supporters' Trust, because we might be needing that down the line! At Shrewsbury, a lot of money has been invested in the good of the club in the long term and for fans. We can be proud of what we can give back to fans on and off the pitch. It would be impossible to be a big Championship team. I could live another 100 years and be 90 per cent sure we'd never get to the Premier League. But every few seasons, there will be a cup run. Some of the best times of the last 20 years have been cup games. I still love my club and I hope there will be a club there in ten years' time.'

In 2018/19, the year Exeter missed the play-offs and Bury went up, Forest Green Rovers – the team with a solar-powered Sun King – finished fifth and qualified for the play-offs. This was only the second season of league football for this small but venerable club. Two years before, the press had splashed the good-news story of their having ended their near 130-year wait across the back pages, largely disregarding the grumbles of non-league fans who pointed out, rightly, the enormous financial support the club has received from their wealthy owner, green energy magnate Dale Vince (they had reported debts of more than £5m on entering the league and had lost more than £2m in each of the previous two seasons).

Having freshly purchased promotion for his team, Vince unveiled plans for a £100m 'eco park', which includes a conference centre and a new 5,000-seater stadium – the world's first to be built from wood. Few people seemed troubled about the unselfconscious showiness of employing Zaha Hadid's firm of architects to design a lower-league stadium, albeit one that will be the smallest in League Two.

Perhaps this is a good thing, though? A sporting statement that small can be beautiful; a deliberate rebuke to modern football? Well, only if you don't recognise the relationship between club size and catchment area. Except when they put out youth teams in the FA Cup, Liverpool are straightjacketed by Anfield, despite it holding 54,000 people. Forest Green, by contrast, aren't turning anyone away at the gates.

Sustainability is the word at the heart of this all. Forest Green's development into an environmentally friendly club, including becoming certified carbon neutral and vegan, has been widely documented. Doubtless, ecologically speaking, Rovers will become the game's first sustainable club. But this is not the kind of sustainability that matters in football.

Eventually the club want to be in the Championship. And that means that, even if their new stadium were full every week, revenues would depend almost entirely on TV money, leaving them at a massive financial disadvantage in a division where the average attendance in 2016/17 was just over 20,000. In other words, Forest Green could only survive at this level by having a series of managers who can outperform their budget every year.

That just doesn't happen in football. Being an extremely well-run club doesn't provide anything like the competitive advantage that it does in other sports for the simple reason that, in any given division, there will be a huge disparity between the highest and lowest wage bills.

Being an ecological club is not the same as being a sustainable one. No matter how business-like you are, you can only defy the financial gravity of football for so long. With FFP rules making it harder for owners to buy their teams an advantage at the top levels of football, all 'ambitious' fans should remember this basic point: if the plan for making your club sustainable is 'TV money, sponsorship and an interest-free loan from the owner', then you don't have a plan.

Even if Forest Green could reach the Championship and stay there for a few years, there is a serious question about if they could ever generate enough organic growth to pay off their already sizeable debt to their owner. Rovers' home is Nailsworth, a large village with a population of 5,800. The modest-sounding capacity of its proposed new stadium is similar to its current one, but the aim is that better facilities and league football will raise attendances much closer to full capacity every week (in Rovers' last season in the National League, their home was rarely above half-full). There is also an option to raise the capacity to 10,000 should this become feasible.

But even this looks massively ambitious. Reports in the week prior to Forest Green's Wembley play-off success against Tranmere suggest that they sold somewhere between 3,000 and 4,000 tickets, for the most important game in the club's history.

It's often been noted that Blackburn have, on occasions, managed home turnouts which implied over a quarter of the town had attended games. This is nothing compared to the task facing Forest Green which, if they're to become genuinely financially sustainable, will need to create new football fans on an unprecedented scale in an area of low-population density.

Excluding the two London clubs, Leyton Orient and Barnet, the average size of towns hosting clubs in 2016/17 League Two was over 120,000 (if London clubs were included, it would be higher). The smallest town represented in League Two that season was Morecambe which has a population of nearly 35,000 – six times that of Nailsworth.

So where will all these new fans come from? The nearest town of any size to Nailsworth is Cirencester, population 19,000. The nearest urban areas with more than 100,000 residents are Cheltenham and Gloucester. Cheltenham, which is about 20 miles from Nailsworth, has its own team, already in League Two. Gloucester, meanwhile, which is a few miles closer, has Gloucester City, who are also building a new stadium and, being in the National League North, are just a few good seasons behind Forest Green.

The nearest biggest city is Bristol, population 450,000 – which explains why the proposed new green stadium will be sited right beside a junction on the M5 – a relatively easy drive from north Bristol – where it will generate additional car journeys.

So Forest Green's stadium will go up. But what then? Rovers are an interesting club, but they ought not to bank on their green credentials proving a significant draw for fans.

Results trump football ethics every time, even in the hipster parts of Bristol (of which that fine, liberal city has many).

Other generally sceptical people give the owner a pass because he's a down-to-earth man with a sincere passion both for his community and the environment. But you can kill a club with kindness as well as with neglect. What he's planning begins to look like a modern fairy story where a king builds an outsized palace to show his excessive love for his queen, dooming her to wander the lonely halls endlessly. Some gifts, even those given in heartfelt love, can be ruinous.

One man determined not to let that happen to his club is Steve Gibson, another local boy made good. When he picked it up, his team, Middlesbrough, wasn't a village outfit with potential, it was a rusting hulk; not a sleeping giant but an expiring one.

It was the late 1980s and the club, with a crumbling ground and major debts, had gone into liquidation. For a town that had seen its manufacturing and heavy industry topple like dominos, the period became part of an ancestral memory that guides Boro, even when they were later in the Premier League.

Gibson joined a consortium of local businesses to re-found the club, becoming CEO and then owner. 'The economy was crashing,' says lifelong Boro fan Guy Bailey. 'The shipyards were closing. ICI was going. Factories were being knocked down. The consortium realised you couldn't lose the club too, it was holding the community together. Middlesbrough is a hard-working, hard-drinking, hard-living area. The work sometimes stops but the living and the drinking doesn't.'

263

Something unique was forged in the hardship of Boro's collapse. Bruce Rioch took over a squad of just 14 players, 12 of whom had come through the ranks. 'Only one local player left,' says Guy, 'the rest stayed. There was Tony Mowbray, Gary Pallister, Bernie Slaven, Stuart Ripley, Steven Pears.' All could've gone elsewhere, and several would become internationals, but they chose to stay.

Later, when he took full ownership of the club, Gibson – who describes himself not as an owner but a custodian – moved the club from the decaying Ayresome Park to a new stadium in the old industrial heart of the docks. Bailey believes that 25 years later it still has a powerful message of rebirth for the town.

'Even if things aren't going well for people, they can look out of the window at the Riverside Stadium, which was built on disused industrial land. It literally stands out as a beacon.'

Going into 2018/19, Boro fans had hopes of promotion. They'd been in the play-offs the season before. There was a sense of urgency; a number of recent signings had proved duds, so fans knew a reckoning was coming.

'We recognised we'd spent badly,' says Guy, 'so we realised this was our last chance for a couple of seasons before we'd need to rebuild. This was our last best shot.'

Boro looked like they might take that chance. They were in the play-offs for much of the season, before a terrible run of six losses on the bounce in March ruined them. In the end, they missed the play-offs by one point, on the last day of the season. Ahead of them were free-spending Derby County, also owned by a local lad who loved his club. Just how much became clear when it emerged that he had bought Pride Park off the club he already owned, at an apparently generous price, to offset the club's massive losses. Promotion at any cost was the goal. Derby were revealed to be the only club in the league amortising their players in a non-standard way – assuming for accounting purposes that their players would have resale value at the end of their contracts (clubs usually write the cost of the transfer fee off over the lifetime of a player's contract and assume he has no value at the end). Meanwhile, a string of high-profile players and managers arrived, including Wayne Rooney as player-coach, with his wages part-paid by a sponsor.

'There was disappointment that we missed out on the play-offs but people are used to disappointment here, sporting and otherwise,' says Guy. 'We were happy to take it on the chin, but what galled us was when the news came out about the financial chicanery that had been going on at Pride Park, Villa Park and Hillsborough.

'We'd also had a front row seat seeing what had gone on at Sunderland, so that took a lot of heat off our manager and board. People weren't saying "spend, spend, spend" because we could see, 30 miles up the road, what happens when you throw money and managers at a problem. But we didn't realise how critical the financial issues were at other clubs, how far out on the gangplank they were going.'

Guy is pragmatic, though. He recognises how fine the margins are and how much Boro cost themselves over the season. 'We're all football fans, we can all find ten extra points from thin air over the course of the season. There's that chance late on, he scores, that's a point right there.'

He's reluctant to be too critical of how Derby and other clubs are run. 'It's not so much cheating, but we all know you can only do it so long and eventually it will catch up with you. The rewards are so high that clubs are quite willing to break rules to get to them. They are literally mortgaging the house, ironically to themselves.'

What would Guy say about a new owner with a much less cautious attitude than Gibson? 'We're wary of Greeks bearing gifts. There's Darlington, a nice, friendly small club which was at one point owned by a convicted criminal, a former safe cracker, who moved them and their crowds of 3,000 to a new all-seater 25,000-capacity stadium on the edge of town. There were gold-plated taps and marble work surfaces.

'The ground is still there but the club went under and a rugby team plays there in front of 700 people. You drive past it on the main road into Middlesbrough, a monument to ambition. Obviously we'd like the promises of more goals and wins, but we remember the liquidation and we see what happens at Sunderland.

'And when I look at what's happening in Newcastle [with the controversial sale by Mike Ashley to the Saudi sovereign wealth fund], it reminds me of the bit in *King of the Hill* when Hank says, "It's like when you get a wish from a genie but ask for it in slightly the wrong way and wake up with a solid gold head."

'There's a lot of fans who've been through the Premier League who would like the money but would be happy to stay where they are from a footballing point of view. I don't get when it became such a good idea to go up and look forward to getting seven or eight thrashings a season in the hope of finishing 17th and banking £100m, even if that means writing off the FA Cup and the League Cup. That's not why you start watching football. That's not why you have a kickaround in the park as a kid. You don't celebrate like you've scored the goal that got you to 15th in the Premier League. No, you're scoring the winner at Wembley.

'On one level, if it was entirely in pursuit of sporting glory – like you used to have the mad Spanish presidents in the 70s and 80s getting elected with huge promises of signings and trophies – that would be one thing. Back then it wasn't to open up new commercial partnerships and sponsorship deals in China. It was always about winning and being the best. It was about the glory not the money.'

There's that word again, glory. Perhaps Guy is right. We've confused money and winning with glory and achievement. Beyond that, maybe there's a bigger issue still, bigger even than sporting equality: justice. When we fans demand success, success at any price and especially success paid for not from fans' pockets, we ignore that promotions, cups and titles are zero-sum games.

If you buy these things, you rob all the other teams trying to honestly earn what they have. All the players giving everything for what may be their one shot at league football or a medal or the title or European football. All the managers running themselves into the ground with stress, knowing even finishing as runners-up could be enough to get them the sack. All the fans, working hard to pay for their tickets, yelling their team on and desperate for one little sniff of success. All of them are robbed when we let teams buy their way to success. It's corrosive to the soul of football.

So, yes, let us criticise the owners of Chelsea and Manchester City, Leicester and Forest Green Rovers – all of whom bought their success in one way or another. And, yes, let us criticise the owners who promised success, but haven't yet delivered it.

But only if we can first say this, 'More than anything, I want my club to survive and to earn everything it has honestly.'

If we can't, then truly we have forgotten the first thing we are taught about sport as children: it's not the winning but the taking part that counts.

18

Not a single fuck is given

*It is a strange thing to feel hunted. To fear
every knock at the door, to be continually
looking over your shoulder.*

YOU MIGHT think that someone awaiting trial for assault
who had also been arrested and interviewed over making
death threats, and whose business was collapsing, might keep
a low profile.

You might expect that, if someone was arrested for the
unprovoked beating of a journalist who had written about his
business, then if, within 24 hours, that same person sent death
threats to the family of someone who has also been writing
about that person's company, this would be a breach of his
bail conditions. And even if it weren't, you'd think the police
investigating the assault would be keen to know about it.

You would be wrong on all counts. It's the classic mistake
of someone who's been fortunate enough to have limited
experience of the criminal justice system.

On Friday, 5 April 2019, the day after Stuart Harvey had been removed from outside the Caves' house by the police, a new Twitter account appeared. The account, which styled itself 'Troll Watch FC', had for its header image a photograph of the Caves' house. It advertised itself by liking a tweet of James's.

Why a like and not a message? As the police would later explain, when declining to take action for further threats by social media, the Malicious Communications Act 1988 requires that threatening messages be sent to the victim. It is not enough that they be made and displayed. And so one is free to harass someone – as posting a picture of their home surely is – provided you don't send it to that person. Instead, you simply draw their attention to a place where the implicit threat is.

As serial harassers know, victims will typically be highly alert for threats, keeping tabs on their persecutor online in an attempt to gain as much knowledge as possible about their movements and keep themselves safe. In this way, the instinct to protect yourself can be subverted, with the harasser able to make coded or ambiguous threats which fall short of the legal definition of a malicious communication, knowing their victim will likely feel compelled to seek them out, redoubling their fear. If there is more than one victim and they are connected, there is a high likelihood that one will locate a threat intended for another and then inform that person, making the work of the harasser even easier, with attempts at mutual support among victims becoming a network for distributing the threats.

On Saturday, 6 April, the Troll Watch account started up in earnest, replying to a few posts about OwnaFC by some of its critics. Once it had attracted attention, it went to work.

Explaining the purpose of the account, its owner said that Harvey had 'made sufficient money from this venture and will move on, but only after he has seen the trolls'. Apparently referencing the attack on Calladine and the harassment of the Caves, the poster claimed, '1 job complete, 2 jobs in process, 5 more to visit and all episodes will be released in a documentary similar to Tommy Robinsons panodrama.'

'Panodrama' was the name of far-right agitator Tommy Robinson's attempt to turn the tables on the BBC journalist who was preparing an episode of *Panorama* about him by covertly filming him and releasing it before the BBC show could be aired. The message to Harvey's critics seemed to be that not only would they be attacked, but that he would have the beatings filmed for broadcast. The reference to Tommy Robinson wasn't simply an expression of admiration for his response to investigative journalists, but seemed to grow out of a sense of political kinship; the account claimed that it 'despise[d] the left and everything they stand for'. Why the account should think that journalists writing about dodgy businesses and customers complaining about mistreatment should be a uniquely left-wing activity was not explained.

Privy to information that only Harvey or someone close to him would have, the account went on to describe the harassment of the Caves as 'a live job on the system', referencing their postcode and Harvey having '[spoken] with the constabulary' when last there. The account also promised a repeat visit to Calladine's address 'in the very near future', saying that a film crew and 'new presenters' would be sent, in recognition of Harvey's bail conditions. Informed about this message by an alarmed Owna, Calladine sent his wife and children out of the house for the day and called the police. They declined to take any action other than to instruct him to call 999 if Harvey showed up.

The account went on to attack another journalist, suggesting he'd been doing the bidding of Supporters Direct. While answering to the name 'Stuart', it threatened visits to several other Ownas, telling one it 'could have your address in 24 hours if I wanted', and setting out a nationwide itinerary of future visits. It then turned on a former OwnaFC Facebook moderator, naming him as number four on the list, making a series of libellous allegations about him, changing the profile image of the account to a photo of him holding his young child and demanding he switch his phone on so he could face questioning. The Owna seemingly complied, as the account later reported having had a long conversation with him.

You might expect, having been beaten up on your own doorstep, that when someone was caught literally red-handed, with your blood on his fists, and was awaiting charging, that you would be, in effect, untouchable. You might expect that the penalties for intimidating your victim would be such that, when the person who attacked you threatened publicly to do it again, the authorities would drop the hammer on them. You might think the police would be concerned that the attack on you wasn't an isolated incident, but rather an escalating pattern of behaviour with implications for the safety of many people. Again, you would be wrong in every assumption.

Several people who were subject to threats reported them to the police. At least one force took a formal report, but none investigated further. The Met Police officer dealing with Calladine's case responded, 'As for the Twitter posts, it's going to be difficult to prove that this is Harvey sending the tweets. I need to give him a call with regards to his property ... and will discuss his bail conditions with him again.'

Proof that you don't look for is, of course, the hardest proof to find.

When the Troll Watch account was finally taken down, it wasn't due to the police, but rather in response to a claim of impersonation by the moderator whose photo had been used as the profile image.

This was far from the end of the intimidation, however. Just a few days later, another Owna reported on the Facebook group that he'd received an email from Harvey saying that he had the Owna's address and would visit him.

For all the energy he put into it, stalking and terrorising his critics was not seemingly a full-time job for Harvey. When not door-stepping people, he was also fighting a rear-guard action to keep hold of his customers' money. Sometimes he seemed to be doing both at once.

Having been seemingly dumped by his law firm and with the football press having turned on him, Harvey's business was already fatally wounded. The coup de grâce was delivered, somewhat ironically, by the same organisation that had given OwnaFC its big break. On 18 March 2019, the BBC ran a piece on its website under the headline, 'OWNAFC: Football fans call for refunds over club app'.[46] Written by a news reporter, the piece highlighted the plight of some of the many Ownas who felt disillusioned and misled, and were trying to get a refund.

Though the piece didn't mention the BBC's own role in having helped promote the business, it was balanced, detailed and factual. And while Harvey had been given a right of reply, the effect was nonetheless devastating. The game was up for OwnaFC. The only question that remained was who would get to keep the cash.

It pretty soon became clear that the authorities were not going to ride to the rescue of the many customers left in the lurch. Before March was even out, Police Scotland had declined to get involved, telling David Anderson, in effect, that it bordered on fraud but that he'd handed his money over willingly. Trading Standards and the Financial Ombudsman were similarly reluctant to act. By mid-May, the National Fraud Intelligence Bureau said they had reviewed complaints and passed them on to Greater Manchester Police, who, a little over a week later, announced they would be taking no further action.

In fact, allegations of criminality were coming in the opposite direction. The Troll Watch account claimed that OwnaFC had won 61 of 64 attempted chargebacks by customers. A chargeback is the process by which a consumer reports a company to their credit card provider if they feel they've been conned, misled or otherwise mistreated and asks to be refunded. If the card company agrees, they will repay the customer and debit the amount from the company – a process that doesn't require the company's agreement. A forced refund, in effect.

Harvey's response was aggressive and immediate. He returned chargeback notices to banks with printouts showing dates and times when customers had downloaded and logged into the app. This, he claimed, proved that the service promised had been delivered. He even went as far as to threaten to take action against a customer requesting a chargeback on the basis they were trying to defraud OwnaFC. 'This shows [customer name] to be inaccurate and trying to claim monies under false pretences,' wrote Harvey. 'We will be looking to seek damages for this false claim.' Another customer who, when denied a refund said he'd leave a bad review in the app store, was told he would be reported to the police for blackmail. Harvey went on to allege that customers seeking chargebacks were part of 'a Facebook campaign by a competitor'. There appears to be no evidence to support this claim.

In many cases, customers simply left it there. Only those who escalated matters with their card provider and were able to get someone to properly look at the terms and conditions of the business and its public promises were able to get their money back.

Others contacted Harvey directly. One emailed to ask when he could expect a refund, only to be told on 28 March, 'Further to your request for information, the business is now entering a process of winding up and is no longer solvent. All of the assets have been sold by the former owner and the licence to OWNAFC Limited to trade was revoked.'

This was the beginning of a new front in Harvey's campaign against his former customers: outright lies.

It was publicly launched in early April, when the official Twitter feed posted a message saying, 'Coming soon under new ownership. This concept is no longer affiliated with

OWNAFC Limited (company number – 11442752). More information will follow.' The information that followed was brief, 'The six-figure deal to purchase the assets from the director of OWNAFC Limited is now completed.' No mention of who might have bought the business or for what purpose.

It's worth noting that, while OwnaFC would later be struck off the company's register at its own request, for its entire life the company remained the sole property of Stuart Harvey. The claim in the customer email that 'the assets had been sold' and the company's 'licence to trade had been revoked' were, respectively, untrue – it had no assets – and meaningless: the company did not have and did not need any 'licence to trade'. It's hard to know how any experienced business owner could have been wrong about these facts.

The day after the OwnaFC Twitter account had falsely claimed that the business had been sold to new owners, a new anonymous account appeared on the scene. Purporting to be a former employee of OwnaFC, the account claimed to have kept hold of his or her work laptop and to be trying to bargain with its contents for the £1,500 back pay they said they were owed.

It went on to make an ever-more lurid series of claims, including that the whole Hednesford Town bid has been a land-grab scheme, with the aim being to acquire the club, move it to a new stadium and redevelop the substantial car park and stadium as housing. The company, the account claimed, had had £1.2m cash available to make the purchase only for the club to call it off – the implication being they had got wind of the fact that OwnaFC was fronting for a major house-building company.

Attempting to give credence to the false claim that OwnaFC had been sold, the account asked, 'Why is no one asking who and why a large software company have paid £185,000 for software that is incomplete?'

No evidence was provided to support either the sale claim or the land scheme, and the figure quoted would be an inconceivably large amount of money for an app with limited, unremarkable features.

Like a character from a Coen Brothers movie putting on different pairs of shoes to walk back and forth through the crime scene in a bid to confuse the cops, the account then upped the stakes, alleging that the company had been a front for organised crime.

'This was much more than an app,' it said. 'The football club was to be used as a laundry for money and then rising up the leagues would have meant no questions ever got asked. Millions and millions were passed openly between this gang. I'm now here to give a statement and be protected.'

'Here' was apparently a police station in the Greater Manchester area. The post included a photograph artfully cropped of an Apple laptop resting next to a glass screen with police literature visible on the other side. The torso of a bulky figure appears reflected in the glass screen and above it a plaque is displayed. Dedicated to a C. Watson, a police officer who was killed at Dunkirk, the plaque hangs in the foyer of Wigan police station.

A further tweet claimed that it had 'Photographs of millions being passed around this gang and evidence of how money was being "washed" and how trips to Asia were for new teeth and large deposits.'

In other words, only the day after Harvey had begun publicly misleading customers about the status of the business, an anonymous account had appeared claiming that a former employee was so scared that the company was simultaneously a front for organised crime's money laundering, a front for a huge housing project with a legitimate building firm and had just been sold to a large software firm for nearly £200,000 that he or she had sought police protection.

The only element of any of this that appears to be true is that Harvey had quite recently had his teeth fixed. A post from the OwnaFC Twitter feed, which claimed that Harvey was working on a business deal abroad, featured a photo seemingly taken at Istanbul airport. Turkey is a popular destination for British people seeking cut-price porcelains, so this might join some of the dots. But there's no evidence that Harvey had any connections either with organised crime, legitimate builders or large software companies. At least, not on the scale suggested by the account.

Was it credible that Asian-organised crime gangs – Triads or Yakuzas – had decided to use a small non-league club in Staffordshire as a way to launder their piles of cash? Would they really choose a club which turned over less than £400,000 a year as a way to insert their millions seamlessly into the British banking system? At the same time, would a nationally famous building firm become embroiled in a secret plan to acquire land for housing development using the same crooked company? And then, with both schemes in ruins, would a legitimate software company pony up for the remnants of the business? Was it possible that someone who claimed to work 'in operational matters' was aware of all of these schemes, indeed had proof on their work laptop, proof so explosive that it would endanger their life? Above all, was it credible that both the legal and criminal conspirators would select Stuart Harvey as the right man to front up these conjoined endeavours? A man with a long history of business failure, an entrepreneur who'd been bankrupt and whose recent business expansion was bankrolled by borrowing from his own family. A man with a short temper, poor judgment, a big ego, limited communication skills, no business plan and a seemingly insatiable appetite for drawing attention to his own activities. In short, was Harvey and OwnaFC the nexus of a global criminal enterprise? It seems decidedly unlikely. Other, simpler explanations for the claims of the former employee may need to be sought.

Disinformation does not, of course, need to be believed to be successful. It just needs to sow confusion and delay. With the waters duly muddied, the account vanished. That was 4 April 2019: the day Harvey first came to the Caves' house and the day before he began the Troll Watch account.

It was also the same day the OwnaFC Twitter account posted, 'We would like to advise all customers of OWNAFC Limited who have made contact with us that they should direct their questions to that limited company. We are a software company and not offering subscriptions to customers.'

The implication seemed to be that the company had now changed hands – with brand and social media channels now under new stewardship. Ownas responded asking for details of who these new owners were who had apparently already got their feet under the boardroom table. No response was forthcoming.

Alarmed by the idea that the business and its customer database might now belong to a new, unidentified company, an Owna emailed Harvey to request clarification. The response, when it came back, was characteristically blunt. 'If your data has been sold then it has been sold,' he wrote, 'and not a single fuck is given.'

Shortly after, several of the most vocally critical Ownas found themselves bombarded with calls and emails from debt-advice companies and other spam. It appeared that someone had signed them up to a number of mailing lists without their permission.

A complaint about misuse of data by OwnaFC was filed with the Information Commissioner, but no action was taken.

While this was going on, the Calladine and the Cave families were waiting for the wheels of justice to turn. Harvey had now been arrested and was on bail for two separate but related offences. In mid-April, while on holiday, Calladine gave a statement to Merseyside Police about Harvey's attack on him. When he returned from holiday, a package was waiting for him. Postmarked Malaysia, but with no other identifying marks or return address, it contained a small packet of powder. Concerned, Calladine emailed details and a photo to the Met seeking guidance. They did not reply.

Eventually, in early May, Harvey was charged with 'assault by beating' and a trial date was set for 28 May.

When the date came around at the local magistrates' court, Harvey didn't show. It became apparent that, contrary to what the police had said, this wasn't in fact his trial but rather a plea hearing. Harvey's lawyer informed the court that he was working away and then on holiday, but intended to plead not guilty. He requested a delay of a week, which was granted.

That evening, Calladine's car was vandalised, with a wing mirror ripped off. Scuff marks from trainers could be seen on the paintwork where it had been kicked. The Met were supplied with photos and a description, but again the police did not reply.

The following week, with the plea hearing rescheduled, Harvey entered a guilty plea. The magistrates sentenced him to a six-month conditional discharge and £20 surcharge to victim fund services.

You might think that we generally send too many people to prison but that a violent, premeditated, unprovoked assault would result in at least a small amount of prison time rather than a slap on the wrist. You would yet again be wrong.

As Calladine jokes, 'If people knew they could come and take a swing at me for 20 quid, there would be a queue round the block.'

To add to the almost overwhelming sense of disbelief at what had occurred, it transpired that, judging Harvey not to be a further danger to Calladine, the Met had not applied for a non-molestation order – what's colloquially known as a restraining order. They had also not invited Calladine to complete a victim impact statement, meaning the court knew nothing of the trauma and further intimidation that followed the original attack.

The next day, Calladine released a carefully worded statement about the attack and the trial. Within 24 hours, a new anonymous social media account appeared and began tweeting abuse and threats at Calladine, Cave and journalists like Will Magee of *i* and Daniel Storey of *FourFourTwo*.

Responding to a post of Storey's in which he said, 'Having also had multiple threats from an anonymous Twitter account for reporting on OwnaFC, looks like I got off lightly,' the account replied simply with a gif that read, 'Not yet.'

19

We will come back better prepared

If March 2019 had been the beginning of OwnaFC spinning out of control, July was when the slow-motion car crash finally came to an end. After months fighting to keep the company on the road, Stuart Harvey hit a wall and, dragging himself from the wreckage, began to hobble away.

MONDAY, 1 July ticked round: refunds day. According to OwnaFC, when trying to resile from the refund provisions in its T&Cs, this was when all customers would be entitled to a 60 per cent refund. By now, no one was very surprised when the second half of 2019 wasn't ushered in by the sound of electronic money transfers jingling in thousands of customer accounts.

Depending on the accuracy of OwnaFC's claims about its bid for Hednesford Town FC and the legality of it unilaterally imposing less-advantageous refund provisions on its customers, the company should've refunded somewhere between 60 per cent and 100 per cent of several hundred thousand pounds to customers. The best-available evidence suggests that the company voluntarily refunded less than £200 to customers, with no more than a few thousand being successfully claimed as chargebacks. That left hundreds of thousands literally unaccounted for.

Despite this – and his violent harassment of his critics – Stuart Harvey continued to insist on his own good intentions and, indeed, to try and cast himself as the injured party. Whether he actually believed this, we can only speculate. For someone who claimed to be concerned about harassment of people's families, he certainly seemed to be doing a lot of harassment – and to be taking pleasure in it. Why us, we wondered. We hadn't accused him of criminality; it was his own customers calling him a conman and fraudster. Ultimately, we came to believe his behaviour was a product of humiliation and rage at his own failure. And, perhaps, the belief we were easy targets. He never knocked on the doors of anyone writing for a national paper. Martin Samuel, who eviscerated his idea and insulted his business, wasn't on the list. And there was no door knock for the BBC journalist who'd reported on customer dissatisfaction or for Will Magee, who'd published the allegations of Harvey's threatening behaviour. But what Harvey's rage lacked in focus, it more than made up for in intensity.

In mid-July, Harvey reappeared in public styling himself a 'Developer of sports club apps focused on fan control/ownership. Currently in ten countries across the world and covering seven different sports.' He claimed to be based in

Dubai. None of it was true. While his new social media handle, @ownaclub, seemed to suggest that he intended to take the idea of OwnaFC and build a global sports consultancy, he was actually in the Wigan area overseeing the winding down of his crumbling empire. The snazzy-looking header image on his account appeared to show his software displayed on three mobile phones. In fact, the image was simply taken from the website of a company that actually did develop apps for sports clubs and then cropped.

Harvey initially claimed to be about to share news about OwnaFC, the company he had been telling his customers was both insolvent and that he'd sold. 'Prepare for really exciting news about how things have developed in the last few weeks,' he said. When OwnaFC customers inevitably turned up to press their cases for refunds, his responses were classically evasive. Alternately confrontational then conciliatory, he flipped between lies, insults and pleas in a matter of minutes.

Despite having promised news about OwnaFC, he instructed people to 'direct any questions relating to [refunds to] that business'. When asked how customers should contact the new owners, he responded, 'Any questions ... should be sent to stuart@ownafc.com and one of the team will respond.'

Who this team was, and why they were now using Harvey's own work email address, wasn't explained. In turn angry then self-pitying, Harvey claimed that, though he had refused refunds to all but a handful of customers, he was 'truly sorry' for people who had lost money. Puzzlingly, having previously claimed to have sold the company for a 'six-figure' amount, he now said that running OwnaFC was a 'failing' that 'cost me everything I had'. How selling a limited liability company for more than £100,000 could've ruined him was unclear. He also claimed that the company had 'continued to meet its ongoing costs', which is true only if you ignore its contractual requirement to refund its customers.

Finally, seemingly forgetting the attention he'd received from the BBC, *The Sun*, *The Times* and Granada TV, he rounded on journalists who he claimed had failed to take up the opportunity to get an insight into the business. As further customers arrived to demand their money back, he alternately deleted and reinstated his account, professing a desire to help but making no effort to do so.

No one took his expressions of regret seriously. From mid-June the OwnaFC account had begun sending deliberately provocative responses to refund requests, posting childish animated gifs saying 'no refunds'.

One customer became engaged in a protracted email debate with Harvey where he insisted that he had sold the company but refused to supply details of the new owners. Just a few weeks before claiming to have lost everything, he taunted the customer that he was 'sat on a beach ... in my new holiday home'. If the customer persisted in demanding a refund, Harvey said, he would come and visit him in person. The customer, Harvey suggested, ought to read up about Calladine to see what happened when he was paid a visit. Harvey then demanded the customer's work address and, having been told he was working shifts and wasn't available to meet during the day, insisted instead that the customer meet him at a nearby park sometime after 10pm. The customer, quite understandably, decided he didn't want to meet an aggressive-sounding man in a secluded area after dark and declined, only to be told by Harvey that, if he didn't come, Harvey would use a private investigator to find his address. The next day came and Harvey didn't show but then, having left it a few weeks, he tried to phone the customer at his place of work. Reaching the switchboard, Harvey demanded to be put through to the customer so he could set up time to meet him the same day. The customer declined and Harvey responded by sending a message to his employer on social media falsely alleging that the customer had been threatening and harassing him. Strange behaviour for one claiming to have nothing to do with OwnaFC by virtue of having sold it. Eventually, the customer reported Harvey to the police.

Around the same time, another news organisation was taking an interest in OwnaFC. Sam Meadows, a personal finance reporter for the *Daily Telegraph*, began gathering Ownas' stories while preparing a piece on the legal situation for people seeking refunds. He contacted Harvey to request a statement on the many allegations he'd collected from unhappy customers. Seemingly tired of denying the evidence of his own malfeasance, Harvey delivered one of the shortest, strangest corporate statements in UK business history. His response to Meadows's questions read, in full, 'Tommy Robinson is a political prisoner and should be freed.'[47]

Like so much of what he did, it was hard to know quite why Harvey chose to use his public platform to endorse a thug of the far right who was then serving one of his many prison sentences. It did not seem completely out of character, however, coming as the second spontaneous mention of his admiration for Robinson – the other being his desire to produce a documentary about his critics as Robinson had.

A month later, left-wing *Guardian* columnist Owen Jones was beaten up by a gang of three men in an unprovoked assault while out with friends celebrating his birthday. Having spotted him in a pub, they lay in wait and attacked him on his way home. The leader of the attack would turn out to have ties to the far right as well as previous convictions for violence. He was convicted of assault aggravated by his hatred of Jones's politics and sexuality.

When Harvey saw the news, he gleefully replied to Jones, 'Chat shit, get banged,' before blaming Jones for his own assault. 'Far left activism,' said Harvey, 'is a cancer that should be closed down at all costs.' He followed it up by calling Jones a 'prick' and a 'vile little rat' before referencing the recent throwing of a milkshake over Tommy Robinson by a protestor with the claim, 'TR was attacked by a muslim male in a race hate attack, the guardian and the left applauded that.'

A few days later, Harvey announced that '17 September cannot come soon enough. [Calladine] will be getting his second visit of the year once the period is over … counting the days'. The date was six months to the day from when Harvey had attacked Calladine, which would mark the end of his conditional discharge period. Despite Harvey still being under sentence for one attack, the police did not feel any action was required by the promise of a second one.

For all his belligerence, behind the scenes things were not going well for Harvey. As he had done so many times before, he called time on his companies and began clearing the decks.

In mid-July he put his house on the market, advertising it with no chain. It would sell four months later for just shy of the asking price, with Harvey moving into rented accommodation and netting a 55 per cent profit on the house in just six years.

A few days after the for sale signs went up, OwnaFC filed a notice with Companies House to strike off the company. The form was, in effect, a declaration that the business had not traded in the last three months and would not do so going forward. While it's a natural end point for a company that has never traded or has been dormant for a long time, it also has the advantage for a business owner of drawing a line under the venture. Once approved, the striking off application negates the requirement of the owner to file with Companies House any outstanding documents – like accounts. It also ends the company's tax liability – as far as HMRC is concerned, once a company is struck off, it ceases to exist and an entity that does not exist cannot owe taxes. Any assets that a company has once it's struck off pass to the Crown – the Queen or the Prince of Wales, depending on where the business was based. In the case of OwnaFC, those assets would not include the brand, as the OwnaFC trademarks – protecting the name across sport, dogs and more – had been registered in Stuart Harvey's name, not through the business (so, in theory, OwnaFC could rise from the grave in future). As a result, when it went under, the company had neither intangible assets nor money in its bank account to offer up.

Once done, a self-striking off removes the need of a business owner to provide a true picture of a company's finances or to settle any debts. It's not a get out of jail free card: business owners are obliged to contact a range of people to notify them of the strike off application, including employees and creditors. The notice is also published in

The Gazette, the government's official journal, to ensure it's widely available. Several Ownas contacted Companies House identifying themselves as creditors – by dint of being owed a refund – and objected to the strike off, requesting instead that the company be formally wound up and a receiver be placed in charge of it. That would've forced OwnaFC to provide details of its finances.

For whatever reason, Companies House took no action and OwnaFC duly ceased to exist at the end of October, taking with it any chance of customers getting refunds or the public getting a clear account of how much money the company extracted from football fans.

OwnaFC was not VAT-registered or, if it was, it failed to display a VAT number on its website and receipts – both legal requirements. The moment a UK business sells more than £85,000 of goods or services which are not VAT exempt, it must register for VAT and begin charging it at 20 per cent – and remitting it to HMRC. Based on Harvey's figures, it seems that at least £100,000 of OwnaFC's income might fall into this category. If OwnaFC didn't charge VAT and pass it on to HMRC, the taxpayer was short a minimum of £20,000. HMRC did not, however, object to the strike off.

What makes OwnaFC's end even more unsatisfactory was that, even though RightTrades was further behind on its filings at Companies House, Harvey waited until he'd put the paperwork in on OwnaFC before he began closing up his other business. Unlike OwnaFC, Harvey appointed a liquidator for RightTrades. Why he tackled the company closures in this order – what the benefit of sequencing them this way – is hard to know.

At the end of August, RightTrades filed what's called a Statement of Affairs – an unaudited outline of its finances showing its assets and liabilities. When it came, it was quite an eye-opening document. Having started out so promisingly, the company now claimed to have no assets and liabilities of over £365,000. A little over £13,000 of this was money owed to the tax authorities and there were dozens of small creditors owed between a few hundred and a few thousand pounds. The most notable entries, though, were sums of £125,000 and £112,500 owed to the companies of Harvey's relatives in Canada and £31,250 owed to two other people with the surname Harvey.

All told, RightTrades was claiming to have gone under owing members of Harvey's family £300,000. Enough to make Christmas dinner an awkward affair.

A few months later, the liquidator confirmed there were no assets for distribution to the creditors and, at the end of June 2020, the company ceased to exist. It meant Harvey would never have to answer the biggest question of all: where had all the money gone? He'd never have to explain, except presumably to his family, how he'd burned through £300,000 of their money with one business and every cent he'd ever taken from his Ownas.

With his businesses closing, Harvey switched into his usual self-defeating reputation management mode. He sent several bilious messages about other journalists, decrying their methods, including two to the BBC reporter who'd put a stake through OwnaFC's heart. For a man who had once courted publicity and complained that his critics didn't want to speak to him, he now spent a considerable amount of effort trying to goad the very people who'd been most keen to hear from him.

In August, an extraordinary spat developed, ostensibly between Harvey and his soon-to-be liquidated company. The OwnaFC Twitter account began to criticise Harvey in eyebrow-raisingly clumsy language and the two accounts became embroiled in a barely credible series of seemingly choreographed tit-for-tat rows that ran for several days. Around the same time, some new accounts appeared and began to attack Harvey, criticising him as 'violent' or a conman before vanishing. One of these, which had zero followers and only ever tweeted at Harvey, was a fake using the Amazon author photo of an American writer who lived in Thailand and who was most notable for having had stories included in *Best of Asian Erotica 1* (3.5 stars, said reviewers) and its follow-up volume.

Shortly after, perhaps in an attempt to present himself as the victim of online harassment, it seems Harvey contacted the police and claimed that the OwnaFC account had been hacked by persons unknown. Whether there was any truth to this, it seems odd that Harvey didn't follow the well-established procedures that social media companies have to help businesses rapidly regain control of hacked accounts. The account continued to post intermittently into the middle of 2020, ceasing to attack Harvey but with no indication that there had been a change of control.

Under his own name, Harvey continued his quest for rehabilitation and revenge. In early August he announced he was starting another charitable project. He was, he said, dedicating himself to raising 'as much money as possible between now and Christmas' for people with cystic fibrosis. How much, if any, he raised was not subject to a similar level of publicity. He also threatened to launch legal action to bankrupt his critics; he would, he said, 'Serve the papers and go for the house. I hope they have deep pockets as we have plenty of donations to play with.' No papers were ever served.

He claimed too that he would be holding 'more meetings' with Ownas, giving a date for an event at the Trafford Centre in Manchester and promising a future one in London, where former customers could meet and discuss the business with him. The Trafford Centre calendar of events showed no such meeting.

Aside from celebrating the attack on Owen Jones and promising visits to Calladine on several occasions, Harvey went quiet for a month, not reappearing until just before he was due at Liverpool Crown Court to enter a plea for the charges of harassment and sending malicious communications to the Caves. Then he managed to have a furious row with some boxing fans that ended with him yet again threatening to track down and attack someone he'd disagreed with. As the row developed, Harvey was asked if he was 'on the sniff', to which he responded that he had given up drugs because they had made him paranoid. Despite his clear head, Harvey went on to threaten to summon members of one of Scottish football's most notorious firms of fans to deal with his disputant. 'Get a fuckin life you sad prick. Trolling people online will end up with someone knocking on your door,' he wrote. 'I will happily knock on your door,' he continued, 'done it many times before and will do it many times again.' When asked if he was making threats, he responded, 'I will act them out mate, not an issue. Cunts like you make my blood boil. If you want to come to Wigan, I will pay your train ticket down.' Unimpressed, the person dug up and posted Harvey's connection to OwnaFC.

Harvey, unable to harass the Caves in person with legal proceedings pending, and finding himself dogged by Ownas wherever he went, finally dropped out of the spotlight and would not be heard from until after his trial in July 2020.

Before he went, though, he left something of a will and testament. One customer caught Harvey in an unusually reflective mode and, when asking what now, was told that he would release a 'report' later in the year on what happened with OwnaFC.

Even for a man obsessed with projecting himself as a success, it seemed strange that Harvey would sit down and spin a tale for a virtual stranger. But spin one he did.

Harvey claimed to have proof that he had completed a deal with Hednesford Town only for Supporters Direct to 'threaten them'. He promised to release his recording of his phone call with Supporters Direct once he 'finished a legal case' against the organisation. He would, he said, release 'all statements and financial information' and went on to claim that the software was 'still there, the clubs still want it'.

He raised the prospect of revising the business. This time, he said, he would take over a club first before going public. 'The concept is flying in other countries in a slightly amended model,' he said, 'and it will work here, just needs to be more strategic.'

He finished, ominously, 'Now we will come back better prepared and better structured.'

20

Be more than a fan

Stuart Harvey was just one person looking to get a slice of the football action. Even as OwnaFC went under, a stream of new ideas were emerging for how to further financialise fandom and reform club ownership.

IT WASN'T so many years ago that being a mascot at a football match was free. It wasn't an especially big deal. Football wasn't glamorous back then, not the kind of place a family would probably want to take their six-year-old kid. Running out with the team was something arranged by a quick phone call to the club. The child would pose briefly in the centre circle for a picture with the captain and then jog back off.

How times have changed. Now teams will typically have multiple mascots, each paying several hundred pounds. To ensure the right look on TV, the kid won't be allowed to turn up in their favourite jeans, trainers and last year's top. The club will insist each mascot is in the full current kit, socks included, and who has those?

At some Premier League clubs, by the time a parent has sprung for the cost of the mascot experience and the kit, they might've spent over £750 – far more than their annual season ticket. And all for a quick run around that is likely to mean more to the parent than the child. There's a line where commercial exploitation blurs into straightforward exploitation. Linking a parent's love of their football team with desire to create a priceless memory for their child and using it to gouge £750 out of them is well over that line, especially when you consider that some large Premier League clubs still offer the chance to be a mascot for free.

Every inch of football is being similarly pored over in search of opportunities for commercialisation. In the 2019/20 season, Manchester United had more official commercial partners (23) than league titles in their history (20). These included brands that had stumped up to be the official wine partner, tyre partner, coffee partner, electrical styling partner, denim partner, digital transformation partner (whatever that is) and forex and online financial trading partner. There was even a global lubricant and fuel retail partner and a global mattress and pillow partner. For the easily influenced, almost your entire consumer existence can be used to express your footballing affiliation.

Laughable as this is, where's the harm? If brands will pay for this nonsense, let them. The worst that can happen is that a marketing manager somewhere gets fired when it turns out that a Manchester United endorsement isn't a major driver of pillow sales globally.

The problem comes when obvious money-making opportunities have been sold to reputable businesses and the next wave turns up. Among these will be lots of decent people with new and interesting ideas. But there will also be others. Private equity, asset-strippers, property developers, digital innovators, get-rich-quick schemers. The vast majority will be acting within the law and many will become successful, sometimes valuable parts of football. Very few will come with a genuine love for the game, though; a belief that, first of all, they should do no harm. The question is how do we tell the good from the bad? Those who mean well from those who mean to enrich themselves? Those who want to remake the game for their own benefit from those who want to return it to fans?

In the same week that OwnaFC missed its final deadline for refunding customers, a new business was launched. Named Socios – after the membership organisations that own some Spanish clubs such as Real Madrid and Barcelona – it promised to use digital technology to allow people to 'be more than a fan'.

It's quite the claim, isn't it? Many of us will have always assumed that there is nothing beyond being a fan – no higher state of grace to aspire to. Players, owners and stadiums pass away, and it is only fans who abide, as custodians; the true spiritual owners of the club. So being more than a fan could logically only mean allowing fans to become the actual owners of their club.

You'll be surprised, then – shocked even – to discover that this is not in fact what Socios (which rapidly inked partnerships with Juventus, PSG, Atlético Madrid, Roma, Galatasaray and other clubs) meant by being more than a fan.

Instead it meant, broadly, a fan engagement app allowing you to vote on matters affecting your club. And perhaps, once you get over the disappointment of not owning a stake in the club to which you've dedicated your life, some better fan engagement and consultation sounds, well, all right.

It's a bit more complicated than that, though.

First, there's the question of what you can actually vote on. We hate to break it to you, it's not whether the manager should be sacked. Nor is it whether the club should cut ticket prices.

What it is, according to examples from Socios's promotional materials, is things like: voting for the man of the match in certain games, choosing which player the camera focuses on pre-match and deciding which music should be played when the team scores a goal.

The last of these actually became a reality in early January 2020, when the first poll of fans using the app decided that Juventus would now celebrate goals to the somewhat clichéd strains of 'Song 2' by Blur. The news received global coverage in many papers looking for a press release to copy-paste and pump out into the ever-hungry football news cycle.

But once the smoke had cleared, and Damon Albarn had quietened down, what had been accomplished seemed decidedly less than revolutionary. Radical, digitally mediated, participatory democracy had spoken. And it had said, 'Play that song they played at 10,000 other sporting events this weekend. You know, with the woo-hoo.'

The event might've had more historical heft if the song had some unique meaning to Juventus. But no, it was simply one chosen from a shortlist of four (drawn up by an unknown person according to unknown criteria), all utterly generic cuts from *Now That's What I Call No Atmosphere! Vol. 12*.

A bit naff, perhaps, but again, where's the harm? Well, there's a great deal more to the Socios business model than just helping clubs poll their fans.

Money, of course, is at the heart of it – in this case, real and imagined. Because to vote in a Socios club poll, you have to own a 'Fan Token' for the club on whose business you are expressing an opinion. And to own a 'Fan Token', you have to have bought it using Socios's own cryptocurrency, 'Chiliz'. And, to own 'Chiliz', you have to have bought them with real money from your own pocket. The blockchain, meanwhile, a sort of digital register of ownership, ensures that only those who've paid for tokens can vote.

Socios's model, then, is one of charging football fans for a say over the actions of the organisation to which they already pay huge amounts annually and of which they consider themselves the true spiritual owners.

For each of its clubs, Socios plans to issue different numbers of voting tokens – the bigger the club, the more tokens will be available. In the case of West Ham – who were supposed to launch in early 2020, but later dropped out of the scheme – the plan was to price the tokens at £1 and give existing season ticket holders and members a free token each.

Unfortunately for the world's 80,000 most-loyal Hammers, Socios intended issuing millions of tokens for each of its clubs – 40m for Barcelona, for example. In other words, just fractions of one per cent of the total number of voting tokens would have been given away free to the kind of West Ham fans who regularly attend games.

Who would get the rest? With whom would the remaining 99 per cent+ of the voting power have sat?

The answer, quite simply, was with whoever would buy them. Because those tokens would be on sale in the app to anyone who had registered with it. They wouldn't necessarily be casual West Ham fans – or even obsessive Hammers in other countries who'd love to go to more games but can't. They might not have even been football supporters at all. Or worse, they could be followers of Spurs, Chelsea or Leyton Orient fans. Imagine.

While many supporters would be horrified by the thought of non-fans or even fans of other clubs having a say over their club's business, Socios was eager to trumpet the number of people living outside Italy who'd voted in the Juventus poll and the number of Socios users who owned two or more clubs' tokens.

That then is the Socios model: using complex tech that many football fans might not understand to sell the right to almost anyone to vote on your club's business. The more tokens you buy, the more influence you have.

Originally, the blockchain was going to destroy government, undermine the global financial system and create a libertarian paradise. Ten years on, it was reduced to something that could have helped Messrs. Gold and Sullivan monetise their much put-upon fans.

With tens of millions of dollars of investment and the backing of global entrepreneurs, Socios has been able to present itself as a glossy, modern football innovator – bringing much-needed tech savvy to the tedious, hand-dirtying business of fan engagement.

West Ham fan groups were not impressed, arguing vociferously that it was unjust that a club which engages very poorly with its fans should be looking to charge for something that it should be giving away free. For many, it was clear that Socios would mean being shafted as well as polled.

An overstretched football press, however, lacked the capacity to interrogate Socios's business model and explain how clubs were allowing their brands to be used to lure fans into buying cryptocurrency. Few outside of sceptical fan groups pointed out that if you were to design an engagement app from scratch, there's no way you'd use the Socios approach – requiring purchase of digital currencies and allowing literally anyone who could afford it to buy voting rights in a football club. You do not need to sell cryptocurrency to determine what colour your third strip should be. You do not need the blockchain to ensure the authenticity of player of the year votes. It's like cracking down on shoplifting by giving security guards machine guns. As one former blockchain developer said when looking at how the technology was being deployed to solve problems, 'You could also use a forklift to put a six-pack of beer on your kitchen counter. But it's just not very efficient.'[48]

But for football clubs, desperate to boost commercial revenue, it was that most attractive offer: a seeming one-way bet. They get the lion's share of the purchase price, while Socios covers the investment in software and promotion. If the scheme is popular, everyone profits; if it's not, clubs face no losses beyond minor reputational damage.

This, perhaps, helps explain why the Hammers, whose owners have a pretty poor record of fan engagement, were the first Premier League club to embrace Socios.

If they really wanted to, clubs could easily survey fans for free – by email or SMS, or by incorporating voting into their own club apps. That would actually reward those fans who devote most time and money to the club.

But the aim here isn't engagement, it's monetisation. It's about new things to sell or new ways to charge for what was previously free. Being more than a fan doesn't mean being an owner of your club nor having a meaningful say in its running. Being more than a fan means owning a portfolio of voting rights in football clubs and trading those rights as and when the spirit moves you. It would be like the next edition of FIFA claiming that gaming makes you 'more than a player'.

No one other than some owners denies there is a huge problem in football with clubs being run with no regard for their fans' wishes. Supporters are routinely ignored on far more fundamental issues than goal-celebration music. You can see it at the top end of the game, where many fans feel the globalisation of football is marginalising them in the dash for cash, or in the middle, where owners are selling stadiums out from under clubs, or at the bottom, where fans are tired of their clubs passing from the hands of one shallow-pocketed chancer to the next.

Solving these problems is a monumental task. It requires radical change to how the game is governed and structured. And it involves hard, costly things like fan ownership, along with unglamorous stuff like structured fan communication.

The danger with Socios, beyond people losing a few quid on digital magic beans, is that, by adopting the language of fan engagement, it undermines real attempts at giving supporters the voice they need in how their clubs are run. It's the promise, not of being more than a fan, but the realisation of fans' greatest fear: that we are now, and will never be anything more than, customers.

One person trying to challenge this, with a much more down-to-earth form of fan engagement, is Scotsman Chris Ewing.

Today, we're all familiar with the idea of young British players like Jadon Sancho, Jude Bellingham or Lewis Baker going abroad to further their careers. But two decades ago, Chris saw the value of getting a football education overseas. He's been spreading the word ever since.

'I first went to the US in 1994,' he says. 'I was 15 and my dad took me to the World Cup to watch Tommy Coyne play.' Coyne, a Scot who qualified for Ireland, was then at Motherwell and was a relation of Ewing.

'I remember coming off the Long Island railroad train and going up the stairs at Penn Station and on to Fifth Avenue and seeing New York open up in front of my eyes,' says Chris. 'It changed my life. I saw there was more to life than just Glasgow; there's something else out there. The love of New York never left me.'

Chris came from a working-class area of Glasgow. He had been a decent player at youth level – good enough to sign with the Motherwell youth system – but had realised he wouldn't make it after he began drifting down the divisions.

Remembering his World Cup experience, Chris decided to use his skills to acquire an education. With a good set of Higher grades, he applied for and won a football scholarship to a New York university. He loved his time there but, sadly for Chris, his dad passed away and, struggling with bereavement, he came home before he could graduate. He later returned to the US, though, studying and playing for a college in Florida before moving abroad again to spend time at the Johan Cruyff Institute.

After that, on a whim, Chris went to Paris, where he started out working in a bar. Having arrived with £40 in his pocket and speaking no French, Chris phoned up Paris Saint-Germain and asked if they needed any help.

'It just happened to be that they were looking for English-speaking coaches for their summer camps,' he says. 'And that was it. I was working in football and could say I'd coached at PSG.'

Chris parlayed that experience into coaching at the American School of Paris and then opened a business helping place French kids in US universities on scholarships. Not every young player will make it as a professional, he reasoned, but they could still use their talents to get an education and broaden their horizons.

For Chris, the next logical step was to open his own academy – the Edusport Academy – which he did in Glasgow in 2011, giving French players a chance to live and play abroad and learn English. 'I'm a proud Glaswegian,' he says. 'I love to bring students here from France and show them what Scotland's all about.'

The academy developed well, but Chris was concerned his students weren't always able to get enough quality playing time, turning out as they were in friendlies and for local clubs. They needed more competitive football, he thought, and that sparked an idea: why not start his own professional club? And so, in 2014, Chris entered a team in the South of Scotland

League, becoming the first private football academy in the world with its own senior league club.

Edusport Academy won the South of Scotland League in 2016/17 and got promoted into the Lowland League – just one division below the SPFL, which had recently opened up the fourth tier to promotion and relegation. He has ambitions, one day, of seeing his team in Scottish Premiership.

'We never planned the club's success,' says Chris, 'it was just about creating playing opportunities.' At every step, his team has faced opposition off the pitch at least as strong as on it. The club was twice refused direct access to the Lowland League on the basis it wasn't a traditional club, with a home ground and fan base. And while it had its UEFA club licence, it was initially refused membership of the SFA.

Stepping up through the divisions brought its own challenges. 'The first year in the Lowland League we understood right away that it was a different standard to the South of Scotland League,' says Chris. 'If we were just going to field young French footballers, we would probably end up getting relegated.'

So Chris decided to supplement the team with Scottish players with a bit of experience to consolidate the position in the league. Even at that level, paying expenses and running a team adds up, creating a strange role reversal. Uniquely, Edusport was an academy financially supporting a senior team, rather than the other way round.

'The academy wasn't set up to provide for the team,' says Chris, 'so I had to think about ways to make it sustainable. We didn't have traditional sources of revenue – fans, sponsorship. We had to think a little bit differently.'

Chris decided to turn the weaknesses into an advantage. 'I thought, we're a brand-new football club. We're not hindered by the traditional way of doing things.'

His big idea was OurFootballClub. Launched in early 2018, Chris envisaged a member-controlled, subscription scheme for the team. Interviewed about it on the BBC, he said, 'This is an online project and you can touch the whole of the world. The dream I have is to have members from France, from Scotland, from England, from Finland, from Holland all pulling together. We're trying to create an online community that can pay a fee of £25 to join as members and they will have decision-making and voting powers to influence the running of the club. The idea is to give fans a unique way not only to support a football club but to be involved in it on a day-to-day basis.'

Over 800 people signed up for the annual membership right away and, with a kind of power Ownas would never attain, decided on a team name, logo and stadium name. The newly renamed Caledonian Braves moved to play at Alliance Park, in Motherwell – a 500-capacity, 100-seater stadium.

Getting this far – creating a club, moving it up to semi-pro level, building an identity and fan base, finding a modest-sized home – has been a huge effort. 'There's a limit to how far one person can take a club,' says Chris. 'Being the owner of a club on your own isn't as exciting as people might think. There's a lot of stress. What football is really about – people and emotion and a sense of community – can get lost.

'But we have something interesting. We don't have a traditional location and fan base. But what I can do is open up and share the club with people all over the world. With technology, we're not limited to any area. We can say to anyone, "You want to get involved? You want to be part of it? You want to have a voice? Decision-making power? Let's go! Let's do it!" I love the idea of a community of people from all over the world, with different religious backgrounds, different ethnicities, different styles and philosophies of football, different ages all being drawn together to see this little club in Scotland succeed. For me, that's what football's all about, and I don't feel there's enough of that in football. If we can use technology to harness that and create a sustainable business model, that's the vision.'

While OwnaFC crashed and burned trying to bring a global digital community together to buy someone else's club, Chris has been patiently building a similar project from scratch, focusing on delivering the fan engagement that existed only in OwnaFC's collateral.

Chris has a clear idea of how he sees fans shaping the club. Running it is the work of professionals, but creating it and contributing to strategic direction is where he feels supporters have something unique to contribute.

'Fans need to be present in creating the identity of the club, its values and ethos,' says Chris. 'Fans are involved in the off-field activities – sponsorship, how we spend money. But you have to draw the line on firing the manager or picking the team. Owners already know how fans feel about the manager – they make that clear in the stadium and on the forums. But you have to give the coach and management team respect. It would be a farce letting people pick the team. Football is about man-management, knowing players.

FIT AND PROPER PEOPLE

'We will create involvement and content that allows anyone in the world to be part of it. We'll get you inside the dressing room, get you to know the players. You'll come to like them and have some affinity to them. But only the coach knows how they'll perform on the park.'

One area he is tentatively exploring is using the global fan base as a scouting network. At the level they're playing, it's perfectly conceivable that supporters might spot someone who could improve the squad. The tricky bit will be working out how to manage fans' input and use limited resources to arrange trials for the players they identify.

'It's a real football club, it's not a computer game. If we want to bring players in for a trial, it costs money. We want to build out a women's team, great, we should. But it will cost money. You want a new strip. Great, but it will cost money. We will have to look at the budget together and understand where the money goes. It'll be up to the fans to try and make the best decisions for the club.'

Like what happened with Ebbsfleet, Chris is keenly aware of the danger of the novelty waning. 'It's like any business,' he says. 'You get people interested, but how do you keep them coming back? Financially, Ebbsfleet had a success in generating the money to buy a club, but they bought a club with an existing fan base and community – it creates a clash of interests. Where we're trying to engage with fans is around emotion. We want them to fall in love with the club. They'll go to games because they have an affinity with and understand the club, staff and other fans. We're going to create something of value, something lasting. We don't just want people to download the app.

'Football's changing, society's changing and we need to address that. Football fans want everything now at the touch of a button, they want to know what's going on right now. Want to build the right way. Have a philosophy, get the right players. We need to create an identity and culture, get players who buy in. We don't just want football mercenaries.'

Chris is excited by how the club is already beginning to put down roots. 'One committee member is a guy who stumbled on the academy while walking the dog. Four years later he helps on matchdays. He's a friend and a colleague. We have fans who help on the pie stall, one who's the safety officer.'

Caledonian Braves offer free entry for kids and £25 season tickets. The club works with University of Strathclyde marketing students to engage with the local community and has made a feature-length documentary.

It's hard work and it requires patience. Chris is continually looking for new ideas, trying lots of little experiments to help the club he built succeed. He doesn't know if it'll work, but you don't get involved in projects like this unless you're one of nature's optimists.

Asked what he'd think of someone doing the same as him, he replies, 'I'd say well done, go for it. There's a need for it in modern football and society. It would be foolish to think we can treat fans the same way we did in the 1980s.'

* * *

Some 400 miles south, in Surrey, there's someone who agrees. His name is Stuart Morgan. A lifelong Arsenal fan, he attracted considerable publicity in early 2020 when he decided to found an Arsenal breakaway club for disillusioned fans.

Named Dial Square FC, in homage to where the club was founded in Woolwich, south London, Stuart hopes the club can mimic the success of AFC Wimbledon and rise up from non-league football and reach the Football League with a purpose-built stadium as near to Dial Square as possible. To start, though, the club will have to play outside the M25.

Stuart started to feel uneasy about Arsenal around the time of the birth of the Premier League. 'The game changed massively,' he says, 'for the better many would argue. When [Arsène] Wenger arrived, Arsenal was beginning to develop into this global brand. Over time, it's built on its success and grown the brand. But as [owner Stan] Kroenke has taken over more and more of the club it's become a massive commercial business. Initially moving to the Emirates, it seemed a logical great move for the club, but looking back now, almost all Arsenal fans say they'd rather be at Highbury. The quality of the squad has gone downhill in the last ten years. The FA Cup wins have just glossed over the massive problems on the field.'

For someone who had dreams of a professional career himself, and who grew up idolising David Rocastle, Stuart finds something hollow in the glitz of modern football.

'For me, the greatest time supporting Arsenal was when we had poor talent and George Graham built a winning side,' he says. 'It was the best feeling I've ever had. All you want to do as a fan is win, it's not about making money. Football shouldn't be primarily about profit. These owners with billions to spend, it's not right. There should be a level playing field. It should be down to what managers can get out of players.'

Stuart knew he wasn't the only one who felt the same way, but was frustrated by the way that low-level dissatisfaction seemed never to translate into concrete action by fans.

'People are quick to make their complaints,' he says. 'You speak to many Arsenal fans who say they won't go anymore. There are a few mini-protests, but it doesn't affect Kroenke. Only losing money will do that. I wasn't the only one thinking this way. But it takes effort, doing something. I understand people are reluctant to do anything about it. I thought, 'Let's try it, see what happens.'

Will it replace the club he knew and loved? Will people want more than a second team? Can the desire for a stake in something ever successfully translate into a say in how it's run?

'I'm an Arsenal fan. That never changes. But there's a lot of fans who've stopped going, not renewed their season tickets. Dial Square is to give those fans something to follow on a Saturday.'

While Stuart is still at an early stage, he has a roadmap for the club. He wants to be in the Combined Counties Premier in five years, the Isthmian Premier within ten years and, in 20 years, to have the club – in its own stadium in London – pushing for entry into the EFL. For his plan to work, he needs to develop a solid fan base. He thinks that to be in the Isthmian, he needs a budget of about £1,000 a week, rising to £2,000 for the Isthmian Premier. He believes that, with enough fans, a new club can take something of a brute force approach to get through the non-leagues.

'Wimbledon had 3,000 fans every week,' he says. 'At any level in the non-league pyramid, that's worth its weight in gold. It creates a significant playing budget.'

Releasing his plans on something of a quiet news day, Stuart wasn't quite ready for the attention Dial Square would receive. Questions rained down on him. Why weren't official fan groups backing him? Why was the club a limited company instead of a community benefit society? How could he claim to be an Arsenal breakaway club as its sole owner? How could a so-called breakaway club work if a significant percentage of the fans weren't planning to go with it?

Stuart's plan, perhaps naively, was to try and energise the process of a breakaway by setting the club up – and deal with the innumerable boring but necessary bits of planning – and then invite fans to get involved. Like Chris Ewing, he believes not in outright fan ownership, but fan involvement. He plans to create what he calls a fan-owned business, which will have a stake in the club and that members will be able to vote on matters of club business. This company will be a company limited by guarantee, meaning it doesn't sell shares but memberships – similar to Caledonian Braves. Initially, the company will own 15 per cent of the club, rising annually to an as yet undecided figure. Membership packages cost £60 to £120 annually, including season tickets, voting rights and a range of merchandise and incentives.

It's striking that both Chris and Stuart believe the finances of football ownership, even several steps down from where OwnaFC were aiming, demands annual investment – either from owners or fans. Neither could reconcile a one-off

£49 fee with what they know about the costs for running football clubs.

Unlike Chris, Stuart is prepared to have fans vote on every aspect of the club, including ticket prices and sacking the manager. Members will vote and the fan company will make its views known to the board, who Stuart expects to act upon them. In practice, at least for the early years, he will still own a majority of the club, giving him an effective veto, though one he hopes never to have to use.

Covid-19 allowing, Dial Square aimed to play their first game in the 2020/21 season, another club attempting to redraw the traditional dividing line between a club and its supporters. Chris, meanwhile, will continue his push for league football for Caledonian Braves.

If you're wondering at this point about the overlap in offer, name and timing of OwnaFC and OurFootballClub, you're not the only one. Chris first heard of OwnaFC in late 2018. 'I came across it and it was more or less word for word what we had said [when we launched OurFootballClub],' he says. Seeking an explanation, Chris got in touch with Stuart Harvey. 'I said, "What's going on here, it seems like you're ripping me off?" and [Harvey] said, "Well, when we saw you do it and you … inspired us to do it and so we came up with the app."'

And so it seems that Stuart Harvey, the self-proclaimed football revolutionary, didn't even come up with his own idea. Was Chris annoyed?

'I found his model a bit strange,' he says. 'He didn't have the advantage I have – I own a football club. I think they were trying to do what MyFC [Ebbsfleet] was trying to do.

I took the view, if I can do a good job and be honest with people then that's fine.'

But then, six months later, in early 2019, Harvey called him up. 'He tried to sell me his app. He was like, "Do you want to buy my app because it's not working." He said there was a problem and that Supporters Direct had sabotaged it and he was going to start again, but did I want to buy the app?

'I didn't want anything to do with it. I asked him what happened to the people who'd paid the money and he said, "Oh well, they only had the opportunity to buy a club." It's that kind of thing that gives projects like mine a bad name.

'There's a lot of passion in football and people do want to be involved, but you have to do it in the right way. I have three daughters and everything I do is so that I can provide for my family, but also I want my wife and my daughters to be proud of me. You start taking money off people and banking it without providing a service, that's not the way I'd do business, that's for sure.'

21

I regret to inform you

With OwnaFC officially dead, the trial
of Stuart Harvey was set to be the final
nail in the coffin.

BY THE time Harvey was escorted from outside the Caves'
home on 4 April 2019, OwnaFC was no longer a going concern.
All the effort that Harvey had been putting into saving his
crumbling business would now be directed at taking revenge
on those he blamed for his downfall. Not just Calladine and
the Caves, everyone, Harvey promised, would get what was
coming to them. Supporters Direct, the Football Supporters'
Federation, the subscribers who had dared to criticise him, the
journalists who had failed to embrace his vision, the footballing
elite who had shattered a man's dream to protect their vested
interests. No one would be safe from his wrath.

The day after Harvey visited Southport, his newly created
Troll Watch Twitter account went apoplectic. Ownas who
had requested refunds were mocked. Cave and Calladine
were promised return visits with a documentary planned.

Journalists were accused of being Supporters Direct shills. Previous moderators of the OwnaFC unofficial Facebook group were told they were on 'the list'.

After door-stepping the Caves, Harvey had claimed to the police that his main concern was that Cave remove all material referencing OwnaFC from his @AgainstLeague3 Twitter account. Cave had immediately refused. It seemed extraordinary that the police would be passing on a request to a journalist to delete accurate reporting about a case with a high-enough profile that the BBC and *i* had already covered it as if this were a six of one and half a dozen of the other dispute between neighbours.

Despite this, the Caves reflected that they would probably have been inclined to let the matter drop had the harassment and threats not only continued but been amped up by Harvey's Troll Watch account.

Officers visited the Caves' home the following evening to take statements, around the same time that Harvey was publishing their full address online. Nicola told officers in an email that it was 'another day spent as a prisoner in our own home'. Attempting to excuse his own behaviour, Harvey also falsely accused Cave of having published his home address. With Harvey's relentless aggression, the Caves felt forced to continue legal action for fear of losing the meagre protection afforded to victims of harassment.

Before they left, officers confirmed to the Caves that a 'TAU marker' (treat as urgent) had been placed on their address in case Harvey revisited. But still the threats came, in a tirade of bile, false accusations and gleeful enjoyment of the distress he was causing.

It's a surreal feeling to watch someone dismantle and belittle your entire existence minute by minute online. The irony was not lost on Cave, who had gained a fair social media following from years of outspoken campaigning about the performance of football's authorities. But this was different. For Cave, his criticism of individuals was often pointed but always factual and relevant. Private lives and families of those he covered were always off-limits.

But every few minutes on what should have been a pleasant Saturday afternoon with his young family, tweet after tweet rolled in.

'Pathetic human beings' would be made 'to answer for their actions', said Harvey. 'This troll is going nowhere' and 'the door knocking will continue' followed.

Eventually, Nicola called 999 again. Still, she was told that no action could be taken unless Harvey attended the premises for a second time. Instead, she was asked to email the new messages over to the police. Try to imagine that. You are just out of hospital where you and your baby have been under extra security and a man who has attacked your husband's writing partner and has already been to your house is threatening to return. And you are told to just send the police an email. At that point, you have the cold realisation that you are very alone and that, in effect, you must hope that, if you are attacked, you have time to summon the police before you are too badly injured. That is the reality for many victims of harassment and stalking.

But, on Monday morning, after a long week trapped at home, the Caves found a sudden shift in the police's attitude. A senior officer emailed to say, 'I am very sorry to hear that this has continued to happen across the weekend. It is very clear that the result of the police interaction with Stuart Harvey has failed to prevent his behaviour. I have also asked that [the officer responsible for dealing with the case] gets in contact with you today as a matter of urgency to try and progress this case as quickly as possible. Hopefully this will be resolved as soon as possible, and this will allow you and James to focus on your family.'

A new officer was assigned to the case and the Caves struck up a friendship with him. David, not his real name, showed genuine care to the Caves, listened to their complaints, understood the lengthy context and agreed that he felt there was a case to answer.

It was a week later when David informed Nicola that the police intended to arrest Harvey.

The initial relief that came with this news – in effect, official recognition that they were the victims of crime rather than simply parties to a dispute – was rapidly replaced by a fresh wave of nervousness. Harvey was a volatile, unpredictable individual and there was no telling what would happen when the police paid him a visit.

As it turned out, Harvey wasn't home when they went to talk to him. The police left him a letter inviting him to an interview as a suspect in a harassment case and strongly advised him to stay away from the Caves while their investigation continued. From this point onwards, any attempt to contact the Caves might be deemed witness intimidation, a severe offence.

What happened next isn't completely clear, but at some point over the course of the next few days, Harvey was arrested for an incident that arose between the police inviting him for interview and actually attending. The police declined to provide any more details when asked and it is not known whether any charges were brought concerning this unknown incident.

Whatever happened, it had clearly left a mark on officers at Merseyside Police. There was a new focus on levelling charges at Harvey and a file was sent to the CPS. Meanwhile, Harvey's impending trial for his attack on Calladine approached. Our hope was that the cast-iron case against him for the first offence would make the CPS more willing to charge him – with serious offences – in the second case.

Despite Harvey's arrest – and the relative protection this provided – the Caves remained concerned about their safety. Ordinarily, someone on bail wouldn't seek to confront or attack their victims. But then ordinary people don't drive 200 miles to commit premeditated attacks on journalists. Anything seemed possible, so the Caves were hoping not just for justice, but also for protection. Assuming Harvey was found guilty, they had cautiously anticipated some sort of custodial sentence. But they were also hoping for a long-term restraining order – or a 'non-molestation order' as they are known in English law.

Hopefully, you have never been a victim of crime. If you haven't, you may have the same attitudes that we had to justice. Just as people shouldn't be able to turn up on someone's doorstep and batter them for writing about their questionable business practices, people shouldn't be able to send death threats to a family with a premature baby just out of hospital, call them repeatedly, come to their house and harass them. Terrorising people ought to attract action.

But justice in England runs ever slower, a victim of long-term underfunding. As the months wound on, both Calladine and Cave consulted lawyers privately to inquire about getting a restraining order against Harvey.

Unfortunately, as so often with the law, money talks. Calladine spoke to a firm which specialised in harassment and was quoted a fee of £2,500–£5,000. The lower end of that would be for a senior lawyer to write a letter to Merseyside Police and ask that they extend any request for a restraining order to cover him as a witness. If actual court action was required beyond that, the costs would spiral rapidly. The sums involved were prohibitive for both families, leaving them to simply wait and hope they wouldn't hear a knock at the door before a trial finally began.

Before we encountered Stuart Harvey, both of us had imagined the criminal justice system as being a bit like the NHS. Not as popular, perhaps, but largely effective. Victims would generally receive justice, while suspects got a fair trial. Of course the system wasn't perfect – more funding was required and high-profile sentences might often seem puzzling. We were totally wrong. The system was broken but we had simply been lucky enough not to be confronted with the reality of being a victim of crime.

While the wait for the CPS to file charges went on, Harvey was convicted for his attack on Calladine. His total punishment of a £20 victim surcharge for a significant assault did not reassure the Caves. The Met's failure to apply for a restraining order for the Calladines convinced them to regularly remind the police that they wished to seek one themselves in their own case. Their failure to request victim impact statements from Calladine also compelled the Caves to submit one.

However, charges were finally filed and, for the Caves, everything went eerily quiet. Harvey continued to post on his new @ownaclub account, but the Caves were no longer the focus of his attacks owing to the legal restrictions against him. To their relief, it seemed even Harvey was not so reckless as to threaten accusers in an ongoing criminal case against him. Like so many serial harassers, he knows just how far he can go. So instead, Harvey used the account to dismiss owners requesting their refunds, threaten those he disagreed with about boxing and, to round things off, throw in some good old-fashioned taunting of Calladine.

It's worth a brief reminder at this point of how the English court system works. If you are charged with an offence, you will first appear in a magistrates' court, the branch of the courts system that deals with minor offences. No matter how serious your charge, whether dangerous driving or murder, you will first be seen by magistrates. If you plead not guilty and a trial by jury is required, your case will then be sent to a Crown Court.

Finally, on 15 October 2019 – almost six months to the day since his campaign of harassment against the Caves had begun – Stuart Harvey appeared at Liverpool Magistrates' Court, facing two counts of 'Putting a Person in Fear of Violence By Harassment'.

The Caves decided against attending court to witness the proceedings. They had received mixed messages as to whether

Harvey would plead guilty or not guilty. The Caves were keen for the case to be resolved as soon as possible, but concerned, following Harvey's slap on the wrist in Calladine's case, that he might plead guilty and walk away without a sentence to deter him.

Harvey, however, pleaded not guilty at magistrates' and so the case was referred to Crown Court, where he again pleaded not guilty as part of his plea and trial preparation hearing, on 12 November. A full trial was set for July 2020.

It was expected that the Crown Prosecution Service would call Calladine as a witness, given that a large part of the Caves' anxiety was caused by what happened in Wimbledon. The assumption was that his unprovoked attack on Calladine and the obvious connection with the Caves' case would make it impossible for Harvey to convince a jury that his intentions had been peaceful and that the Caves had no cause to fear for their own safety and that of their baby.

Several days ahead of the trial, the Caves were informed that Harvey's defence team had made an offer to submit to a year-long restraining order in exchange for dropping the charges. It was a curveball. The trial had already faced significant delays due to Covid but rather than a delay tactic, this felt like a last roll of the dice from Harvey to avoid a guilty verdict.

James's only recollection of hearing the news was that it came via a phone call from his wife while he was walking in a park on a bright day. The Caves talked and decided to refuse the offer. To accept would be to essentially let Harvey get away with it, and frankly, he'd done that once before. Moreover, they believed that as Harvey had been convicted of attacking Calladine, there was a real chance of Harvey being properly punished with the Caves receiving some form of permanent protection at trial. The offer had been put to the Caves by the police on behalf of the CPS rather than the CPS themselves. There was no pushback when they decided to go to trial and so the Caves braced themselves for court.

Reading through the mountain of evidence they had accumulated, the Caves felt cautiously confident. This was despite the failure of the CPS to contact them in the months before the trial and to involve them in discussions about how the case would proceed or even prepare them for the tough cross-examination that they would face. No one knew the case in the detail that Calladine and Cave did, yet that depth, we feared, would also provide opportunities for Harvey's barrister to seize on isolated elements and try to discredit us and our work.

But no conversation ever took place on any of those subjects. The best that Witness Care were able to manage was to send over a brief, generic pamphlet.

Two days before the trial began, when only essential travel was permitted and no hotels were open, Calladine had still not heard if he was required in Liverpool for a 10am start. James and Nicola were told to be ready should they be called as witnesses, but in the end no one was called.

James went to work as usual on the morning of the trial while Nicola, now pregnant for a second time, worked from home. The Caves' liaison officer, David, phoned Nicola for a catch-up and to provide reassurance that it was surely the day when Harvey would face the consequences of his actions. A little later, James noticed on a court schedule website that Harvey's trial had begun and concluded in just seven minutes.

Seven minutes. Over a year of torment and psychological abuse had apparently been dealt with by the courts in just seven minutes.

In the hours following, Nicola received calls from Witness Care and David confirming that Harvey had walked free after the prosecution 'failed to produce any evidence'. It made no sense. To the Caves, there was plenty of evidence; reams of it. Shortly afterwards, Calladine received a call from Merseyside Police standing him down. An officer told him that they couldn't believe what the CPS had done. The Caves were left trying to make sense for themselves what the legal jargon meant. Despite several phone calls, it took a letter from the CPS, which arrived over a week later, to establish what had happened.

Sent by a CPS representative, who didn't have the courtesy to disclose their full name, the letter said, 'I am the prosecutor in the case of Stuart Harvey and I am writing to tell you I have taken the decision to stop the case. The prosecutor at the court hearing on 14 July 2020 offered no evidence and the court formally found the defendant not guilty. I reviewed the evidence again together with the prosecution barrister and we were both of the view that there was not a realistic prospect of a conviction in this case. The decision was reached because of the way the contact was made and when he was spoken to by the police and told not to go to your address again he did not return.'

In the absence of a trial, the court had imposed a restraining order on Harvey for 12 months. It felt like a complete betrayal. Having pushed the Caves to accept a voluntary restraining order in place of criminal sanctions, the CPS had turned around and simply ignored their instructions, dropping the charges.

Harassment (fear of violence) is defined within the Crime and Disorder Act 1998 and the Protection from Harassment Act 1997. The sentencing guidelines suggested that Harvey, upon conviction, could have faced a starting point of 12 weeks of custody with substantial additions for the aggravating factor of Nic, a new mother, and Daniel, a premature baby, being classed as vulnerable.

The realisation of what had happened – that the criminal justice system had delivered even less in the second case than in the first – was a massive blow to the Caves. Even the 12-month restraining ordered little comfort. Having been let down by the CPS, they no longer felt they could have confidence that any breach would be policed and punished. And what when the 12 months were up? Having expressed a desire to revisit Calladine the moment his conditional discharge expired, what confidence could they have that Harvey wouldn't knock on their door on the 366th day?

This, then, is the all-too-common experience of being a victim of crime. You expect – of course – that the police will protect you. In fact, you may have great trouble getting them to take your case seriously, even when you have credible evidence you are in physical danger. You will face a continual struggle to find out what's going on and be left to do most of your own research to help make sense of what's happening. And, after being made a prisoner in your own home by a violent man, you may be consulted on the direction of the case only for the authorities to ignore your response and do precisely what you instructed them not to. Justice, if it happens at all, is something that is done to you, slowly, carelessly, and rarely with any sense of satisfaction.

There are 'double jeopardy' restrictions in the UK, meaning that (barring exceptional circumstances) a suspect cannot be tried twice for the same offence. So there was no appeal to be made; Harvey would never stand trial.

Victims do have a 'right to review' decisions with the CPS in cases like these, but this is largely meaningless because no further criminal action can be taken even if a failing is found. In effect, the CPS simply review the file and say if they are or aren't satisfied with their own actions. Nonetheless, the Caves did seek a review.

And that's how the sorry saga of OwnaFC drew to a close. A rather soggy apology came from the CPS, where they admitted it was a mistake to stop Harvey's trial. 'Having reviewed the evidence in this case,' the CPS staff member said, 'I have concluded that it was appropriate to present these charges for the criminal court to consider as there was a realistic prospect of conviction. It is my view that the case should have continued to allow a jury to determine whether Stuart Harvey was guilty of the offence with which he was charged. I am very sorry that this approach was not taken in this case. Unfortunately, I regret to inform you that as no evidence was offered, I am unable to reinstate the charge as the case is at an end.'

And that was that. One person's mistaken decision had cost the Caves a chance of justice.

It was the end of the line. Harvey is innocent of harassing and threatening the Caves. His restraining order against them has now expired. His criminal conviction for attacking Calladine is spent and doesn't need to be declared on future job applications. For him, it's as if nothing ever happened. We wish we could say the same.

In a way, it seemed fitting, inevitable even. This was the same man who'd run riot, abusing his customers and then walked away with unknown hundreds of thousands of pounds after having delivered nothing. He sailed off into the sunset with the total consequence of his actions amounting to nothing more than a £20 fine and two more closed companies.

* * *

It was May 2019 when Calladine and Cave first discussed creating some sort of project, likely a book, on OwnaFC. By that time, many of the events described hadn't yet happened. Nevertheless, the saga had a profound effect on the pair, enough that the need to tell the whole story outweighed the personal risk in telling it.

Too many people were threatened, and too many people lost their money, to allow the chronicle of OwnaFC to slowly dissolve into the Companies House filings of history.

It's a far bigger story than just football. There is plenty that OwnaFC can teach us about the responsibilities of the media. There were excellent writers and journalists who covered the story with distinction: Will Magee, Daniel Storey, Ian King, Seb White. Honourable mentions too to Jessica Labhart and Sam Meadows who recognised this wasn't just a 'sports story'. But that is too small a list when you consider that the company had used the media as a launchpad, with many media organisations presenting marketing and PR as news. A few days after the collapse of OwnaFC, Magee wrote on his Twitter, 'As a further footnote to the story, should note that multiple OWNAs who contacted me said they became aware of OWNAFC after the BBC ran their feature on the app. A reminder that, when reporting on stuff like this, more careful examination is needed.'

There is much that could be learnt about how our judicial system protects victims of crime. Aside from Calladine and Cave, both of whom were left with a strong feeling they were let down by the authorities and left to fend for themselves, the authors were unable to find a single action taken against Harvey for any of the threats and abuse he orchestrated, despite conducting dozens of interviews. By our estimation, at least 15 per cent of UK police forces received a complaint in relation to OwnaFC.

OwnaFC shows us that there must be improved legislation and consumer protection when allegations of fraud are made. That's not to say that fraud was committed, but ask any Owna and they'll tell you that their complaints were received and dealt with in a cursory way. All we can say for sure is that the company was reported to Action Fraud and several police forces and that they all deemed no further action was necessary. The actions of OwnaFC were judged perfectly lawful, if they were judged at all.

We began the book talking of the revolution OwnaFC promised. But, in truth, nothing that the company did tried to overturn or change any aspect of how the game was run. It was a perfect illustration of what was possible within the rules – of how much a genuine popular revolution is required.

OwnaFC underscores the long-standing critiques of football reformers. The poor, opaque, unaccountable governance. Owners ruining clubs, unchecked by leagues. A lack of actual supporter representation. Harvey embodied them all. And while most would agree that football would be a far better place without the Steve Dales, the Roland Duchâtelets and the Karl Oystons of the world, Stuart Harvey added a different dimension. A genuine threat of violence and a deliberate culture of fear.

Behind his glossy promises to give control of the game back to the working class, Harvey was a man interested in nothing but himself and lining his own pockets. OwnaFC was a symptom of football's crumbling system, attempting to fill a genuine void created by the sheer refusal of clubs and governing bodies to engage with the game's key stakeholders: the fans. OwnaFC was so successful at attracting subscribers because it fed off this dissatisfaction at the state of the game. Many fans have grown weary of being asked to support their club through thick and thin despite ludicrous ticket prices, ridiculous kick-off times, unsustainable spending and no real say into how their team sport is run.

On the flip side, and horribly clichéd as it sounds, the Ownas we encountered were the best of football. The vast majority wanted to help a club and give something back to the game that they loved. It was one of the few successes that Harvey had – to tap into an almost infinite source of energy and enthusiasm that, if channelled properly, could yield incredible results. The Ownas deserved better. Many of the people named in this book, along with many who aren't for reasons of their own privacy or protection, went above and beyond in trying to repair the damage wrought by just a single man. Indeed, this book would not have been possible without the incredible assistance of so many people who told us the true story of OwnaFC, despite their fear that they could be next for the door knock.

If football really is the beautiful game, it's not because of tiki-taka, or incredible goals, or mazy dribbling. It's beautiful because of the people. Your friends and family not on a sofa but on a pitch, or in a stadium or at a freezing field hundreds of miles away. In November. On a fucking Tuesday night. Football is beautiful because someone has been making the tea, god-awful though it may be, or marking the lines (slightly wonkily) for 60 years. Football is beautiful because you'll jump up and down shouting with someone you've never met. Football is beautiful because it can bind communities together even when it feels like everyone else has forgotten the town. You can't bottle that, stick it in an app and sell it. You can't value it or buy it or trade it for shares. All any fan really wants, whether they realise it or not, is that way of life to be protected ahead of any one club or any one owner's commercial interests. It's a battle that can never really be won, but one that could be lost the moment we cease to fight for more and better representation for fans.

That's what football is all about

*As it did to the rest of the world, Covid-19
brought football crashing to a halt. And,
like every crisis, the wealthy and powerful
immediately began trying to exploit it.*

WHILE SMALLER clubs were desperately trying to figure
out where the money was going to come from to keep them
afloat, football's authorities were already collaborating with
the Premier League's Big Six on a stitch-up called Project
Big Picture (PBP). Premised on the effective privatisation
of the top flight, the proposals aimed to radically change
the Premier League's decision-making process. The current
system – where the two-thirds supermajority required for all
major changes meant the Big Six could be frustrated by a
group of just seven smaller clubs – was to be replaced. Instead,
under the new scheme, any measure could pass if just six of
the nine longest-tenured clubs voted in favour. In effect, the
Big Six would be able to pass or block any measure they liked

regardless of what two-thirds of the Premier League thought. B teams, changes to revenue distribution, membership of a European Super League – nothing would be off the table. It was disaster capitalism writ large – the wealthiest, most powerful people had seized on a crisis to press demands that they could never hope to achieve in normal circumstances.

Leaked before it was ready – presumably by a non-Big Six Premier League club – PBP was torn apart as the media, fans and clubs united in outrage at the attempted power grab. Notably, though, some of the people present in the smoke-filled room when PBP was cooked up didn't represent the Big Six. Astonishingly, senior officials in the FA, EFL and Premier League had all, at least initially, been involved in shaping the plans. Indeed, even after it collapsed, EFL chair Rick Parry defiantly declared it a 'good deal'. Not all his members felt the same way, having not been consulted on his support for this secret plan to introduce two-tier football to England.

Most of this had happened after Covid had struck but before a bailout had been agreed, meaning that PBP was carefully timed and calibrated to take advantage of the then existential crisis that football was facing. In return for the voting changes, desperate club owners were promised financial support – with the unspoken threat that refusal would mean the Premier League letting mass bankruptcy rip through the pyramid.

Ultimately, the scheme collapsed because the smaller 14 clubs in the Premier League, who'd had no involvement in the negotiations and were being offered nothing in exchange, made it clear that they'd never support changes to the league's constitution that so drastically and permanently disadvantaged them. With no quid pro quo on the table, the 14 were being asked to effectively surrender their voting rights without even the slightest fattening of their wallets.

Perhaps if the plans hadn't been leaked and PBP's proposers had had time to sweeten the deal for the rest of the Premier League, it would've passed. Football had dodged a bullet, but the underhand way that PBP had developed – and the clandestine involvement of the FA and EFL leadership – showed that football's decision-making processes had been drastically undermined by the growing influence of the Big Six.

Football's senior bods were called before parliament for a dressing down, at which point FA chair Greg Clarke put in a gaff-strewn performance so full of offensive stereotypes that he had to step down the next day. But behind the headlines about Clarke's career suicide, there seemed still to be limited appetite in government to force radical change on football. The Premier League made it clear that the Big Six would not accept the status quo and discussions would continue behind the scenes about a Project Big Picture II.

As it turned out, something else even bigger was already afoot. Just a few months after PBP crashed and burned, the prospect of a European Super League returned, increasing pressure on UEFA to guarantee bigger clubs more game and money in a reformed Champions League.

It was a threat that Europe's largest and greediest clubs had rolled out repeatedly, with UEFA always capitulating and so most people took it as just a negotiating position.

Only this time – for the first time – it wasn't an idle threat. Late one Sunday evening, in a move that will live in infamy, the Big Six and their co-plotters put out a brief press release announcing they were actually launching a Super League right then and there.

Fury greeted this betrayal – with marches on the grounds of several Big Six clubs by their own outraged fans – and, briefly, there was some unity around calls for change. The league itself folded within 48 hours, like a bouncy castle with a slow puncture, although some of its more cash-strapped Spanish and Italian members refused to admit defeat. (While the launch had been a disaster, many people interested in the business of football believe that a Super League, in some form, is all but inevitable in the long term.)

Eventually, UEFA fined the clubs a nugatory amount, while the Big Six found their people removed from key Premier League committees and, a few weeks later, faced collective fines of £22m. And that, English football's authorities stressed, was that. Time to draw a line under the matter.

But, from a long-term perspective, the most notable outcome of the plea deal that the Big Six accepted was that, in laying down a financial and points penalty for joining a Super League, the Premier League accepted that playing in a future venture *was* compatible with retaining membership of the English pyramid. While many people had argued that teams joining a Super League should forfeit their place in English football, the Big Six had somehow managed to use the punishment negotiations to secure an agreement that actually made a repeat more likely. Before, there had been uncertainty about what would happen; now, however, they could plan for it. This is the kind of outcome businesses love. There would be a one-off £25m fine – less than these clubs might spend on a single marquee signing and far less than a future Super League would expect to deliver over and above existing UCL revenues.

Beyond that, there would be a 30-point deduction. Why 30 points and not, for example, automatic relegation? Simple: 30 points sounds a lot but, such is the dominance of the Big Six that only once in the five seasons between 2016/17 and 2020/21 would it have resulted in any of the Super League plotters going down (in 2019/20, Arsenal and Spurs would both have been relegated). In other words, the Big Six agreed to a tough-sounding sanction that, in reality, would be unlikely ever to materially inconvenience them. What was fanfared as a deterrent to a future Super League is, in fact, a major incentive to form one. The Big Six now have it in writing that they can join a future Super League for a one-off £25m fee and only limited prospect of even spending one season outside the Premier League. It's the greatest judicial change of fortunes since Colonel Blood, on being caught stealing the Crown Jewels and facing execution, insisted on speaking personally with the King. He did so and somehow was pardoned, given a cash lump sum and had his ancestral lands in Ireland restored to him. Even Manchester City's lawyers aren't that good.

In a move it probably regretted almost instantly, the government responded speedily to the Super League announcement, denouncing the scheme and immediately launching its long-promised 'fan-led review of football governance'. Where it will go isn't clear at the time of writing, but even as the terms of reference were being announced, Rick Parry popped up again to call for the revival of Project

Big Picture. By the time you read this, the findings of the review will have been announced and, hopefully, despite a panel 90 per cent composed of the great and good, it will have produced some radical reform. We remain sceptical about the willingness of the government to sanction any fundamental changes to the game that would chip away at the power and value of the assets accumulated by some of the world's richest people, but we hope to have been proven wrong.

Not least because, elsewhere, like water on stone, money was lapping relentlessness away at football, wearing it down, reshaping it.

In late 2020, a company called Football Index, which had grown rapidly by offering punters a chance to trade on players' values – like shares on a stock market – ran into trouble when, concerned about its liquidity, it rewrote some of its terms and conditions. Many customers who'd believed they were sitting on profits running into the hundreds of thousands of pounds saw their 'portfolios' crash by more than 90 per cent as trades dried up. By early 2021, the company was in liquidation.

The problem, it emerged, was an opaque business model that was only partially understood by many customers and barely regulated by the authorities. The suddenness of the collapse brought accusations that the Gambling Commission was asleep at the wheel, having been warned in January 2020 that there were questions about Football Index's sustainability – some people having referred to it as a 'pyramid scheme'.

What the company presented to the public as a player trading stock exchange was, on closer examination, simply a gambling platform. In effect, customers made (and could trade) long-term bets on the performance of players against set metrics. But, rather than winning points – as in fantasy football – customers got regular cash payments for top-performing players in which they owned 'shares'. These payments – which the company called 'dividends' – could amount to 30 per cent of the player's value weekly, producing a handsome return and driving up those player's notional value on the index. The company also provided a guaranteed purchase option, where it would buy any 'shares' in any player for a figure slightly below market price. Both these factors – the high returns and the guaranteed ability to cash out – drove wild inflation in the value of players, creating massive notional profits and encouraging customers to put in more of their money.

At some point, it became clear to Football Index that it couldn't sustain the level of 'dividends' it was paying or continue to stand behind a promise to buy any 'shares' for sale, and so it cut the value of dividend payments by about 90 per cent and withdrew from the player share market. Customers were faced with a massive cut in returns and would now only be able to sell players if they could find someone to buy them. Predictably, the market crashed. Football Index denied any wrongdoing and promised that customer funds would be ring-fenced. But this applied only to unspent cash in customer accounts, rather than holdings in player shares. In the fall-out, the papers carried stories of unwary people who'd seen their life savings wiped out.

Meanwhile, buoyed by surging values in Bitcoin, Socios's cryptocurrency rocketed. People who'd owned currency units at launch in July 2019 could've sold in mid-March 2021 for a 400 per cent profit. The company unveiled further club signings, including its first Premier League partner – Manchester City – as well as international football teams and NBA sides. Fan token owners were invited to vote on the name of a Leeds United training pitch, the title of the Argentinian national side's Qatar 2022 World Cup song and the most appropriate spontaneous expression of joy that Radamel Falcao should display next time he scored a goal.

Excitement began to grow about Socios, but like so many other applications of technology and finance to the game, the coverage was largely superficial, failing to interrogate in any depth the principles of monetising club voting or the practical implications of tying tokens to wildly fluctuating cryptocurrency units.

However things play out for Socios, the most likely result is people profiting off football with fans getting no meaningful say in the game in return. The company for its part doesn't deny that its polls are often for relatively minor issues, but believes it is building something of much greater value. It told *The Athletic* that, 'Creating opportunities for the fans is our mission. We are still educating both clubs and fans to understand the countless opportunities we can create for them.'[49]

Internationally, things were no different. Before the tears had even dried on England's magnificent summer 2021 performance at the Covid-delayed European Championship – a display of character and skill that delivered pride and joy on and off the pitch – money was whispering that things needed to change internationally. Having been suspiciously muted in its condemnation of the Super League, FIFA poked UEFA with the other tine on its fork when it used a friendly confederation to fly a kite for the idea that maybe one World Cup every four years wasn't enough. What if we had one every two years, FIFA suggested, wouldn't that be even better?

Usually, if you're looking for encouraging signs in English football – reasons to believe that fans can ever again be more than customers – you need to look a bit further down the pyramid. And, despite the epic collapse of the 2020/21 season in the National League, where the campaign was cancelled part way through and clubs and administrators turned on each other like a circular firing squad, there were some reasons to be cheerful.

With Chesterfield saved from relegation by Covid's curtailing of 2019/20, the club was transferred to the fans, allowing Stuart Basson to return from his self-imposed exile. The days of running regular, substantial losses would have to end, but so, hopefully, would the financial chicanery and the setting of different factions upon each other.

In south-west London, AFC Wimbledon finally opened their new stadium. It wasn't quite how Charlie Talbot had imagined it; he was there as part of the media team, with his joy tempered by restrictions which meant that, while football could be played at Plough Lane for the first time in decades, fans couldn't be there to watch it. They would eventually, though, and the people who'd put so much time and love into their club would have something to celebrate.

The Caves' team, Southport, were caught up in the great National League debacle and fined for failing to fulfil their fixtures, and the club changed hands again. Calladine's Reading, meanwhile, faced a points deduction for long-term overspending in breach of FFP rules.

Hednesford Town were finally sold too, to a pair of local businessmen. The consortium that competed with Harvey's OwnaFC bid did assume control of the club for a short period, but owner Steve Price ultimately went in a different direction. At the time of writing, early in the 2021/22 season, the club look set to challenge for a promotion place in the Southern League.

Arsenal protest club Dial Square FC only got six games into its debut season before it was cancelled. Frustrating as it was, it gave founder Stuart Morgan time to work on his plans for fan involvement. He set up a company which fans can subscribe to and transferred an initial 15 per cent of the club to it – a figure he promises will rise over time. One of the fans' first acts was to vote down a proposal to change the club colours to the familiar bright red of Arsenal. Instead, they voted to retain the maroon of the original Dial Square team from the late 1800s. As a perk of membership, Stuart had the names of the first 40 fans who subscribed woven into the new season's shirts. Having signed a new manager and players, he's feeling confident about the future – and somewhat vindicated in starting the club by Arsenal's decision to join the Super League. The morning after it was announced, the number of Dial Square subscribers jumped from 80 to 120.

In the Lowland League in Scotland, Chris Ewing was busy with Caledonian Braves. The club voted to allow so-called colt teams – B teams – for the Old Firm into the league on a one-year trial. Chris spoke publicly in favour of the move after 60 per cent Braves fans voted to support it. On the pitch, though, the team effectively had two seasons kiboshed by Covid. None of it could dim Chris's passion and energy. 'I didn't set out to do this,' he says, 'but I feel very privileged.' Interviewed the day after England had knocked Germany out of Euro 2020, he spoke of his belief in the power of football.

'Look at the Euros,' he says, 'the Spain-Croatia game, the France-Switzerland game. And then in England, you'll be able to feel the buzz in the streets and the pubs and you'll go and buy a paper this morning and there's a smile on people's faces. That's football that's done that, that's what football's all about. It's England today, but it could be anybody, anytime. Our project's trying to harness that and bring people together and drive the project forward through passion and hope, which is something we have again after the last few years.'

One person no longer trying to harness that passion is Stuart Harvey. Despite having pleaded poverty when OwnaFC collapsed, he found the money to set up yet another new business in the middle of 2020, buying the franchise to run a gym in Lancashire. Some might question the wisdom of moving into a sector that would be among the last to reopen during a pandemic, but Harvey embarked on a complete refurbishment of the gym and remained bullish about its potential. Perhaps this time things will work out for him.

Before publication, we contacted Harvey to put the most serious allegations in this book to him. He did not respond.

OwnaFC's erstwhile legal representatives Gunnercooke also popped up in mid-2020 when *The Athletic* disclosed that the firm appeared to have acted for both parties in the calamitous sale that led to Wigan being put into administration less than a month after the new owners had received EFL approval for the takeover.[50]

A year later, the firm was in the headlines again when Al Jazeera broadcast a documentary about a British businessman who they claimed was willing to help would-be club buyers circumvent the EFL's Owners' and Directors' Test. Caught on camera apparently boasting about how he could deceive the league, the businessman named a Gunnercooke partner as his go-to legal representative for brokering club sales, claiming the lawyer had worked on several previous deals, including the purchase of Aston Villa and Reading. The businessman denied being willing to help criminals get around the ODT. As for Gunnercooke, who are not accused of any wrongdoing, they told the programme that they 'comply strictly with all legal and regulatory obligations at all times.'[51]

For Ownas, life goes on.

David Anderson is now the proud father of his first child and last year competed for Scotland in the Fantasy Football World Cup. 'I don't know if my attitude to football has changed during Covid,' he says. 'I think it has shown how important fans are to the game at all levels, not just on a financial level, but they add to the spectacle. Clubs shouldn't take them for granted.'

Liam Crowe was promoted at work, but admits he had a tough year. Football without fans lost a lot of appeal for him and, unable to gather with friends, he no longer followed West Brom so closely.

Michael Nye saw his team, Morecambe, promoted to League One for the first time in their history. 'It's been amazing,' he says. 'Covid has made me realise how much I take football for granted. I'm still helping out at my grassroots club, we've recently installed fencing around the pitch and made a sports bar to boost matchday revenue. I'm also doing my coaching badges this year and I have started coaching at another grassroots club. I think the whole OwnaFC experience has opened my eyes to grassroots and lower-league football.'

Martin Roberts, meanwhile, recalled with sadness his excitement at the thought of OwnaFC remembering that he used to get told off by his wife because he'd even set up a special tone on his phone for the app notifications, so he wouldn't miss a thing. Speaking about the end of the company, he says, 'I felt this isn't real, this doesn't sit right with me, I don't really want to be involved. I lost faith in Stuart before I lost faith in the concept.'

Martin is now a school governor and the national chair of the charity he volunteers for. Ever tireless, he's also embarked on writing a series of children's books based on the bedtime stories he would tell his kids.

Like so many millions of fans in the UK, his love of football is undimmed. No matter how commercialised it gets, there remains a part of it that no money can tarnish, a purity that transcends the chancers and plutocrats who seek to remake the game for their own purposes. Something will endure beyond the ambitions of broadcasters, billionaires, sportswashers and venture capitalists.

It expresses itself in the joy and passion we feel on matchday and in the unreasonable amount of mental space and actual hours of the day we spend thinking about football. And behind that, stirring now after Project Big Picture and the Super League and the Big Six domination of football, there is a primal urge to own a part of our football clubs.

A calling to turn fans' deep love for these institutions into decision-making power, to guard and protect clubs for their communities – for their children and grandchildren – so that clubs can survive the next century and remain recognisably themselves. These, then, are the true fit and proper people.

And so, while this has been a story of institutional failure – of fans shut out of owning clubs while a stream of obviously unsuitable people destroy them. Of a media that often doesn't interrogate the businesses they are inadvertently promoting. Of administrators asleep at the wheel or actively working against football's interest. Of a criminal justice system so understaffed and underfunded that it's unable to protect people from unethical business practices, harassment or violence – it's also a story of hope.

People will always try to exploit the instinct of fans to want a piece of their club. They will try to make money by twisting that dream and then selling it back to fans. But fans have woken up. They know the game has been taken from them; that the unspoken agreement between temporary owners and permanent fans has been broken. And so we must believe that, eventually, the commercial tides will turn and the dream of ownership will come to fulfilment.

When it does, doubtless there will be an app involved, perhaps even with voting.

Let's just hope someone does it right next time.

Endnotes

1 Davis, Matt, 'OWNAFC: Non-league football club could be run by supporters using a phone app' (BBC, 28 February 2019) www.bbc.co.uk/sport/football/47386953

2 Goldstone, Jack A., Revolutions: *A Very Short Introduction* (Oxford University Press, 2013)

3 Herbert, Ian, 'The Brazilian job: How Morecambe's supposed saviour left them staring into oblivion' (*The Independent*, 26 January 2017) https://www.independent.co.uk/sport/football/football-league/the-brazilian-job-how-morecambe-fcs-improbable-saviour-left-them-staring-into-oblivion-a7548206.html 'Morecambe FC ownership fight may soon end' (*The Visitor*, 2 May 2017) https://www.thevisitor.co.uk/news/morecambe-fc-ownership-fight-may-soon-end-1-8522914

4 'Stuart Harvey both nervous and excited about his consortium's plans to takeover at Whitehaven' (*News & Star*, 14 June 2018) https://www.newsandstar.co.uk/sport/rugby-league/whitehaven-rl/latest/16740800.stuart-harvey-both-

nervous-and-excited-about-his-consortiums-plans-to-
takeover-at-whitehaven

5 'Titans coach optimistic in their inaugural season'
   (USARL, 24 May 2011)
   http://www.usarl.org/news/2011/titans-coach-optimistic-in-
   their-inaugural-season--/

6 'Titans coach optimistic in their inaugural season'
   (USARL, 24 May 2011)
   http://www.usarl.org/news/2011/titans-coach-optimistic-in-
   their-inaugural-season--/

7 'Stuart Harvey both nervous and excited about his
   consortium's plans to takeover at Whitehaven' (*News &
   Star*, 14 June 2018)
   https://www.newsandstar.co.uk/sport/rugby-league/
   whitehaven-rl/latest/16740800.stuart-harvey-both-nervous-
   and-excited-about-his-consortiums-plans-to-takeover-
   at-whitehaven/

8 Cole, Sean, 'What happened to MyFootballClub – the
   club where fans decided everything?' (*The Guardian*, 26
   October 2017)
   https://www.theguardian.com/football/2017/oct/26/what-
   happened-to-myfootballclub-ebbsfleet-united

9 Cave, James 'Our 9 Hour Twitter Conversation with
   OWNA FC (Against League 3, 3 March 2019)
   https://web.archive.org/web/20190511081036/http://
   againstleague3.co.uk/2019/03/03/our-9-hour-twitter-
   conversation-with-owna-fc/

10 White, Seb, 'OWNAFC is not the answer to non-league
   football's problems' (*Mundial*, 4 March 2019)
   https://mundialmag.com/blogs/articles/ownafc-non-
   league-club-opinion-7th-tier

11 Statement on OWNAFC and Hednesford Town' (FSA, 4 March 2019) https://thefsa.org.uk/news/statement-on-ownafc-and-hednesford-town/

12 Badcock, Matt, 'Football is not just a plaything – Online app OWNAFC raises questions' (*Non-League Paper*, 6 March 2019) https://www.thenonleaguefootballpaper.com/features/26059/online-app-ownafc/

13 Samuel, Martin, 'Giving power to a bunch of cyber nerds is fatally flawed' (*Daily Mail*, 7 March 2019) https://www.dailymail.co.uk/sport/football/article-6783611/MARTIN-SAMUEL-Giving-power-bunch-cyber-nerds-fatally-flawed.html

14 Storey, Daniel, 'OWNA FC was supposed to change how football is run – but if it looks too good to be true…' (*FourFourTwo*, 11 March 2019) https://www.fourfourtwo.com/features/owna-fc-was-supposed-change-how-football-run-if-it-looks-too-good-be-true

15 Magee, Will, 'OWNAFC: How a fan ownership "revolution" descended into disaster' (*i*, 13 March 2019) https://inews.co.uk/sport/football/ownafc-app-fan-ownership-scandal-268642/amp

16 'Soccer club boss jailed for fraud' (BBC, 22 September 2005) http://news.bbc.co.uk/1/hi/england/derbyshire/4272022.stm

17 Chaudhary, Vivek, 'How Mr Bean's team unravelled the financial web at Chesterfield' (*The Guardian*, 13 April 2001) https://www.theguardian.com/football/2001/apr/13/newsstory.sport3

18 Hughes, Stuart, 'Brown cuts Steelers ties' (BBC,
16 March 2001)
http://news.bbc.co.uk/sport1/hi/other_sports/1225946.stm

19 'Soccer club boss jailed for fraud' (BBC, 22 September 2005)
http://news.bbc.co.uk/1/hi/england/
derbyshire/4272022.stm

20 Conn, David, 'Chesterfield fighting for the right to be the
ultimate community club' (*The Independent*, 10 October 2011)
https://www.independent.co.uk/sport/football/news-and-
comment/david-conn-chesterfield-fighting-for-the-right-
to-be-the-ultimate-community-club-563425.html

21 Chambers, Matthew, 'Athletic fire Fitzgerald' (*Oldham
Evening Chronicle*, 21 February 2017)
https://www.oldham-chronicle.co.uk/news-features/10/
oldham-athletic-news/102202/athletic-fire-fitzgerald

22 Current Suspensions List – As of 1 August 2017 (The FA,
1 August 2017)
http://www.thefa.com/-/media/files/thefaportal/
governance-docs/agents/intermediaries/current-suspended-
intermediaries---1-august-2017.ashx

23 Nursey, James, 'Notts County in fresh crisis as "advisor"
is convicted fraudster living under new name' (*The
Mirror*, 7 June 2019)
https://www.mirror.co.uk/sport/football/news/notts-
county-fresh-crisis-saviour-16478871?12

24 Findlater, James, 'John Fenty responds after details emerge
of company set up with convicted fraudster Alex May'
(*Grimsby Live*, 13 December 2020)
https://www.grimsbytelegraph.co.uk/sport/football/
football-news/john-fenty-alex-may-grimsby-4794965

25 'Barnsley Football Club coach sentenced for bribery'
(BBC, 17 January 2020)

https://www.bbc.co.uk/news/uk-england-51154992

26 'Player payments issue "referred to the FA" say EFL'
(*Derbyshire Times,* 6 September 2017)
https://www.derbyshiretimes.co.uk/sport/football/player-
payments-issue-referred-fa-say-efl-53245

27 'Chesterfield ordered to replay FA Cup tie with
MK Dons over ineligible player' (*The Guardian*, 15
December 2014)
https://www.theguardian.com/football/2014/dec/15/fa-
cup-chesterfield-mk-dons-ineligible-player

28 'Chesterfield issue apology to fans over faked winning
raffle entry' (*The Guardian*, 19 July 2016)
https://www.theguardian.com/football/2016/
jul/19/chesterfield-issue-apology-fans-faked-
winning-raffle-entry

29 'New owners of Chesterfield football school still
discovering historical debts but say they can turn it
around' (*Derbyshire Times*, 13 December 2016)
https://www.derbyshiretimes.co.uk/news/new-owners-
chesterfield-football-school-still-discovering-historical-
debts-say-they-can-turn-it-around-1171631

30 'Player payments issue "referred to the FA" say EFL'
(*Derbyshire Times*, 6 September 2017)
https://www.derbyshiretimes.co.uk/sport/football/player-
payments-issue-referred-fa-say-efl-53245

31 'EFL demands answers over Orient's pay dispute with
Francesco Becchetti' (Sky Sports, 24 April 2017)
https://www.skysports.com/football/
news/11742/10849311/efl-demands-answers-over-orients-
pay-dispute-with-francesco-becchetti

32 Wright, Duncan, 'DALE STAKES: Who is Steve
Dale, what's the Bury FC owner's net worth, and

which companies has he owned previously?' (*The Sun*, 31 August 2019) https://www.thesun.co.uk/sport/football/9783813/steve-dale-bury-owner-net-worth-companies/

33 The Regulatory Reform (Fire Safety) Order 2005 https://www.legislation.gov.uk/uksi/2005/1541/note#text per cent3Dreplaced hsttps://www.fireassessmentservices.co.uk/fireregulations-html

34 Steven, Keith, 'Homecall Plus in Liquidation (Update)' (Company Rescue, 19 May 2011) https://companyrescue.blogspot.com/2011/05/?m=0

35 Brignall, Miles, 'Alarm bells ring over Groupon discount deals' (*The Guardian*, 11 November 2011) https://www.theguardian.com/money/2011/nov/11/alarm-bells-groupon-discount-deals

36 Good, Alastair and Morgan-Bentley, Paul, 'Action Fraud investigation: victims misled and mocked as police fail to investigate' (*The Times*, 15 August 2019) https://www.thetimes.co.uk/article/action-fraud-investigation-victims-misled-and-mocked-as-police-fail-to-investigate-wlh8c6rs6

37 'Fraud victims "failed" as criminals "operate with impunity"' – report (BBC, 25 January 2020) https://www.bbc.co.uk/news/uk-51246926

38 Conn, David, 'Majority of AFC Wimbledon fans oppose private investors in new stadium' (*The Guardian*, 10 December 2019) https://www.theguardian.com/football/2019/dec/10/majority-of-afc-wimbledon-fans-oppose-private-investors-in-new-stadium

39 Conn, David, 'AFC Wimbledon fans raise over £4m to keep Plough Lane return alive' (*The Guardian*, 13 February 2020)

https://www.theguardian.com/football/2020/feb/13/afc-wimbledon-fans-raise-over-4m-plough-lane-stadium-

40 Conn, David, 'New breed of owner typified by Hammam' (*The Independent*, 11 January 2002) https://www.independent.co.uk/sport/football/news-and-comment/david-conn-new-breed-of-owner-typified-by-hammam-9255934.html

41 Ozanian, Mike, 'The World's Most Valuable Soccer Teams: Barcelona Edges Real Madrid To Land At No. 1 For First Time' (*Forbes*, 12 April 2021) https://www.forbes.com/sites/mikeozanian/2021/04/12/the-worlds-most-valuable-soccer-teams-barcelona-on-top-at-48-billion/?sh=4d5650bc16ac

42 Lane, Barnaby, 'A Spanish newspaper claims FC Barcelona is on the "verge of bankruptcy" after it reported a $117 million loss and failed to pay players' (*Insider*, 27 January 2021) https://www.insider.com/fc-barcelona-financial-results-lionel-messi-loss-debt-2021-1

43 Morris, Patrick, 'The Simple Reason Warren Buffett Will Never Buy an NFL Team' (The Motley Fool, 1 February 2014) https://www.fool.com/investing/general/2014/02/01/the-simple-reason-warren-buffett-will-never-buy-an.aspx

44 Maguire, Kieran, *The Price of Football: Understanding Football Club Finance* (Agenda Publishing, 16 January 2020)

45 Markham, Tom, 'What is the optimal method to value a football club?' (University of Reading – ICMA Centre, 22 March 2013) https://www.sportingintelligence.com/wp-content/uploads/2013/03/Markham-paper.pdf

46 Labhart, Jessica, 'OWNAFC: Football fans call for refunds over club app' (BBC, 18 March 2019) https://www.bbc.co.uk/news/uk-england-stoke-staffordshire-47527747

47 Meadows, Sam, 'Investment scheme gave fans the chance to own a football club – now they are left with nothing' (*The Telegraph*, 17 July 2019) https://www.telegraph.co.uk/money/consumer-affairs/investment-scheme-gave-fans-chance-football-club-now-left/

48 Frederik, Jesse, 'Blockchain, the amazing solution for almost nothing' (*The Correspondent*, 21 August 2020) https://thecorrespondent.com/655/blockchain-the-amazing-solution-for-almost-nothing/86649455475-f933fe63

49 D'Urso, Joey, 'Special investigation: Socios 'fan tokens' – what they really are and how they work' (The Athletic, 18 August 2021) https://theathletic.co.uk/2774492/22021/08/18/investigation-socios-fan-tokens-what-they-really-are-and-how-they-work

50 Crafton, Adam and Hughes, Simon, 'How Wigan Athletic were torn apart by an invisible owner' (The Athletic, 4 July 2020) https://theathletic.co.uk/1907722/2020/07/04/wigan-athletic-royle-efl-paul-cook-hong-kong-yeung/

51 Harrison, David, 'The Men Who Sell Football' (Al Jazeera, 9 August 2021) https://www.youtube.com/watch?v=ldgTCXpDEgk